CV

Handbook

Forthcoming from PhD Books

A PhD's Guide to the Academic Job Search: An owner's manual for your academic job search for PhDs, MDs, MFAs, and other's with a whole lotta brains. (In Press, Spring 2012)

A Graduate's Guide to ePortfolios: An owner's manual for ePortfolios for professional development, job seeking, and career advancement in the academy. (Spring 2013)

Get the latest on additional publications, white papers, and other resources at: www.phdbooks.com

Also from Anthony & Coghill-Behrends

Getting Hired: A Student Teacher's Guide to Professionalism, Résumé Development & Interviewing (2010). Kendall Hunt Publishing. www.kendallhunt.com

Books by R. Anthony and G. Roe

101 Grade A Résumés for Teachers, Barron's, third ed.

The Curriculum Vitae Handbook: How to Present and Promote Your Academic Career, Rudi Publishing, second ed.

From Contact to Contract: A Teacher's Employment Guide, Sulzburger & Graham Publishing, Ltd., second ed.

Over 40 and Looking for Work? A Guide for the Unemployed, Underemployed, and Unhappily Employed, Bob Adams, Inc.

How to Look Good to an Employer, Pearson Education.

Educators' Passport to International Jobs, Peterson's Guides.

Finding a Job in Your Field: A Handbook for Ph.D's & M.A.'s, Peterson's Guides.

CV Handbook

A Curriculum Vitae Owner's Manual

The best reference on the market for those with a PhD, MFA, MD, DDS, and a whole lot of brains.

Will Coghill-Behrends & Rebecca Anthony

PHD BOOKS

PhD Books LLC

PhD Books, LLC, Publisher

For Inquires about this publication or about the services available through PhD Books, please visit www.phdbooks.com or email: phdbooks@gmail.com

PRINTED IN THE UNITED STATES OF AMERICA

ISBN 9781461090519

For: Frank & Fred

Contents

Contents

*Professional Résumé

Foreword

I first met Rebecca and Will at a national conference when I happened upon their presentation on a unique doctoral retention and success program they had created and were piloting at The University of Iowa. Their presentation compared the large numbers of doctoral students in the academy to the reproduction cycle of rabbits, and was both funny and intelligent. Will and Rebecca managed to convey a really powerful message and captivate a room full of folks from ivy leagues, large state research institutions, and all others in between. Their fundamental knowledge of higher education, including: recruitment and retention; market factors; the academic job search and self-promotion in the academy; as well as the social and emotional needs of graduate students, was incredibly evident. One such fundamental was that if we're not having fun, it's not worth it. They've captured that spirit once again in this book as the "Click and Clack" of CV writing. Who knew it was possible for two people to spend this much time talking about CVs, but it's worth it – their advice is solid, and their recommendations academy tested. Thank goodness they've thought about it this hard so you don't have to.

The CV Handbook is an indispensible tool because of both the depth and breadth of the information covered. It's an encyclopedia of information – from the first half that deals with what you'll need at various stages of your graduate or academic career to the last section that provides a sample for just about any discipline out there.

The CV Handbook provides readers a launch pad to create a powerful and effective CV. Let us at Interfolio take care of the rest. Interfolio hopes you'll use this book to achieve your goals. Interfolio is proud to offer you this handbook and be your partner in your life's work.

Frank Fessenden, Vice President, Interfolio

Preface

The academy is in a state of transformation as it responds to the new demands of the political, economic, and social climate of the day. While we would like to believe that we could help every PhD who reads this book get the job, we are aware of some pretty staggering statistics: we produce more folks with PhDs than there are jobs, and new PhDs are looking at a vastly different job market than the one in which many of their mentors emerged. PhDs need more than smarts to land a job and we'll show you how to demonstrate the skill and experience critical in the new academy.

This book is organized into three main sections. The first section, THE CV OWNER'S GUIDE, to quote Fräulein Maria from the Sound of Music, starts at the very beginning, because it is a very good place to start. Start here if you are a true beginner to the art of CV writing. The second section, the CV STYLE GUIDE, provides folks with all the requisite tools and advice they'll need to start drafting, or redrafting, a CV. The final section of the book, CV SAMPLES includes multiple CVs from just about every discipline imaginable. We've even included interdisciplinary examples, professional résumés, dual program CVs, as well as condensed and transformed CVs to meet candidate's special needs (not all CVs are used for job seeking). Find a CV in your discipline, or find one with a look and feel that appeals to you and make it your own. There's no right or wrong way to use this book, so find whatever section is most useful to you and begin the work of creating or recreating your CV. If you already have a job and are using this book to recreate your CV for tenure or other purposes, we say welcome and skip ahead to whatever section you'll need to begin your work.

We're excited to help you through this process. We've helped hundreds of doctoral students across the entire academy transform their identity and bring their strengths and talents to life. We know that the process of getting an advanced degree or going up for tenure is abusive, exhaustive, and downright stupefying. Let us help; we promise this little book will make things easy for you.

Will & Rebecca
Iowa City, 2011

Introduction

Welcome to your curriculum vitae owner's guide. If you are reading this book, we know two things about you: 1) you're smart; 2) you're pragmatic. We know that you are smart, because most people who need to write a curriculum vitae have, or will soon have very important letters behind their name (PhD, MFA, MD, DDS, MBA, MA, to name just a few). We know that you are pragmatic, because *The CV Handbook* offers guidance to future academics, researchers, and specialized professionals who have spent time in the academy earning terminal degrees and now find a reason to have this document called a CV. Within the pages of this book, you'll find what goes into a CV, how to make it look like you picked up a minor in graphic design as an undergrad, and for what occasions you may be asked to share your CV. This no-nonsense handbook is going to help you set your record straight, will offer you sound advice and guidance for whatever stage of CV authorship you claim and we promise we will do our best to waste none of your time. We know that you have more important things to do: like publishing and finding a job. Therein lies our caution: your CV is among your most valuable assets, for it's your academic chronicle, your legacy, and, in many ways, the authentication of your academic career. Take it seriously – you're gonna need it, and you're gonna want a good one!

At a recent seminar for doctoral students, we were introduced as "The CV-Experts of the Universe." Then the speaker went on to talk about our CV-writing super powers. We don't have super powers, but we are super heroes to the hundreds of doctoral students we've helped along the way. We've tailored thousands of CVs from myriad disciplines. We've seen CVs from all corners of the world intended for all of the world's academic disciplines, from the biological sciences to the physical sciences, and from folks in English to just about every other language taught in the modern academy. We're convinced you'll be able to find yourself in this book and launch your first, or maybe your newly re-envisioned curriculum vitae. By the way, we hope you have a little fun while working on your CV. Life is hard enough, try not to take this all so CV-ious.

1

CV Owner's Guide

The Curriculum Vitae

To most, the term *curriculum vitae* sounds like something the doctor recommends once a day along with 1200 mg of Fish Oil and a big glass of orange juice. Turn to its more widely recognized name in the vernacular of the academy, *CV*, and you end up with something that easily rolls off the tongue but poses a high risk for certain forms of skin cancer. Indeed, most everyone reading this book knows that a curriculum vitae is not to be confused with a daily supplement, nor are they at all as dangerous as the sun's UV rays, though many young academics would argue they know more about both of those topics than they do about drafting a meaningful CV. This document goes by many names, but most commonly: curriculum vitae, vita, résumé, or CV. For the remainder of this handbook, we'll strive to just call it a CV, thereby saving a few dozen pages of paper.

Your CV needn't compete with Pulitzer Prize winning authors for rosy language, but the problem is that most CVs read like the financial section of the newspaper: endless lists that are legible only to those with degrees in business, and that can put just about anyone into a state of boredom-induced coma. When did academics become bean counters anyway? To fully capture all that one does in a one- or two-page résumé would be nearly impossible: the CV is born. The CV is the document to capture all that is expected in the modern academy: teaching and research responsibilities; publishing; presentations; student advising and mentoring; service; and consulting to name just a few. All of this work has a dramatic and profound effect on our economy, our health, our social and educational outcomes, though much of it occurs in forums, venues, and publications scarcely known by the general public.

> *"Academics have the unusual and difficult task of having to make what they do into rocket science for their peers and into basket weaving for the public in an effort to be relevant. There's no way to be 'relevant' to everyone, but you can give them something from which to find relevance. That document is called a CV."*
>
> ~Associate Professor of Economics

The CV as Lifetime Investment

A CV is an academic's perpetual – though forever unfinished – companion: a paper-mate, a scholarly shadow, a constant on your 'To Do' list. At most every major professional milestone and accomplishment, your CV will be there. You'll revisit this old friend regularly to make updates for career and professional purposes, and for the occasional pep talk: those times when the academy makes you feel like you haven't accomplished anything. Just haul out your CV and you'll be reminded that yes, you have accomplished something (or you'll remember that you really need to get to work on more publications). As a grad student you'll need your CV to land assistantships, get funding, and help establish your professional trajectory. Eventually, you'll turn to your CV for help getting a job, landing a speaking engagement, and even getting published. Your CV can get you raises or a higher starting salary, a reduced teaching load, and that multi-million dollar grant. Yep, your CV is potentially worth millions, so don't screw it up. Your CV is an indispensible tool of your academic career.

Your CV is worth millions, so don't screw it up!

For many, the CV is an unknown quantity. Across the pond the term curriculum vitae, or CV, is used to describe what is commonly referred to as a résumé in the United States. Not only are its distinguishing features unrecognized, even its name is misspelled, mispronounced, and otherwise mistreated. Our friends in linguistics fully appreciate the etymology of the Latin word used in its genitive form and translated as, "(my) course of life." The word is often mispronounced, with the accent occurring over just about every possible vowel. The last word, vitae, is often concluded with an, 'uh', 'a', or 'ee' sound. Which one is right? At search committee meetings when one is indeed looking at multiple CVs, it's not uncommon to hear multiple renditions of the plural of the word (which is: curricula vitae) as curricular vitas, curricula vitarum, and we'll stop there. I often wonder if CV, or the singular, vita, isn't often evoked because one's just less likely to mess it up and that's one thing all academics hate…making a pronunciation mistake.

Let's go back for a moment to the translation of the Latin, "course of life." Perhaps, you can appreciate the romantic origin of the expression as it is used in the academy: a lifelong pursuit of knowledge, and the thought that the course of one's life, could be devoted to a singular academic endeavor. It's beautiful almost. Of course, we know a lot more than we did then, and the romantic notion of academy has been replaced with the realistic demands of today's world. It's just much easier to text "CV" than "curriculum vitae."

CV and Résumés Defined

The need for academics to engage in the work of the mind has always come under scrutiny from those outside the academy who recognize the importance of universities and colleges as a training ground for a productive workforce but who criticize the perceived inflated salaries and work hours of its faculty. The CV has most certainly evolved in its most exhaustive and comprehensive forms to fully acknowledge and account for the incredible workload and increasing responsibilities of its owner. More and more college and university departments require that their faculty submit an updated CV annually, documenting the past year's teaching load, research accomplishments, and service to the department, institution, profession, and community. It's not uncommon for a seasoned faculty member's CV to be dozens of pages long, full of presentations, publications, course descriptions, reviews, consulting services, and other professional activities. To chart one's life is to establish a trajectory, to affirm one's commitment to the profession and indeed the institution.

So are there differences between a CV and a résumé? Are academics just trying to sound different or smarter than the rest of us? The answer to both of those questions is, yes. There are substantial differences between CVs and résumés, and yes, though you don't just sound smarter...you are smarter, honey. You deserve a premiere career document with a multi-syllabic non-English loan word. Own it! Work it!

The CV is an academic version of a résumé.

To be completely crude, a CV is an academic version of a résumé that details education and experience related to teaching, research, and service: the mission of the Ivory Tower. A CV, unlike a résumé, distinguishes you as a member of the academy. A résumé is primarily a job-seeking document used outside academe.

Some consider the differences between a résumé and a CV minimal, yet to us they are substantial. CVs are used in academe to describe and detail academic-type accomplishments and accolades. Résumés are used outside of academe and are conventionally shorter summaries of professional accomplishments with the goal of securing a particular position by highlighting functional skills. More academic departments are seeking to hire individuals with substantial and varied skill-sets, commonly in teaching, technology, diversity education, applied research techniques, interdisciplinary partnerships, and, of course those skill-sets related to student success: student retention, program marketing, and career placement. So while the CV has typically been limited to more traditional academic notions of productivity, we're seeing more and more individuals find greater success on the market when their CVs include information that addresses the ways in which the academy is changing to better meet the needs of today's economic, social, and conceptual realities. Here's a quick summary chart.

Curriculum Vitae

Other names:
CV, Vita

Plural:
curricula vitae

Pronounced:
Curriculum vee-tay, vee-tie, or simply vit-uh.

Latin for *Course of My Life.* An academic's résumé or chronicle of everything that one has done in the academy. The distinguishing feature is that the CV is intentionally meant as a professional archive of all work completed related to scholarly endeavors. CVs address academic preparation; teaching, research and clinical responsibilities; publications, presentations, and performances; and service to the profession, institution, and community. A CV is often multiple pages in length, and can have multiple functions beyond job seeking, including: professional archive, obtaining grants and funding, and for tenure and promotion.

Résumé

Other names:
Work History, CV

Plural:
résumés

Pronounced:
reh – zoo – may

Document that summarizes education, experience, qualifications, skills, and functional or special talents as well as other items related to your employment objective. Legitimate entries could include particular coursework, non-academic pursuits, and civic or community activities. Typically, a résumé is one to two pages in length, although this can vary with degrees, life-experiences, and industry-type. Used typically outside academe, and typically only for job seeking.

You might consider posting this conspicuously at home so you "sound" like a member of the academy by using the correct plural of CV!

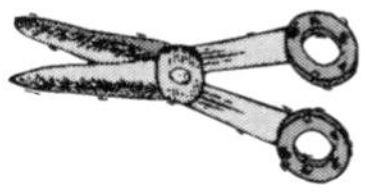

Functional skills aren't the only difference between CVs and résumés. Résumés often include more detail about how the past relates to a particular posted job opening, and past outcomes are made very evident with statements that speak to the job posting. CVs, on the other hand, are less descriptive listings of relevant accomplishments that let the reader make their own conclusions about a scholar's ability. To quote one academic, "You either got it or you don't." You might think, "I let my CV do the talking." And, yes, individuals can have both a CV and a résumé – indeed, most astute professionals do.

Length and other CV Myths (Headaches)

You've probably seen the CV of an advisor or some other accomplished person in your field. Don't beat yourself up if their CV is dozens of pages long: they're using the CV as a professional archive, and that professional archive CV you're seeing probably isn't the same CV that they submit for grant applications, for sabbaticals, and the like. They share this humongous version with you to demonstrate how much work lies ahead and the kinds of work you should be thinking about. Don't worry, though, if your CV in its infancy doesn't amass to more than a few pages. We don't expect that it will.

We're not going to lie, size does matter when it comes to a CV: too big and you'll overwhelm and bore your audience; too small and you'll look inexperienced and unqualified for the position. Unfortunately, too many candidates either leave off all sorts of defining qualifications and experiences or they give us too many details – TMI! If you're getting a PhD or other terminal degree most will assume you fared well in high school, and if you didn't it makes a great interview story, but it doesn't go on your CV. We discuss length before delving into too much detail about content because some folks are so preoccupied with length, that size becomes the overarching mindset. Let it go. Let content determine length.

Let content determine CV length.

The size of your CV is dependent on the amount and depth of your experience. Some experiences are worth writing about on your CV, and others belong in your journal. There are some good rules of thumb with respect to length. If you're writing a CV you're in a discipline that values experience. With that said, many of you, in fact, most of you have had limited experiences in graduate school, so you might feel that your CV's length is inadequate. Remember, it's how you use the CV that counts.

Use your CV as a professional archive and remember to add all relevant details regardless of how significant (or insignificant) they may seem in comparison to your faculty advisor. You are new to this. We know it. Like the seasoned and disciplined academic who takes just a couple of seconds every few months to update with the most recent presentations, publications, course offerings, campus and departmental service obligations, you too should get in the regular habit of updating your CV with important "minutiae" that you might forget or inadvertently leave off when you really are in a crunch to get that CV out the door for that grant application that closes today!

It's an old cliché that sometimes getting started is the hardest part. In the instance of drafting your first or modified CV, that cliché rings so true. Not only are the demands of a graduate program sometimes overwhelming, but many new academics find themselves in the precarious situation of having to draft their first CV on the fly. Hopefully, you're reading this book at a time when you have at least some brain space to give your first attempt your best college effort. Be warned: the first stab at a CV generally results in a night of binge drinking and self-loathing. Most new academics question their relative worth and ability to be successful because their attempts at creating a CV based on some arbitrary standard have yielded little more than a page or two of seemingly meaningless padding. If you feel like this characterizes you, don't worry. For starters, there is no unwritten rule that folks new to graduate school need to have a multi-page CV. In fact, we would argue that *most* new graduate students would be hard pressed to fill two pages with completely meaningful and relevant experiences.

My CV in 3: Why are you here?

Over the course of your professional life, you'll use your CV for multiple occasions with multiple goals in mind. Do you know the immediate purpose of your current CV? Are you reading this book for fun or for a particular goal? Are you on the academic job market? Are you facing a tenure review?

Take three minutes to think about the three most important things you hope to communicate on your CV. Are you hoping to accentuate your activity as a graduate student leader? Maybe you want to highlight your teaching experiences? Maybe you're hoping they pick up on your vast experiences working with international students and scholars? What are the three most important ideas you want your CV to communicate?

1	
2	
3	

The Life of your CV

Search committees, review boards, funding agencies, publishers, nominating committees, your students, colleagues and department chair, even your family! Yep – even your family might find it necessary to use your CV – so make it a good one. There's nothing more embarrassing than misinformation in your obituary. Your CV will pass through the hands of many individuals, even after you pass on from this earth! So take each moment seriously and treat each accomplishment as another excuse to haul out this career companion and update your CV. As your representative, your CV must convey a consistent professional image, whether it is merely glanced at, or very closely scrutinized.

We promise that more with more regularity than Metamucil you'll be in need of an updated CV throughout your career. There's nothing worse than a last minute and rushed CV: updates typically have typos, misspellings, botched dates, missing punctuation, and irregular formatting (our biggest pet peeve). Keeping an up-to-date CV is critical because you'll find numerous occasions to submit a comprehensive or condensed version of this versatile document. You can update and keep track of your CV yourself, or you can simplify the process and use online services like Interfolio to store and distribute your updated CV. Let's take a look at your CV through the ages.

Your CV: BCE (Before Comprehensive Exams)

Your CV is, perhaps, one of the most important documents you will publish throughout your career, and during graduate school, it may be the only thing you "publish." Treat it with care and don't assume that you won't find reason to use it before your job search. Take a look at all the occasions for which you may be asked to share your CV and pay attention to the style tips on making the most of that occasion.

Program Admission

You'll probably use a document that looks more like a résumé to get into your graduate program. Make sure it highlights information that won't be captured on your application form or in your GREs, GMATs, MCATs, LSATs, or any other standardized examination. Did you volunteer at the Beijing Olympic Games? Maybe that was you passing out hot chocolate on NBC during the winter Olympics? What about your summer research experience in South America? You probably took away more from that experience than just malaria. Don't forget to add significant undergraduate accomplishments, student groups, selected coursework, and work experiences. If you're headed to graduate school, there's a good chance you've had some experience in the discipline, or related discipline. Make sure that specific experience is highlighted and don't skip the details. Take this document seriously; it is a search committee's first impression of you.

On that note, if you are applying to multiple graduate schools, consider using an online recommendation letter and application materials service like Interfolio. By keeping your materials organized online, you'll find it easier to submit them professionally and on-time. The last minute rush and chaos during the application process can be much simpler and you'll improve your chances of getting into the program of your dreams when your materials arrive as intended.

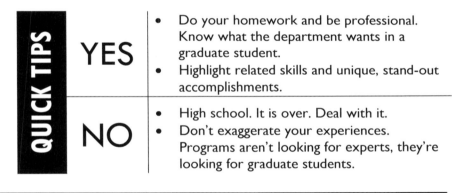

QUICK TIPS		
	YES	• Do your homework and be professional. Know what the department wants in a graduate student. • Highlight related skills and unique, stand-out accomplishments.
	NO	• High school. It is over. Deal with it. • Don't exaggerate your experiences. Programs aren't looking for experts, they're looking for graduate students.

Graduate Assistantships and Funding

Your admissions CV may be useful as you apply for assistantships and other funding for graduate school. The biggest recession since the Great Depression has seriously redefined the funding landscape for graduate students. Funding is tight these days and in some programs, funding goes to those with the best credentials, not necessarily everyone in the program. Your CV can be strategically used to win funding and secure your ability to complete your program. If you are applying for an assistantship that involves research, technology, or teaching, make sure your CV speaks to those respective areas. Don't expect the reviewers to read your mind. Do your homework about the department or funding agency, ask colleagues for advice on the kinds of experiences that would make your CV stronger, then be sure to highlight those and related experiences on your CV. Key annotations should address experiences relevant to the assistantship, be it teaching, research, or program management and operations.

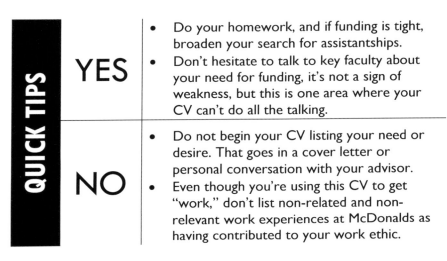

QUICK TIPS		
	YES	• Do your homework, and if funding is tight, broaden your search for assistantships. • Don't hesitate to talk to key faculty about your need for funding, it's not a sign of weakness, but this is one area where your CV can't do all the talking.
	NO	• Do not begin your CV listing your need or desire. That goes in a cover letter or personal conversation with your advisor. • Even though you're using this CV to get "work," don't list non-related and non-relevant work experiences at McDonalds as having contributed to your work ethic.

In these tight financial times, it's also worth mentioning that missing out on an assistantship in the first year or so of graduate school does not determine the rest of your future, although funding is the biggest factor in program completion rates. Do your best to keep your head up. Keep adding good experiences to your CV and something will come to you.

Research and Study Opportunities

Research and study opportunities that enhance your academic credential are advantageous for graduate students to pursue. Many of these experiences are offered off campus or through campus partnerships and frequently a CV is required as a part of the application process. Often a one-page or abridged version is acceptable. Consider adding categories like, "Supervised Research," or "Coursework," to highlight the kinds of research and study you've already experienced, even if it is through coursework as opposed to a paid assistantship. Research methods courses are valuable in many disciplines and some universities have rigorous research methods curricula that will make students of those programs more competitive than students with less background in research methodologies. These opportunities exist in the form of volunteer clinical experiences, mini-grants, service-based learning, and even internships.

QUICK TIPS		
YES		• Do your homework, understand what the search committee is looking for (experience, knowledge, leadership) and make sure it's on your CV! • If a one-page CV is necessary or requested, cut out non-essential sections that aren't directly related to your goal.
NO		• Don't send materials that aren't specifically requested: sometimes candidates go overboard when trying to mask inexperience.

Establishing Your Trajectory with an Annual CV Update

Most graduate programs are rigorous enough to keep students pretty busy, but it's imperative that you are keeping track of everything somewhere, from supervised research projects, to workshops and presentations you have attended, to class projects. It never fails during a CV workshop session with our graduate students that someone exclaims, "Oh I forgot about that!" By keeping a regular and up-to-date archive of your accomplishments, trainings, seminars, classes, and research projects, you'll also spend less time when it really matters getting your CV ready for a particular deadline. As is the case with most application deadlines; they always occur at the most inconvenient times.

> *"You're too busy in graduate school to remember everything. Take three minutes weekly to recap any of the week's accomplishments, or activities that belong on your CV. Those three minutes here and there will really pay off over a lifetime."*
>
> ~Associate Dean, Graduate & Professional Programs

It's not uncommon for faculty to request that graduate students participate in an annual review of sorts (similar to what you might expect as a junior faculty member). At this review, faculty will expect an updated CV to highlight the past year's accomplishments. This helps to establish your trajectory for success in the program and beyond. Additionally, most individuals are required to submit an updated CV in advance of significant program milestones like comprehensive examinations, proposal meetings, and when establishing your dissertation committee.

If you've done your homework throughout your graduate program, an annual or semiannual update of your CV has hopefully been on the to-do list. A regular update to your CV makes your life a whole lot easier when the time comes to prepare a document worth sharing. It's easy to miss important details, one-time presentations, or that obscure article or book review you wrote for that barely known and even less often read graduate student publication. Hey, it's a publication, though, so don't be afraid to list it. It never fails during a professional consultation that a doc students says, "Oh yeah," or, "I forgot about that!" or "I didn't know I could include that," or my personal favorite, "Search committees want to know that?" With particular emphasis on the word "that." Our answer is YES! Just bare it all on your CV, but remember no pictures please!

The immediate use of your first CV will determine the kinds of content you include. If you are required to submit your CV at some point during your first or second year as a graduate student you might feel pressured to stretch your information to make the CV appear larger. Understand that CVs collected at this point by departmental advisors or faculty are truly aimed at gauging your trajectory and assessing the accomplishments of your first year. In this sense, the CV is used to explore your emerging identity as a graduate student and future professional. Benchmarks are good, and we'd be remiss if we didn't mention the tendency for many graduates to extend doctoral studies beyond the typical 4-6 years or the less than 50% completion rate.

Make the most of your CV in its early stages, and establish your professional and scholarly trajectory by considering the following categories and ideas as valuable information on your CV:

- *Coursework*
- *Thesis Summary*
- *Conferences Attended*
- *Research Posters*
- *Supervised Teaching*
- *Research Methods*
- *Clinical Experiences*
- *Meetings Attended*
- *Student Engagement*
- *Workshops Attended*
- *Professional Development*
- *Supervised Research*
- *Departmental Service*
- *Literature Reviews*
- *Memberships*

Your CV: AD (After Dissertation)

Once you near the completion line, your CV will be an important document to help you land your first academic or clinical position. You will need your CV for a whole slew of occasions following your dissertation. You're going to be glad you got so good at writing one in graduate school.

Dissertation Review and Defense

Your CV will likely be required at several intervals in the post-comps period. Of course, you will want to remain a top contender for the departmental and collegiate assistantships and research opportunities that come your way. You will also need to submit one to apply for awards and fellowships which are often geared toward individuals who are seriously working on their dissertation research. These awards are highly competitive, so make sure your CV is as polished and professional as possible. Most committees will also require that your CV be submitted along with your dissertation proposal and at your dissertation defense. Include the terminology, "PhD Candidate" under your PhD program to highlight to individuals that you are post-comp and in the final stages of your program. Your post-comps CV should still include significant reference to coursework of interest, supervised research projects (through coursework), presentations (both on campus and off), and a more clearly defined research and teaching agenda.

QUICK TIPS

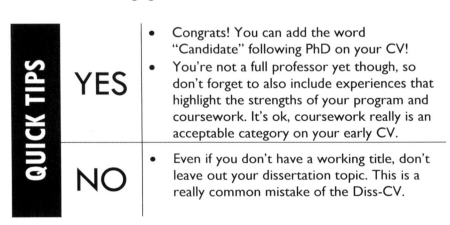

YES	• Congrats! You can add the word "Candidate" following PhD on your CV! • You're not a full professor yet though, so don't forget to also include experiences that highlight the strengths of your program and coursework. It's ok, coursework really is an acceptable category on your early CV.
NO	• Even if you don't have a working title, don't leave out your dissertation topic. This is a really common mistake of the Diss-CV.

Employment CV

Nary an academic job is posted that doesn't require candidates to submit a CV as a part of the application process. It's almost always the first document search committee members will see, aside from perhaps a cover letter. The CV you use for job seeking must be as up-to-date as possible, must be completely flawless (meaning without typos or formatting gaffes), and with all indications that you will be the next professor of the year! Do your homework about the posted position and try as best you can to understand what the responsibilities of the new position will be. In doing so, you are able to make minor tweaks to your CV that will highlight what the employer wants in a new hire.

Although search committees will have certainly seen your CV, never leave for an academic interview without several copies of your CV. Your CV is equivalent to a Wall Street executive's business card. It identifies your pedigree, your promise, your potential.

Your CV will be scrutinized as thoroughly as your dissertation.

Every member of the search committee will examine your CV as though it is your thesis. Since much may have happened since your CV was originally submitted during the application process, make sure your interview CV is updated and reflects any and all of your most recent accomplishments. Not to mention, taking the time to update your CV in advance of your campus visit is a great rehearsal for your interview.

Many institutions require that newly-hired faculty and researchers submit an updated CV that reflects completion of the dissertation and the granting of the doctorate or advanced degree. It is also good to update even if not required so that you have one ready to go once you hit campus (with your new position and employer listed). Once on campus or in your new position you will likely have the opportunity to compete for seed money, grants, course releases, to be appointed to campus-wide committees, and the list goes on. Be ready to present your most professional and accurate self to your new colleagues and, again, don't forget to add your new employer and title to your CV. You made it.

Reference Writers

Share your CV with your reference writers. Most faculty advisors and others drafting meaningful references can do so without too much assistance. Unforgettable as you may be, dates and details are not always correctly recalled. Having your CV at the recommenders' fingertips enables them to write effective letters or to respond to email or telephone inquiries with ease and without hesitation. It's like having Cliff's Notes about you.

Post Appointment CV

It goes without saying that an academic's CV is never done; it's always a work in progress. Your CV is paper job security if you've done it right. Consider the following occasions for which you'll be required to update and submit your CV. Don't forget that we're living in precarious times: public funding for higher education is under assault across the nation. Your CV helps you demonstrate your accountability to various constituencies.

Yearly Merit & Tenure Review

Department chairs are charged with evaluating faculty members yearly for the purpose of determining salary or merit increases. Each institution or even department may vary in what is expected or required but, typically, thorough documentation of all teaching, research, and service activities needs to be provided. As a new faculty member, you will likely be surprised how busy you are with commitments that seem to keep you from what matters most (especially if you're trying to get tenure). This record of your activities (as minimal as they may seem) is indisputably critical to demonstrate on paper what you hope people recognize and know about you off paper, which is that you are 110% committed to the work of the institution, department, and your own research and teaching agenda. Your first years in the academy will be so busy that keeping a good record of your committee work, curriculum development, and early research activities (including on/off campus presentations, publications large and small, and community outreach) is key to substantiating your bid for tenure and promotion.

> *"When you go up for tenure, don't forget that even though you've been here for a while, there may be people reviewing your materials who don't know you, or who are off campus. A well-polished CV is so important to the tenure and review process. We're counting on you."*
> ~Department Chair, Educational Measurement and Statistics

Your college or university will have very specific guidelines for materials to be submitted for tenure considerations. Each department will adhere to mandated steps and procedures. Your CV will demonstrate publications, presentations, research activities, funding, honors, service contributions, and teaching responsibilities. Tenure decisions are typically not only made with folks who know you, though, and remember that provosts, external examiners, and others up the pipeline will review your CV. Make sure your CV is accessible to folks outside the discipline by providing relevant annotations, user-friendly design principles, and a substantial record of work productivity.

Funding Applications

Your CV will accompany requests for internal or external support for research grants or project development opportunities. Funding agencies routinely require CVs from principal investigators, project managers, or for supporting key personnel listed in the proposal. Often, the funding agency limits the CV to one or two pages in length. This requirement dictates that you will need to condense your multi-page CV to a condensed CV.

Consulting

Consulting opportunities provide academics considerable benefits both in reputation and financial terms. Most of the time, faculty are initially recruited because of their reputation or professional network. Not all involved in the project may be familiar with your credentials. If asked to share your résumé you might consider sending a condensed or transformed CV. See examples in CV SAMPLES for more assistance transforming your CV into a professional résumé. Consulting CVs are typically only one page long. Commonly, an overview section provides the audience with a sufficient idea of your areas of expertise. Publications should be shared in abridged format, as should presentations. You can always provide a more detailed list of these items if requested.

Leadership Roles

Nominating committees frequently request background information from candidates seeking office or top committee appointments. Identifying specific leadership opportunities in your department, college, or research community can be an important selling point. Transform the *Research and Teaching Interests* section of your CV to include *Leadership* experiences. The major overhaul of higher education as a result of the near collapse of the market has provided considerable learning opportunities for individuals responsible for the realignment of institutional budgets and departmental missions. Even graduate students, perhaps hit hardest by the transition, have certainly learned a lot about the way we do Higher Ed in the US. If you seek leadership, plan to answer and address these topics and issues; better yet, be proactive and address them immediately in your CV. Leadership CVs should allude to your vision, commonly in a section called *Leadership Skills and Interests*. Save lengthy statements for your cover letter or interview.

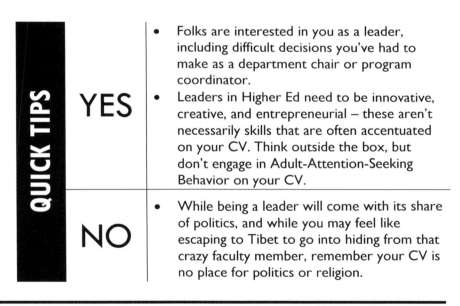

QUICK TIPS		
	YES	• Folks are interested in you as a leader, including difficult decisions you've had to make as a department chair or program coordinator. • Leaders in Higher Ed need to be innovative, creative, and entrepreneurial – these aren't necessarily skills that are often accentuated on your CV. Think outside the box, but don't engage in Adult-Attention-Seeking Behavior on your CV.
	NO	• While being a leader will come with its share of politics, and while you may feel like escaping to Tibet to go into hiding from that crazy faculty member, remember your CV is no place for politics or religion.

Special Accolades

Individuals or selection committees who are charged with reviewing nominations for honors, prizes or special accolades will review your record presented on the CV. Clearly identifying your scholarly and creative record will make a significant difference in how you are evaluated. For their sake, consider removing material that may not be relevant to the particular review committee. A condensed CV is generally sufficient when it highlights your most prestigious accomplishments.

Sabbaticals

As a supplement to required application materials for a sabbatical, submit your CV to document scholarly achievements and requisite competencies. A CV that has been dutifully cared for can offer details not specifically requested as well as reinforcing information that you have provided on required forms. Your post-sabbatical CV should also not make it look like you took an extended vacation at taxpayers' or student tuition expense! Document your scholarly productivity (the reason for sabbaticals) during this period and work to remain active in a verifiable way through annotations and additions to your CV that address publications, book or article reviews, submitted articles, and manuscripts in progress.

Your CV Legacy

Academics continuously update their CV. A publication, presentation, honors, new committee assignment, or any professional development necessitates an update. A continuously maintained draft can eliminate the pressure of hastily reconstructing your professional history to meet a deadline or a special request. Remember, your CV is your lifelong companion. Treat it as such and you'll never have a poorly-constructed CV to blame for a missed job opportunity or promotion.

My CV in 3: Where am I?

For this three minute reflection, think about where you are in your program, career, life...are you still in graduate school or on your way to being tenured? Pick three goals you have for using your CV now or in the near future and jot them down. Maybe it's landing an assistantship, maybe you're going on the market this year, are you hoping to get hired as the Department Chair, Provost, Dean? Putting your goals on paper may help clarify what ends up on your CV.

1	
2	
3	

CV Content

Ask any experienced member of the academy and they'll probably all tell you just about the same few things that should be on your CV: degree information, teaching, research, publications, and service experiences. After those few things are mentioned, there's quite a bit of variance among members of the academy about what truly constitutes relevant information in a CV and which additional information should call this document home. Depending on your discipline, level of achievement, and institution, you'll find all kinds of items are worthy of inclusion on your CV. Here's some advice on the standards as well as some ideas on what else might be relevant.

Part 1: Your Name and Letters

No matter what the end purpose of your CV, the first two basics that everyone reading it will want to know is what's your name, and what are your letters. Letters, of course, referring to the letters that represent your academic identity. You've probably already noticed, that often in this setting on printed or web material, office directories, and even your syllabus, most every academic who's earned a terminal degree, has added a few letters to their names, almost like Jr.'s or Sr.'s. From now on, you're Jane Doe, PhD, or Art Jobs, MFA, or Megan Moeller, DDS, or, U. Will B. Fine, MD. You get the picture. We have lots of fun with those names.

Contact Information

Including contact information seems like a no-brainer for sure but as you thumb through the various CV samples in the back of this book you'll notice that while each CV contains common contact information, there is some variation. Aside from layout, you'll notice that some CVs include multiple addresses, phone numbers, or emails. Some CV samples also include professional websites or blogs that direct the reader to additional information or work samples. Your name and contact information never needs a category header like the other sections. Your name is a sufficient introduction. You should, however, avoid the common mistake of using *ego-sized font* (meaning a font that is significantly larger than the rest of your text).

Always list your full legal name: even if you go by another name in daily life. You can inform individuals of your preferred name upon making their acquaintance. Avoid using nicknames, overly-simplified and anglicized versions of a non-English name (name modification is common among individuals from some geographic regions), or non-English orthographic characters on your CV. It's beyond the scope of this book to get into the sociological and societal implications of this practice, but we will offer a caution that your legal name should be the only name used on your CV. If you are an individual who prefers to go by a different name, just share that with search committees or others when you meet them or in an introductory paragraph of your cover letter.

Some CVs offer cell phone numbers, office telephone numbers, and home phone numbers. Some samples include a campus address and a home address, or PO Box. We recommend you list the phone number and postal address that is most accessible and least likely for you to lose materials or miss calls. Shared TA mailboxes, for example, aren't the best place to receive official correspondence from a potential employer. If you are using your CV for job seeking, it is probably best to avoid using your present employer's address, and instead list your home address. Chances are, you won't necessarily get anything sent to that address during the screening process, but your offer letter will be sent there. Make sure you list an address that you check often.

Your email should be professional and not necessarily associated with your current employer especially if you are using your CV to land another academic job. Privacy in the job search is imperative. If you are using your CV for internal reasons, tenure review or promotion, annual review, or for an assistantship within your department, you can omit the contact information altogether and simply list your name, followed by department, and your internal email address.

QUICK TIPS

YES

- Do provide your legal name at the top of your CV – avoid nicknames, using foreign characters, or ego sized font. Attention seeking isn't a good idea on your CV.
- One address is typical, two are acceptable, and three is a crowd.
- Date your cover letter, not your CV.
- Use a phone number that's yours and yours alone (like a cell phone).

QUICK TIPS

NO

- Never use attention-seeking email addresses (brown nosing the search committee, making reference to your sex life, or other potentially provocative tricks will likely automatically exclude you from serious consideration: smartkitty@email.com futureprof@hotmail.com sexyprof@gmail.com)
- For CVs that are posted to open webpages never list all of your contact information: this is identity theft waiting to happen (academics aren't known for their street smarts).
- If you use a professional web portfolio or website, avoid including personal information and pictures, especially from your honeymoon, or your bachelor(ette) party.

Degree Information

The hallmark of any CV is the section that deals with academic training and educational achievement. It is the one section that, with few exceptions, will always be on the first page of your CV. This section often immediately follows your name and contact information. We are in the business of degrees, so go figure that folks would want to know where you got yours. Not to mention, without that terminal degree – or progress towards it – you are usually not going too far in academe. Your academic pedigree, namely where you earned your credentials, is hugely important to search committees or others who may be making your first acquaintance over a CV. If you have made it this far in academe, even if you are just in your first year of graduate school, someone has decided that you have what it takes to make it through a terminal degree program, that should be assurance enough and you should be proud of that. List your terminal degree even if you are not yet finished or if you have just started a PhD program. Take a look at the samples in the back for how to address your early program status effectively.

"I have to be able to get a sense of what kind of student you were from your CV so I know what kind of teacher you'll be."
~Professor of Religion, Chair Faculty Search

You'll find multiple ways to format this section with regard not only to positioning and page layout, but also the nature of the information that is presented in CV SAMPLES. In all instances, however, two bits of information must be very easy to find: degree and institution. Other information is important too—dates, dissertation and thesis topics, cognate areas, and other areas of interest, so don't rush through this section and leave out some important details. Depending on where you are in a program, or in your professional journey, the needs and value of information in this section changes. Someone just completing their dissertation will certainly want to address this here or in another prominent area on the CV. A fully-tenured professor might decide to remove now-forgotten or irrelevant cognate areas from a graduate program many years in the past. Think about what information is valuable to your identity at this particular moment (related to degree and institution) and include it here.

QUICK TIPS

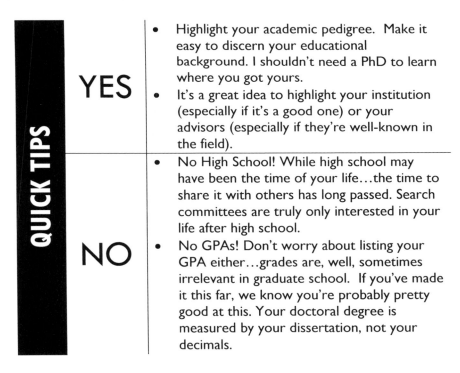

YES	• Highlight your academic pedigree. Make it easy to discern your educational background. I shouldn't need a PhD to learn where you got yours. • It's a great idea to highlight your institution (especially if it's a good one) or your advisors (especially if they're well-known in the field).
NO	• No High School! While high school may have been the time of your life…the time to share it with others has long passed. Search committees are truly only interested in your life after high school. • No GPAs! Don't worry about listing your GPA either…grades are, well, sometimes irrelevant in graduate school. If you've made it this far, we know you're probably pretty good at this. Your doctoral degree is measured by your dissertation, not your decimals.

Part 2: Your Professional Brand

While often a premier consideration in determining your academic credentials is your degree granting institution, individuals interested in making important decisions about you including whether to give you a job and especially whether to grant you tenure will look more at this part of your CV than the first part. It's great that you're smart enough to do this work, and even that you have a clever name, but do you have the work ethic and the discipline to do the work of the academy? It's easy and not all that uncommon for new faculty members to grow a little too accustomed to Post-Dissertation Relaxation Disorder. Part 2 tells us what you can do, and whether you've been doing it.

Teaching, Research, & Clinical Interests

It's a good idea to frame your professional identity by following your academic background with some solid teaching, research, and/or clinical interests/areas of expertise. Many posted faculty positions will list specific areas of teaching, research, or clinical competence that are required or considered highly-desirable among qualified applicants. This is your place to make the claim that you're the next junior faculty member of that department. Likewise, more experienced faculty members may find this particular section of their CV as a useful place to highlight areas of expertise for the purposes of landing a consulting gig. Faculty applying to work in administration, or who are using the CV simply as an archive or promotional tool, find that this section is less necessary, but may instead choose to highlight leadership strengths, philosophies and major accomplishments. A specific section devoted to more precisely defining your academic talents or professional identity is rarely problematic. This also helps focus the reader's attention throughout the rest of your CV on specific experiences that support your areas of interest.

Teaching, Research, & Clinical Experiences

Your experiences form the basis of your unique academic identity. These experiences will likely be the icing on the cake for search committees – the reason they favor you over other candidates – the reason you get promoted to associate or full professor and the reason that you get that assistantship or fellowship you've always wanted. Our experiences, perhaps more than any other information on our CV, have to be formatted in such a way that draws attention to your particular strengths. The difficulty about "experiences" is that it's basically your entire CV! No worries. We're going to break it down for you into manageable chunks so that each inch of your CV is a power-packed punch of academic goodness.

A good way to frame your experiences is to go from broad to specific. Immediately following your academic background and teaching, research or clinical strengths section, you should delve into your experiences that support those claims you made in the section prior. There are multiple examples of this in CV SAMPLES – find one that suits you both in terms of your level of experience and your intended outcome. If you are seeking a faculty position, you'll certainly want to characterize yourself as someone capable of carrying out the mission of your particular institution. Some institutions place great emphasis on teaching, while many others focus (sometimes exclusively) on research. It is a matter of institutional preference: find your fit.

> *"I look to your cover letter to see how you synthesize the teaching and research experiences you have described in your CV, but I usually form an opinion of you the teacher, researcher, and potential colleague based on the experiences you share in your CV. It's always clear to me which individuals don't have a clear sense of what their strengths are because their CVs are all over the place. Tell me a coherent, cohesive story."*
> ~ Associate Professor of French & Director Language Lab

You must also consider the richness of your experiences: you will be hired on the basis of your strengths, not your areas of potential or needed growth, so make sure you remain true to who you are, and highlight those strengths. Teaching experiences should address the kinds of teaching you have been able to do (as a teaching assistant with full recourse over your classes, as an assistant to a big time faculty member, as a guest lecturer at a local community college, etc.). Research experiences should provide sufficient detail about your level of engagement with the particular study or paper. Clinical experiences should certainly include mention of client population, while being sensitive to issues of confidentiality.

All entries, regardless of whether they are teaching, research or clinical in nature, should provide the audience sufficient information (sometimes in the form of annotations) to help you achieve the goals of your CV: to get to campus for an interview, to pass your third-year review, to grant you tenure.

QUICK TIPS		
	YES	• Go from broad to specific: begin with the most relevant and typically the most current experiences you've had. • Always play to your strengths.
	NO	• Never begin with your first job out of high school. No one cares that you were a supervisor on the detasseling squad. If you don't know what detasseling is, you're lucky. • Don't go into boring details and certainly don't be repetitive for each course that you taught. We get it: you taught, graded, and provided feedback (and your students hated you for being the world's most boring TA).

Publications, Presentations, Performances

The expectation that faculty and professionals publish and participate actively in their profession is widely regarded as the hallmark of how our jobs differ from folks who work outside of academe. For most disciplines, publishing in recognized peer-reviewed journals is the modus operandi. We recognize, however, the great variation of what is considered scholarly work among our peers across campus, and how new venues of publication and knowledge-sharing are having a profound impact on scholarly productivity. Take, for example, folks in the fine arts, where recitals, invited performances, workshops, or exhibitions might be the ticket to faculty productivity. Regardless of your area, all major and not so major publications, presentations, and performances should be included on your CV.

You must be familiar with the hierarchy of scholarly productivity. Know what is valued in your field to get a job, tenure, or be promoted. Traditions die hard. Get busy doing what matters.

There are still time-honored conventions of what's considered more valuable and certainly a hierarchy exists. If you are new to this world, it is important that you begin to learn and understand this hierarchy so your hard efforts pay off in the end.

QUICK TIPS		
	YES	• Include all publications, but don't treat them all the same. Create a hierarchy and use subcategories to distinguish between publication and presentation types (peer-reviewed articles vs. newsletters, national conferences vs. local meetings). • Make sure it's very clear what kind of presentation you gave (poster, invited address, etc.). Several candidates have had offers rescinded because of unethically representing their work.
	NO	• If you have been a prolific publisher, you don't need to begin each publication with your name. Just start with the title. If you've published with other authors, be sure to include their name(s) e.g. "with INSERT NAMES." • Don't include work you don't want people to see.

Service

In the modern academy the very notion of what constitutes noteworthy service is in a tremendous state of transition. For a long while, most academic disciplines considered service to the profession and service to the institution the only notable forms of service. In addition, several disciplines placed great value on "consulting" type activities that were provided as a benefit to the recipient. In this model of service, academics were seen (or hoped to be seen) as the experts providing some great insight or knowledge that only they possessed. In today's world, a greater emphasis and value is being placed on the kinds of service activities where the academics are not only "experts" but also participants in the service activity. In this sense, service then also includes volunteer experiences, experiences that extend beyond the academic discipline, or that are not related in the slightest to the discipline but where the personal benefit is the value of having an experience working with individuals one may have not typically encountered in the course of an academic or scholarly pursuit.

Service activities might also include student recruitment efforts, public speaking engagements not related to the academic discipline, service learning type experiences, and other sorts of community involvement and engagement. In this interdisciplinary academy, much can be said for experiences that enrich us as humans and that help connect us to individuals outside our academic cubicles, see the bigger picture, and realize a greater good.

> *"Graduate students should actively begin serving their profession by volunteering at professional conferences, assisting faculty with departmental commitments, and seeking out graduate student leadership opportunities for these are the experiences out of which publications, presentations, and assistantships are born."*
> ~ Professor of Mathematics

Additional Category Headings

Since there is no "industry" standard CV or a "one size fits all" possibility, there are multiple categories and details that can be included on a CV. While the categories we mentioned above are found on nearly every CV, there are certainly occasions when very detailed and specific information is relevant. For example, folks applying for special grants or fellowships to provide for teaching or research opportunities abroad, an International Experiences Overview might be relevant. For individuals applying for grants or seed money, relevant research in the funded area is particularly germane. You may have multiple categories on your CV but be aware that excessive or padded use of categories is not to your advantage.

Sometimes unique skills can be tucked in "traditional" CV sections, and other times, those skills will be highlighted in sections of their own. The CV of a new academic, however, cannot depend upon quantity or cumulative effect to convey the strengths and skills of its subject. The significance of selected categories and their arrangement may be inversely proportional to the amount of experience. Lacking the documentary evidence of extensive experience, it is often necessary to make explicit statements of teaching or research interests and competencies. Bottom line: through intentional and deliberate attention to effectively using CV categories and descriptive content, you'll arrive at your necessary goal.

The following list represents a range of category headings and section titles that one might choose when crafting a CV. Many of the terms represent slightly different ways of saying the same thing, for example, Academic Background and Education. If you are in the process of just getting started with your CV take some time carefully going through the more comprehensive listing found in the CV STYLE GUIDE and make notes of any and all relevant information from your past that can be included. Grouping key activities in meaningful categories draws attention to education, experiences, background and scholarly activities. Take a quick look at the myriad of category headings and identify the ones that *most* represent you and your work.

Academic Background
Degrees
Education
Educational Overview
Professional Studies
Clinical Training
Study Abroad

Research Areas
Teaching Interests
Teaching & Research Areas
Clinical Competence
Areas of Expertise
Consulting Experience

Graduate Appointments
Teaching Assistantships
Research Experience
Clinical Appointments
Fellowships
Non-academic Appointments
Postdoctoral Appointments
Graduate Fieldwork
Graduate Practica
Applied Research Techniques

Funded Projects
Grants
Grants & Contracts
Research Grants
Sponsored Research

Cognate Areas
Competencies
Professional Development
Professional Interests
Proficiencies
Specialized Training
Lab Protocols

Presentations
Publications
Publications in Progress
Papers Presented
Poster Sessions
Reviews
Scientific Papers

Articles/Monographs
Book Reviews
Books
Chapters
Lectures and Colloquia
Conference Participation
Workshop Presentations

Arrangements
Exhibits/Exhibitions
Group Shows
Patents
Performances
Guest Conducting
Juried Shows
Solo & Group Exhibition

Service
Campus Activities
Committee Leadership
Community Outreach
Interdisciplinary Collaboration
Departmental Service
Professional Activities

Blogs
Technical Applications
Technology Integration
New Media in the Classroom

Awards
College Distinctions
Fellowships
Honors
Prizes
Recognition
Special Awards

Affiliations
Memberships
Professional Organizations
Scholarly Societies

International Projects
Language Competencies

My CV in 3: Categories

Take three minutes to jot down the three most important areas of expertise and experience that will become the foundation of your CV. Remember, CVs are built around three common areas of experience: teaching, research, and service. If you haven't had any experience to speak of in one or more areas, are there past experiences that have given you skill-sets consistent with those commonly valued under Teaching (training, developing materials, study abroad and diversity experiences, customer service, group leadership); Research (analytical and experimental experiences, sales, academic honors and awards); Service (volunteer experiences, charity work, student group leadership, organization participation)?

1	Teaching:
2	Research:
3	Service:

The Job-Search CV

The CV that you use for your job search is markedly different from the one you used during your graduate program in terms of both the content and the nature of your formatting. By the time you make it to the academic job market, topics such as coursework take a backseat to the courses you've been actively teaching as a TA. Hopefully, you've taken full advantage of all that graduate school has to offer and built an impressive set of credentials to wow your audience. It goes without saying that we are in a tremendous state of transformation across academe. Some of you reading this book will be applying to large R1 institutions, while others prefer the environment and atmosphere offered at a smaller liberal arts college. Both come with their rewards and challenges. Expect your CV to speak to the unique demands of the institution to which you're applying if you hope to make the final cut.

For those of you hoping to be competitive based on your research experience and potential, make sure that all relevant information to strengthen your candidacy is included. Graduates from large research institutions are at a distinct advantage because of their training. They are able to highlight their research skills immediately in the first section of their CV where they describe their formal doctoral and clinical training at the institution. These candidates might include the following under their academic background section:

- *Institution Name*
- *Program Area*
- *Cognate Areas*
- *Dissertation & Committee Supervisor (Particularly if high profile)*
- *Dissertation Title or Topic*

Additionally, astute researchers will be well aware of the research requirements and reputation at the institution to which they're making application. Consider research areas that might be particularly valuable to the hiring department. Include relevant lab or clinical experiences, and use annotated entries that highlight research skills and lab experiences, clinical populations, or settings which might be advantageous to your application but not necessarily assumed without such description. Take a look at the list of additional category headings that might improve your candidacy if making application based on your research credentials.

Common Research Headings

- *Research Interests*
- *Clinical Experiences*
- *Publications*
- *Lab Experience*
- *Presentations*
- *Supervised Research*
- *Grants & Awards*
- *Submitted Articles*
- *Dissertation*
- *Cognate Areas*
- *Honors/Awards/Fellowships*
- *Research Overview*
- *Professional Associations*
- *Statistical Software*
- *Research Applications*
- *Papers in Preparation*

Folks looking to capitalize on their teaching experience or those who hope to land a position working at an institution that places an emphasis on teaching over research, likewise, should emphasize experiences and interests relevant to teaching and student interaction. We mention student interaction because unfortunately, not all graduate students are able to secure teaching experience before they graduate, but most do have some sort of experience related to or working with undergraduate populations in other arenas. Individuals wishing to highlight teaching experience should emphasize some of the following categories on their CV.

Common Teaching Headings

- *University Teaching*
- *University Experiences*
- *Teaching Fellowships*
- *Teaching Interests*
- *Teaching Workshops*
- *Lectures*
- *Master Classes*
- *Teaching Assistantships*
- *Teaching Responsibilities*
- *Courses Taught/Highlights*
- *Technology Integration in Teaching*
- *Mentoring*
- *Graduates Supervised*
- *Clinics*

Applicants at institutions with a teaching mission should be prepared to demonstrate skills as researchers as well. Rarely are positions posted or filled with individuals who possess only one skill-set. Individuals in these institutions may also be required to fulfill more departmental committee obligations, work as undergraduate student advisors, provide specialized seminars and colloquia, and may even have some obligations to reach out to the community more than their peers at larger research institutions might. Be sure you're familiar with the expectations and culture at the institution to which you're applying. The only way to know is to do your research and ask your advisors and mentors what advice they might have or what they might know about the target institution.

Additional Application Materials

If you look through the pages of the Chronicle of Higher Education, or at their online job bank, you'll notice that just about every institution requests materials be sent, uploaded, or forwarded to the chair of the search committee. Many institutions require that applicants send more than just a CV, cover letter and letters of recommendation. In fact, many institutions require multiple artifacts to represent a candidate's full qualifications and potential for success. Searches are very costly and academic departments and organizations are willing to make a major investment in order to get the right candidate. It's important that you communicate a consistent message in all the materials you send. Start with your CV and cover letter. Are they written in the same or similar font? Do you use the same convention for bullets, dates, naming and numbering pages after the first? Additional application materials, when sent as a part of a complete dossier, should look like they all came from the same store. Have you ever had the experience of getting dressed in the morning in the dark and realizing once you got to work that you had put on both a blue and a black sock? Yes, it's ok for your dossier to be matchy-matchy, in fact, it demonstrates you've got class. Here's a list of additional application materials that you may be asked to submit along with your CV:

- *Philosophy Statement*
- *Research & Teaching Agenda*
- *Service Agenda*
- *Syllabi*
- *Student Evaluations*
- *Transcripts*
- *References & Letters of Recommendation*
- *Research Papers*
- *Writing Samples*
- *CDs & DVDs of Performances & Presentations*
- *Publication Abstracts*
- *Certificates & Licenses*
- *Portfolio of Work (Web, Slides, DVD) (arts, writing disciplines, music)*

Some documents in the list above like transcripts will typically be sent directly to the institution – you can't really make these guys matchy-matchy or you'll do time in jail. But for all other documents that you create, control, and submit on your own, do your best to make it look like they "go" together. Search committees appreciate attention to aesthetics and consistency.

Submitting Application Materials

Read all job announcements carefully and follow directions exactly as they are written. Do not call the committee chair to ask if they accept applications electronically if they request that your dossier be sent to a postal address (good online services can also deliver paper copies for you). Likewise, if your materials are requested electronically or if you are asked to upload to a secure application portal, don't call to see if they accept paper copies. The answer is "No" and you have just lost a job opportunity. It comes up quite frequently during candidate reviews that someone's missing a letter or writing sample, or someone called a million times to check on the status of their application materials, or called to ask seemingly nonsensical questions. Follow directions. You learned this in 4th grade.

The bottom line is this: you've come this far, and after reading this book will have an amazing CV. Don't screw it up by getting sloppy at this stage in the game. Chances are, you're also writing your dissertation, struggling to keep your marriage and other personal relationships a priority, in addition to keeping your undergraduates happy and productive while you're juggling the impossible.

You've come this far. You only have one chance to make a good first impression – whether it's in paper or in person.

If you're like most candidates on the market, you'll be applying to multiple institutions and organizations. Keep your records straight. We recommend making separate folders, either manila or electronic, to store all your application materials. Your CV should remain relatively unchanged regardless of where you're applying, with the exception of the minor tweek here or there to highlight this or that. Your cover letter, on the other hand, should be written to the specific position, addressed to the specific person, and written as if it's the only job to which you're applying. Each year dozens of search committees chuckle when they read a cover letter addressed to another competitive search in the field. Guess what happens to your application if you do this. First they laugh and make fun of you, then they toss your materials in the recycling bin. What if we told you we had a complete solution to this headache?

Using a Credentialing & Dossier Service – Interfolio

In the not so distant past, many graduate colleges and universities offered their graduates assistance in the process of applying for faculty positions. They had a vested interest in this process – the more PhDs they had working in the field, the higher the rankings and reputation, and, quite honestly, the more likely alumni were to give generously to the foundation. The value of student placement with regards to rankings, reputation, and recruitment hasn't changed, but in these austere times, the onus has fallen on the graduates themselves to organize, print, send, and keep records on their applications. That's ok, you can do it, remember you're a smarty pants.

The problem is that many of you, while incredibly intelligent, are a complete mess when it comes to organizational skills. We know this to be true. Remember the crazy life you have: dissertation, family, teaching, work, job-seeking? We get it: applying for jobs, at least until the campus visit, can be kind of tedious, menial (given the heady stuff you have to think about), and prone to disaster. We have an idea. How about giving your job search a spa day? How about letting someone else take care of the dirty work? Let Interfolio help.

Give your job search a spa day; use Interfolio for the management of your dossier materials & breathe easy.

Interfolio is the premiere credentialing and dossier management service. They take care of everything, except writing your CV and cover letter. Interfolio provides a complete document collection, storage, and delivery solution for account holders. Imagine forwarding your entire dossier (CV, cover letter, writing sample, transcript, and, and, and) with a few clicks of the mouse.

There is nothing worse than collecting and formatting writing samples and research papers, and then having your computer crash two days before the application deadline. By publishing your CV and all other materials to the Web via a secure service like Interfolio, you will have access to everything you need, regardless of the time of day, fried hard drives or Internet viruses. You can set up an account at www.interfolio.com, which is inexpensive and will give you peace of mind as you juggle multiple job opportunities and application requirements.

Many of you reading this book will be required to submit confidential letters of recommendation. Interfolio specializes in managing confidential letters for you. Letter writers can submit confidential letters to Interfolio in a variety of ways and then you have complete access to package and send. The only thing you can't do with your confidential letters is read them. It's an absolute life-saver for busy folks like you.

Interfolio is cost effective, professional, and more and more graduates, search committees, and institutions are partnering with them to offer a sleek and easy-to-use application process. To learn more about Interfolio and the multiple ways they can make your life easy (and trust us, you need more of this) press the Staple's easy button and visit Interfolio's website at: www.interfolio.com.

Experienced CV

Earlier in this book, we outlined a number of occasions for which one would need a CV. During graduate school and while on the academic market there are some CV standards and basic categories that must be included, not to mention there are simply fewer occasions when one is required to submit a CV. Unfortunately, not all programs require their graduate students stay on top of it and maintain an ever up-to-date document, nor do all graduate students take full advantage of the myriad opportunities that occur during an academic program (writing grants, seeking a more competitive assistantship, conducting volunteer research). For these reasons, it's important to revisit your old friend once you finish ordering your new computer equipment, hauling all of your old textbooks to your office (nothing says, "I'm smart" like bunches of books lined up on stained wooden bookcases), and sending your first syllabi as Dr. You to the print shop. There's quite possibly nothing more satisfying than adding the words Assistant Professor, Research Scientist, Post-doc and the like to your CV.

Key CV Categories for the Working Prof

Don't wallow in self-jubilation for too long – you have work to do! You need to seriously begin establishing your research and teaching agenda, or that program you promised to start, and those new classes you were planning to develop. Your work is just beginning. Once you're hired, you'll find multiple occasions to represent yourself with an updated CV. Take a look at some additional categories that might be useful as you apply for external grant funding, fellowships, leadership appointments, speaking engagements, and new projects:

- *Grants*
- *Teaching Appointments*
- *Consultantships*
- *Funded Projects*
- *National Boards*
- *International Projects*
- *Collaborative Projects*
- *Research Publications*
- *Research Projects*
- *Research Overview*
- *Advisory Committees*
- *Leadership*
- *Invited Presentations*
- *Faculty Development*
- *Research Presentations*
- *Professional Service*
- *Committee Leadership*
- *Scholarly Works*
- *Editorial Appointments*
- *Campus Leadership*
- *Appointments*

If you need your CV to do the legwork to help you get that big grant, don't forget the lessons you learned earlier in this book: highlight qualifications relevant to the particular institution or organization. For example, a community non-profit might value your service, whereas the National Science Foundation will expect a serious attempt to highlight relevant research. The presiding officer in charge of introducing you at a meeting or conference needs to be able to glance quickly and tell the audience who you are and what is special about you. Know your audience, respect your audience. This also means following guidelines for length. Several organizations and agencies expect a condensed one page version of your CV. We have one-page CVs for you to review in the CV SAMPLES section of the book.

Once hired, you'll find multiple occasions to represent yourself with an updated CV. Stay on top of it, so you can always be on top.

From CV to Résumé

We apologize if you feel like this book has been unevenly slanted to help folks seeking employment in academe. We know, though, that many of you will find work outside of the academy both voluntarily, and, unfortunately, some of you will be forced to look for related positions as a result of the poor academic market. We strongly encourage you to remain as focused and committed as possible when drafting your best job-seeking materials regardless of the audience. You might recall the first paragraph of this book, which poked fun at the name Curriculum Vitae and its obsolescence outside the academy. Academics who find themselves with an opportunity to apply for work outside the academy, or within the academy for non-faculty, non-research positions, should begin the process of transforming their CV into a résumé.

This does not mean returning to the drawing board. With a few simple modifications, you can take your most significant and relevant experiences from your CV and effectively market them to a potential employer. Your new résumé is not, by the way, any less important or significant than your CV: release all guilt or self-consciousness you possess about working outside academe if you happen to feel a bit beaten up by the job search. For fun, let's call this new document your CV-sumé! In the CV-sumé, outcomes are clearly identified and related to the specific job. Great news for you: we have an example that you can use to help you craft your CV into a functional résumé in the CV SAMPLES section of the book.

> ***CV-sumé***
>
> (cee: vee: zoo: may), noun, *A CV in the transition to a résumé. A document that combines elements of the CV and résumé. . "My CV-sumé is going to be useful when I apply for that position in student services."*

Applications outside the academic setting require a résumé. The process of transforming your multi-page CV into a one to two-page résumé is less daunting than you might think. You just have to let go of a few things. There is nothing degrading about using a résumé instead of a CV. Employers outside the academic environment have different needs and expectations. All of this makes sense if you remind yourself that job-seeking documents must be appropriate to the setting and to the responsibilities of the position. Even within the academic world, certain types of positions generally call for a résumé rather than a CV. An example of this might be a position as a student services advisor or counselor. Your PhD in religion is certainly not irrelevant, but your specific teaching interests and experiences, and exact details of your scholarly activities are likely to be of lesser importance than other skills.

> *"Reluctance to make the transformation sends a clear message to non-academic employers: either you're unable to recognize the differences between academic and non-academic environments or unwilling to adapt to the reality of the situation. We like to hire folks who know the ins and outs of the academy, but who also understand that they're not in graduate school anymore nor are they being hired as faculty. They're here to work with students – that's their talent."*
> ~ Associate Provost & Director, Student Advising Center

Whatever academic degrees you hold, if you are seeking a position outside the realm of teaching and research, a résumé can be a better choice than a CV. Simple adjustments may give your CV a new look. On the other hand, major revisions, even a complete restructuring, may be more helpful than a superficial touch-up.

Résumé Transformation Strategies

The easiest part of the transformation process is cutting or deleting information. Because you need to shift the focus from one area, i.e. teaching and research, to another area, like student services, advising, or private industry, the task can be accomplished through judicious trimming/slashing/cutting, all really harsh sounding words, we know. For example, annotations about your research assistantships or your teaching assistantships are an important component of your CV. A simple employment history may be sufficient in a résumé that emphasizes other capabilities or interests. A CV typically lists all publications. Your résumé can be selective, listing only the most recent, most relevant, or most prestigious. If you've presented workshops on technical subjects meaningful only to your peers, you can cover presentations with a summary statement, such as: "presented papers at two national and five regional scientific conferences, 201x-201x." Outside the Ivory Tower, dissertation topics or titles, advisors, research agendas, principal teachers, and teaching evaluations are not so important or even understood.

There are several categories not generally seen on the typical CV that can be important components of a résumé. Let's start with a Job Objective Statement or a Special Skills Statement. Why? Beginning with a statement of your job objective is one way to give your résumé focus and direction. Another option for capturing the reader's attention is to begin with a statement of relevant skills, for example Special Skills and Competencies. If you want to have this category on your résumé, it needs to be at the top. Placing it near the bottom is a space-waster and will often go unnoticed. Unlike a CV, your résumé must abide by the 30 second rule: many employers report that they can tell within about 30 seconds whether they're reading the résumé of someone of interest.

Your résumé has about 30 seconds to convince the reader that you're worth it.

Résumés can include information that is not all academic. Civic activities and community service, usually omitted as irrelevant to academic pursuits, may be of real interest to potential employers. If you are transforming your résumé for small business, education, industry or social service agencies, your civic activities will undoubtedly be of value. As you rearrange and reformat your CV-sumé, you'll want to lead off with your strengths related to the new position. The most important point to remember is that a résumé, like your CV, reflects your education, achievements, accomplishments, skills and your career progression – just miniaturized, condensed, and not verbose. Transforming a good CV into a good résumé will help you promote yourself to employers in specific fields. In the CV SAMPLES section, you'll see a number of examples of professional résumés that can be used in a variety of settings.

It's easier said than done, we know, especially since many of you weren't necessarily planning on applying outside of the academy when you started graduate school last decade, and because many of you view your CVs as the "Chronicles of You," but don't light a match to it. Create a new document that is your condensed CV-sumé, your separate résumé. You never know when you're going to need that CV again.

My CV in 3: CV-sumé

In this three minute reflection activity: 1) define your goal and target career move; 2) pick three things on your CV that already support your qualifications for this position; 3) write down an area of growth or strategic marketing.

1	Desired Position: Notes:
2	My existing strengths and qualifications: 1 2 3 Notes:
3	Areas of growth or strategic marketing: 1 2 3 Notes:

The Digital CV

What's out on the internet about you? Have you ever Googled yourself? What were the top five results that came up? Chances are your search results would yield a mixed bag of both personal and professional information. You might find both a reference and picture to a paper you presented last year at the MLA, and in another, pictures of you at your daughter's school fundraising 5k. In one picture, you're standing next to some of the leaders in your field; in the other you're a disheveled sweaty mess with your daughter standing next to you. Unless you're applying for work in physical education only one picture is relevant given your professional objective, i.e. to land the assistant professor position at your state's flagship institution. Search committee members know we have lives outside of our workday and most of our colleagues will know some details of our personal lives, but the astute job seeker realizes not to mix the personal and professional because there are some in high-ranking decision-making positions who would question a "working mother's" ability to get tenure. Don't jeopardize your future or your career by leaving too much information to the beholder.

"We've moved to an almost entirely online search process. In the beginning there was some resistance. My response: if you can't handle this online application, you probably can't handle the job."
~ Dinosaur Professor, Paleontology

The Digital Application Process

More and more institutions require that candidates submit application materials electronically, including: CVs, cover letters, letters of recommendation, writing samples, teaching statements, and research agendas, among other relevant materials. It's no surprise considering the tremendous number of applicants that any position posted within academe can draw. Electronic application databases allow committees to quickly scan and document the process, providing a greater deal of transparency while still upholding the highest levels of confidentiality in the process. Not to mention, it's just easier to manage this enormous paper trail online. It's actually more likely that you'll be asked to share your CV digitally versus providing paper copies.

Wondering why institutions are going digital? There are many reasons ranging from saving on paper costs to savings on staff time. Here is one example: in the Rutgers University English Department, all faculty application materials were sent to the Senior Administrative Assistant to the Chair. In the past, she has collected a cover letter and CV from each applicant by mail or email, and filed hard copies in a box for each open position. The Assistant says the process for accepting applications was time intensive and paper heavy, especially with a large number of applicants for every search. "We typically receive around 180 applications for each open position, sometimes many more," she says. "If I have three searches going on at once, my mailbox gets extremely full and the boxes of paper become cumbersome."

In the Fall of 2010, the Rutgers English Department used Interfolio for the first time in the search for two new faculty members. More than 260 applicants submitted materials through Interfolio for the first two faculty searches. Once the materials were submitted as PDFs, the Assistant gave faculty search committee members easy access to the web portal.

"With Interfolio, all of the application materials are digital and our search committee can review them in their office or even at home, at any time," she says. "In the past, they had to make time to visit my office and read paper files. The new process is a much better fit for our faculty."

You shouldn't feel bashful about checking in on the other end to ensure your materials have arrived and are on their servers, in their email, wherever that final destination is. This is a completely legitimate thing to do and also provides you an opportunity to connect with a "real-human." Don't try to use this, though, as an opportunity to score bonus points. Be a professional and a good colleague: use these sorts of connections as a way to get the information you need.

Applying for academic jobs in the Digital Age is easier than you think, especially if you're using Interfolio to help you manage the tremendous digital paper trail and dozens of applications.

As you share yourself digitally, here are three critical recommendations:

1 Follow Instructions

- It's not that hard, really, to just follow instructions – search committees and others rely on you to do just that. If they want three recommendations, send or upload three. This really goes for all types of applications, but sometimes with email/online processes, people can get kind of carried away or informal.
- Upload documents with recognizable file names.

2 Share only PDFs of your Documents

- Your CV is a grammarian's worst nightmare. When search committees open your Word document, anything might show up with a green or red squiggly line. Those red and green lines send messages to your brain – ERROR!
- Your CV is formatted to the nines. Glue everything in place with PDF. You'll be grateful you did.

3 Skip Steps 1 & 2 and Just Use Interfolio

- We don't know why this happens, but folks really get nervous when they apply online – maybe it's that lack of seeing the Postmaster throw your letter into the mail bag. Interfolio manages your applications for you, so all you need to do is tell them where to send your materials (all of them – even your confidential letters) for one low price. They put together a nice looking and professional dossier (even with a table of contents- wow, you're an author).
- Save headaches, save trees, save your marriage, and use Interfolio.

ePortfolios and Digital CVs

Internet connectivity has dramatically transformed our work processes. Individuals are accustomed to having information at their fingertips. This desire to have "anything I want, anytime I want," is beginning to transform the academic job search process as well. As search committees look through pages upon pages of application materials, occasionally they'd like to dig a little deeper, or take a few minutes and read the abstract of your dissertation, or view a few of your presentation slides from your recent AERA talk. Guess what – you can do all of this in your Digital CV (also known as an ePortfolio), a hyperlinked, power-packed document (albeit, electronic) where each annotation and entry is linked to the information it represents.

Digital media allows us to create a web of documents and mixed media file types that are connected via meaning, dates, discipline, methodology, and institution. We like the ability to structure information in a flexible and meaningful way. It's what academics do really well and why they make, (well, sometimes) the big bucks. ePortfolios or Digital CVs aren't new. In fact, the predecessor, the paper portfolio, has been a standard part of the academic job search for a very long time (also goes by: teaching portfolio, dossier, research portfolio). Disciplines all over campus have used portfolio assessment to document growth, outcomes, and student products. All that's happened to these materials in the last decade or two is they've been electrified and moved to the web.

We could devote an entire volume to the topic, but for now, let's just focus on the ePortfolio as it relates to your CV. Search committees or tenure and promotion review committees make their decisions, both positive and negative, based on a body of evidence. Your CV, even if you've used the most clever design principles, well annotated descriptive statements, and comprehensive listings, only goes so far in telling your story.

Your ePortfolio adds richness both in content and media variety that is unavailable in your CV.

ePortfolios allow you to provide more information to search committees in a way that's super convenient. Imagine that long list of articles linked to the publications themselves. Or what if your presentation titles fascinate me, but I want to know more than just the titles – BINGO – link them to a PDF version or podcast of your presentation. Your ePortfolio adds richness both in content and media variety that is unavailable in your CV.

Building an ePortfolio or Digital CV

The sky's the limit when it comes to how to design and what to include in an ePortfolio. The first consideration that drives your design is what are the goals of the ePortfolio – career enhancement, learning, job seeking. We're interested in helping you build a tool to supplement and complement your CV, so most of our suggestions will be focused on using the ePortfolio for job seeking, career development, or promotion purposes. With your CV in mind, the information you include in your ePortfolio should enhance the kinds of information you share in your CV. This includes examples of your work that will help make you a more competitive applicant. In other words, your best papers, presentations, and other examples of teaching and research experience are the best sorts of items to include.

Take control of your web identity and build a professional portfolio with Interfolio – it's the first thing search committees see. Nice!

Most ePortfolios use simple web design principles for the presentation of skills, talents and experiences. Since most of us aren't web designers, the best place to start building your own web portfolio is by using a service that provides simple-to-use templates – consistent themed web pages (only go professional please – no butterflies), document storage (since you'll be linking to documents you've created – presentations, papers, etc.), and security. You don't necessarily need to lock down your ePortfolio like Fort Knox, but depending on the kinds of information you have out there, you might want some level of security. Interfolio offers users a professional web portfolio with lots of options and loads of professional tools to help you put your best foot forward. One added bonus of Interfolio's portfolio system is that they use clever page-ranking tools so that you can be assured your Interfolio Portfolio will be one of the first, if not the first, link that pops up when people Google you.

How's that for taking control of your web identity? You can always include your professional web portfolio address on your CV, so that search committees can access your ePortfolio. Committees like the richness, the depth and the breadth of the information they can get out of a portfolio. So what kinds of information should you include? Take a look at this abbreviated list:

- *Publications*
- *Presentations*
- *Performances*
- *Syllabi*
- *Student Evaluations*
- *Lab Protocols*
- *Teaching Philosophy*
- *Expanded Research Agenda*
- *Abstracts*
- *Presentation Slides*
- *Teaching Videos*
- *Lecture Podcasts*
- *Graphs, Charts, Summarized Research*
- *Bibliographies*

Again, we could go on and on about the kinds of "artifacts" that you could use as evidence that you're the next best junior faculty member. The bottom line is that your artifacts have to serve the purpose. If they're supposed to get you a job, don't use your worst paper for your least favorite professor. Use artifacts and examples of your work that you are excited about, that you feel tell your story, and that communicate your passion.

Your ePortfolio and CV should not look alike. Understand these two documents serve different purposes. Long bulleted lists of publications with endless hyperlinks make users wish Al Gore had never discovered the internet. Keep your links simple, use TinyURLs (tinyurl.com) where possible. Some folks even just link the title of the publication or presentation so that they're not staring at an entire page of underlined text. Be careful not to make your professional portfolio a scrapbook. Keep it professional, focused on your career, and avoid the relatively common mistake of getting too personal. There are consequences when that line is crossed. This includes pictures, links to lists of hobbies, poems, and cute fuzzy animals unless your field is Rodentology (sorry we don't have a CV sample for you…yet).

My CV in 3: ePortfolio

An ePortfolio is a powerful job-seeking identity and organizational tool. Interfolio offers users a powerful tool designed to maximize the professional impact of your documents while delivering them in a format that is both fresh and secure. For this three minute CV, take three minutes to think about which artifacts of your professional work would be usable under the categories: Teaching, Research, and Service.

1	Teaching:
2	Research:
3	Service:

CV Ethics, Integrity & Sense

Honesty during the job search and particularly the academic job search is imperative. Consider your career GAME OVER if you're caught embellishing the truth. Colleges and universities are under greater pressure and scrutiny than ever to make sure that the folks they're hiring are who they say they are. After a series of scandals in the early years of the new millennia you can be pretty certain that just about every detail of your application materials – from dates to deeds – will be double checked by someone. Never forget this wise adage shared by a faculty member: "If you crawl out on that branch someone is going to cut it off." Don't go there. There are some trees you just shouldn't climb, and don't forget, academics get paid to be meticulous.

> *"Even the smallest exaggeration can hint of a dishonest individual. Search committees seek colleagues who are trustworthy. If they discover somewhere in the process that you haven't been honest or that you've exaggerated your experiences they may have to immediately remove you from consideration."*
> ~ Director of Affirmative Action Programs & Professor of Art

The academic market has never been more competitive with fewer jobs and more applicants. It's easy to see why folks would want to stretch the truth a little bit just to get noticed. Remember that tree we were talking about: a little white lie here, a little embellishment there and pretty soon you're halfway to the top of that tree. Trust us, when this proverbial tree falls in the woods, everyone will hear it and it is typically the end of your academic career. Misrepresentation of the facts generally surfaces at the most embarrassing time: meetings, conference presentations, and interviews, as well as other occasions where your CV has been shared to some professional end. You've worked too hard to throw it away because you decided to misrepresent your skills. Be honest, be you; it's all you can be.

Of Crime and Punishment

While the CV is not the place to list infractions against the law, it is important to maintain academic honesty and integrity in *all* materials. Candidates can expect to submit paperwork authorizing a criminal background check. Most applications provide some area to list criminal offenses; make sure you're forthcoming with this information at the appropriate time. The time you peed in the bushes outside the student union and got caught by the campus police woman will probably not bar you from getting an interview or even the job. Some colleges and universities have policies in place requiring that the intentional omission of criminal offenses, regardless of the severity, automatically invalidates your candidacy. There are few exceptions to policies like these.

Personal Information on your CV

Some folks simply over-do-it when it comes to the content they include on their CV. Your CV should be as comprehensive as possible considering the desired outcomes of your use: the job search, tenure and promotion, grant funding, etc., but most search committees aren't interested in knowing that you were a member of German Club in high school. A relative beginner usually needs to capitalize on each professional activity within the scope of one's emerging identity as a scholar. Traditions die hard, but a CV is not an autobiography. Not so many years ago, it was standard practice to include date or place of birth, or information about sex, race, religion, spouse or significant other, number of dependents, health, height, weight, or color of eyes and hair, nationality, citizenship or resident status. While this sort of information is often used (perhaps inappropriately) for employment outside the US, it's just plain illegal for employers to request it and just plain silly for you to include this sort of information.

Providing personal information on a CV, including your picture puts you and the employer in a precarious situation. Don't do it.

A CV containing personal data appears either naïve, old-fashioned, or consciously calculated. Regardless of age, experience, or professional status, listing vital statistics is unnecessary, unsophisticated, and usually unwise. Equally out of place on a CV are categories featuring leisure interests; avocations; or political, religious, and civic activities. All of these are irrelevant unless they are somehow connected to scholarly endeavors. Relevance is not constant, however, and while personal information is never relevant, be mindful that your

CV will evolve as your career develops. Items related to teaching, research or practicum experience as a graduate student need to be reviewed and evaluated in light of postgraduate opportunities, responsibilities, service and special activities. Let's face it, once you've been hired, tenured, and settled as a professional, the rules change. Indeed, the entire system of tenure was developed to protect academic thought. We thrive in an environment that encourages discourse, affiliation, and participation in forums that aren't always mainstream. Carefully consider the full ramifications of complete disclosure of identity characteristics that some might use against you: sexual orientation, gender identity, political affiliation, and religious identity, among others. Some will celebrate your identity and some will find it unrelated to the needs of your job. Complete documentation of every activity, interest, participation, or accolade of personal rather than professional interest usually is met with an eye roll.

> *"Candidates who go overboard with personal information during their job search are viewed as unsophisticated. We are facing more scrutiny than ever in the academy to maintain the highest levels of professionalism, civility, and ethical behavior. We need professionals in our ranks who understand context and the difference between the personal and professional and who can represent us well."*
> ~ Professor of Engineering, Chair Faculty Search Committee

Though personal information is sometimes requested and often required on the international job market (outside of the US), we never recommend that you include personal information not related to your qualifications to perform the tasks of the job. This includes: Social Security Number (or other legal documentation numbers), visa status, national origin, citizenship, age, gender, political affiliations, sexual orientation, religious or spiritual convictions, gender identity, weight, height, first language (sometimes called 'mother tongue'), even a portrait may be requested. Since most of this information has little to nothing to do with your ability to perform the job, just remember to avoid mention of it. More often than not, this type of information is used inappropriately.

Licensed Professionals

We live in a world of numbers, codes, and licenses. At some point in the employment process, you'll be required to submit some of this information, which includes: Social Security Number or other documentation of residency/work authorization status, license and certificate numbers for folks in professional programs (education, social work, medicine, law, and other clinical fields), and other types of work related qualifications (permits, clearances, and the like).

Don't be the next victim of identity theft – be smart, be selective, be aware of what you're sharing and with whom!

Wait until this information is specifically requested before providing it to individuals and never should it be listed on your CV. While your CV should be detailed, you can avoid providing enough detail to make you the next victim of identity theft! You can certainly list licenses and specialized certifications on your CV, just don't provide specific numbers, folders, codes, or special identifiers that lead to your license or certificate.

International Applicants

Some institutions now require that candidates demonstrate a legal authorization to work in the United States as a condition of employment. It's best to still save this sort of information for the campus visit or other negotiations. Listing this information on your CV obfuscates the other important and relevant information you have to share about yourself. In academe, anything is possible, and departments will do just about anything to get the candidate that they want, even if that means assisting you with necessary visa requirements (a long – but typically not difficult – process).

> *"Some candidates consider it dishonest to withhold information about citizenship or work authorization and go as far as to list it right away on their CV before we've even had a chance to get to know them. Nowadays, we have to rationalize all of our hires and all aspects of the job offer, including sponsoring the legal work authorization process. We are willing to do it, but give us some ammo by means of a research and teaching based CV, before I have to go dodge the bullets on your behalf.*
>
> ~ Professor of Cardiology, College of Medicine

QUICK TIPS

NO

- NO picture, even if you think your looks will get you the job.
- NO personal information (age, sex, race, sexual orientation) even if the chair is also gay.
- NO information about family, place of birth, children, spouse, or significant other, even if you want to join a play group with some of the faculty members.
- NO physical data (eye or hair color, weight, height, ability status). If they don't want to hire you because of the way you look, do you want to work there anyway?
- NO political or religious affiliations unless relevant to the particular institution.
- NO "personal interests" section. You can talk about your passion as a numismatist during the on-campus interview, take a cool coin then, too.
- NO footers with your favorite Indigo Girls quotes; this just looks, well, immature.

Search committees are searching for your potential and promise on your CV, not your personal details. Not to mention, it's simply illegal for employers to keep personal information about you and most will do all they can to avoid it. Keep the focus on you. Your CV is not your autobiography. Tell employers only what they need to know because biases exist.

We often get the question about how to address significant volunteer and service related experiences that are tied to religious, political, or groups and agencies that offer social advocacy: LGBT groups, women's reproductive health agencies, family planning organizations, PETA, graduate student unions, Greenpeace...you get the picture. It's a difficult question to address, because on the one hand, these sorts of experiences tend to be the kinds of things that we are most passionate about, or that go to the core of our identity. Once it's out there though, it's difficult for folks to parse out you-the-budding-academic from you-the-Greenpeace-advocate. It's also possible to share these types of experiences in person, where we have more control over discourse and context. On a CV, everything is left to the eyes of the beholder; make sure the image of you they get from your CV is one that will take you places.

My CV in 3: Ethics

Scan your CV for information that's not relevant, and double check for accuracy in all information: dates, annotations, position titles and descriptions. Make sure it's the R.E.A.L. Deal: Relevant, Ethical and Accurate, and Legitimate.

1	Do I include non-relevant personal information?
2	Are all of my dates and descriptions accurate?
3	Can I provide legitimate proof of all I list on my CV?

Editing and Feedback

We're not going to belabor this point too much, but the 30 minutes it will take you to seriously go over your CV and cover letter with a fine tooth comb pales in comparison to the missed opportunity for a lifetime of employment in a tenure track position. Would you invest 30 minutes for the prospect of 30 years? We guess most of you answer "Yes," to that question. Don't blow it by skipping this important step. Since you'll likely be one of dozens – maybe even hundreds – of applicants, search committees need quick and easy ways to decide whether you're a Yes, No, or Maybe. Trust us, glaring typos will certainly catch the attention of many-a-member of a search committee, after all, it's what most academics do for a living: paying attention to the details, the minutiae, the obscure.

> *"Understand that we get hundreds of candidates for each position we advertise in English. During each search I am absolutely amazed at the number of candidates with glaring typos in their work. I mean, come on people, we're in English for Pete's sake. We won't go any further with your application materials if they contain typos or are poorly formatted. Like you tell your undergrads, "Proof your work."*
> ~ Associate Professor, English and American Studies

Don't forget: programs, particularly those hiring in tenure track positions, are preparing to make a lifetime commitment to you. On some level, spoken or unspoken, you will become a representative of that program, department, college, or university. If it's a state-funded institution, you might even consider yourself a representative of that state. No matter how you slice it, there's no room for error.

CV Editing Checklist

It goes without saying, but spell check isn't the only guarantee that your CV is set to go. For some of you in the humanities – particularly in the foreign languages – the thought of unleashing a spell checker on your largely non-English document brings back horrific memories of that sadistic 3rd grade grammar teacher who butchered (pun intended) your Language Arts homework with her red pen. Remember that many spell checkers allow you to switch languages. Since English will probably be on your CV, we even recommend just dealing with it, and going through all the red underlined words to see if, indeed, there are any English orphans who might need attention. Even the winner of the national spelling bee makes mistakes.

Pay close attention to grammatical correctness. Newer editions of common processing software now come with the capability to offer suggestions to improve your grammar. This is a grammar checker's worst nightmare, especially on a CV, where you're encouraged to write in fragments (no pronouns please!). That's OK though, because while the statements themselves should be action-oriented (brief descriptions of your abilities), you'll still want to make sure that you're using apostrophes in the right places, and that the most appropriate past tense choice for write is wrote.

CV CHECKUP CHECKLIST			
	Dates (degrees, presentations)		Spelling
	Grammar		References (names, numbers)
	Updated contact information (name, phone, address)		Checked your cell phone voice mail greeting
	Even margins		Page numbers
	Categories begin and end on same page		Relabeled categories if more than a page is necessary

Common Errors of the CV

- Candidates frequently fail to spell check or fact check contact information – your spell checker won't know that you mistyped your email address, or gave an old phone number.

- Make sure all technical names, non-English vocabulary, or specialized terminology is correctly spelled. Languages other than English can be included where appropriate, but if you're applying for work in the US, you should probably provide English translations, or simply use a "translated" CV.

- Dates – there are two areas where correct dates are of the utmost importance: publications, presentations, and degree dates. Many institutions are required to verify the accuracy of degree information on your CV. Don't blow your chances of employment or get started on the wrong foot by having to explain an incorrect date as a typo. It sets up a dynamic that most would prefer to avoid.

- Use consistent punctuation throughout your CV. If your descriptive statements end in periods, make sure that all of them do. If you are using APA or MLA formatting for publications and presentations, make sure that's applied consistently throughout. All entries should have consistent formatting across the entire CV. Know whether your field uses MLA, APA, or other formatting guidelines and use them.

- Double check the information you are providing on your References page. This includes: appropriate titles (faculty can be very particular about their titles, especially as it involves rank), contact information, home vs. work phone numbers (be sure to ask!), email, and other important contact information.

- Most colleges and universities now grant students "permanent" email addresses. It's our experience though, that once you've graduated it's a good idea to make the switch to an email address from a provider who can and will provide consistent service. Of course, make sure your email is some iteration of your name that's professional.

Feedback from Mentors and Faculty Advisors

If you've made it this far in academe, you've probably figured out one indispensible fact – it's not only what you know, but whom you know. Along the way you've probably learned that there are some key players in your development as an emerging PhD and these folks are often the same key players with whom you should be sharing your CV. In an ideal world, advisors and program mentors would require students to submit to an annual review throughout graduate school that requires an updated CV. If you are in a program that doesn't require this, consider making this an annual ritual.

It's never out of line to ask a mentor or advisor or even a close faculty member to take a look at your CV and offer guidance on content and also for suggestions on areas which deserve greater attention in your development as an emerging faculty member. Understand that many faculty are strapped for time these days, and with growing programs, and increased pressure to serve on campus committees, among other professional responsibilities, your faculty might not initiate this sort of progress review. They might also expect you to initiate this type of professional development when you feel ready. Don't be afraid to ask for this sort of assistance from faculty. A yearly review and CV critique session gives them the opportunity to give you instrumental feedback.

Someone might offer feedback on the way your CV looks. If you've used the formatting essentials provided in this book, you can rest assured that your CV at least looks right. The best and most relevant feedback for you is content. Do you look like someone in your field? Do you look like someone your faculty would like to meet and hire? What can you bring to a department? These are all critical questions that search committees want to answer by reviewing your CV.

Does your CV look right? Do you look like someone in your field? Like someone your faculty would like to meet, to hire?

Take faculty feedback as professionally as possible and offer your thanks. Your advisors and key faculty have a vested interest in seeing you through: you are, in the end, a reflection on them. Here are a few more occasions where it's wise to send your CV to your faculty for review.

Grant Applications

Many faculty see it as their role to get doctoral students engaged in a rigorous program of research. The most common way is to involve you in some research of their own. You've probably figured out by now, that grants are key to a successful and vibrant research agenda in most disciplines. In order to secure grants, principal investigators and participants have to provide CVs to demonstrate they possess the credentials to receive funding. Most grant applications typically require a one-page condensed version of your CV (see the CV SAMPLES). Make sure you're aware of the size and nature of the CV that your faculty needs if asked to provide one for a grant application.

Graduate Assistantships/Departmental Appointments

Graduate programs are under increased pressure to do their best to fund – or at least employ – graduate students so they can afford the paper with the PhD on it. Most graduate teaching assistantships or research assistantships require a CV as a part of the application process. Depending on the nature of your position (research assistant or teaching assistant) locate the right CV in this book to help you demonstrate you have the requisite skills to fulfill the duties of the position. Confer with faculty before you apply about the kinds of experiences and strengths they're looking for in graduate teaching and research assistantships. Use the information they give you and make sure you speak to it on your CV. If you're struggling with how to annotate, describe, or validate your past experiences see the CV SAMPLES for tips on enhancing your CV to meet your employer's needs.

Scholarships, Fellowships, and Awards

If your advisor asks for your CV to consider you for a departmental or collegiate award or scholarship, make sure you take some time to update it. Include all relevant "emerging scholar" category entries, including supervised research, relevant coursework, departmental and collegiate leadership, undergraduate awards and honors, papers submitted, course and seminar presentations, specialized workshops and seminars, etc. Don't be bashful; this is an opportunity for you to shine.

Conferences & Professional Association Memberships

If a paper or presentation you've submitted has been accepted at a professional conference, be prepared to also submit, or at least take along with you, an updated CV. Generally, a condensed one-page CV is all that is necessary. Conferences are an opportunity for you to network with potential employers, meet future research partners, and connect to others who share your academic interests. The one-page CV is like an oversized calling card that serves as a discussion guide with important talking points. It's a great reference as you discuss your experience with colleagues. It's also a useful tool to compare notes with other graduate students to see what your future competition has on their CV that you don't.

Commercial Résumé Writers

Consulting a commercial résumé writer is often frustrating and unproductive; in a world of business résumé writers, a CV can quickly become a two-page résumé. Commercial résumé writers aren't always familiar with the nuances of the academy or in the ways in which it's changing, nor are they familiar with the language of your discipline. Save the money on a commercial résumé writer and instead use it to take a much-deserved post-dissertation defense vacation to Trinidad and Tobago, or Toledo.

My CV in 3: Proof it!

This CV in three might actually take you more like 30, but you can break it into three ten-minute segments. Take this time to proof your CV considering the following three most important variables.

1	Are all my words spelled correctly?
2	Are all of my dates and descriptions accurate?
3	Can I provide legitimate proof of all that I list on my CV?

Your Academic Buddies

Some things never change and this is one of them. Your academic references continue to play a vital role in helping you get to where you want to go in this world. While stereotypes of cooped-up professors still persist, collaboration is the name of the game. You'll need to be a good collaborator, colleague, mentor and mentee to make a name for yourself and your research. Using the academic buddy system and keeping dibs on one another for mutual benefit is well worth your while. Keep folks who helped you get this far close to you and thank them for their service to you. They deserve your respect and reverence.

Reference Listing

The last and completely separate page of your CV is a listing of key references. It's a good idea for graduate students and active job seekers to maintain an up-to-date listing of important references the entire time they are in graduate school and on the academic market.

> *"Recommendations continue to be a vital part of the screening and selection process in academe. From undergraduate to post-doctoral levels, written references document academic training, professional abilities, scholastic achievement, and professional history."*
> ~ Associate Dean & Professor, English Language & Literature

Faculty members on the tenure track are often also required to submit the names of professional references who can speak to the scholarly productivity and potential of tenure candidates. Those references must be familiar with your academic work as their sole purpose will be to assess your potential for a positive tenure decision. Job seekers, as well, will want to make sure that their reference listing includes significant and, frankly, expected individuals in their development as doctoral students (advisor, mentor, dissertation advisors, thesis committee members, and sometimes graduate student supervisors to the extent that they've had direct supervision over your teaching or research activities). It's a good idea to highlight the references' role in your development.

Alec Sample
Reference List

Advisor:	*Dissertation Co-Chair:*	*Mentor:*
B.E. Example, Ph.D.	Reed A. Lott, Ph.D.	Ken Duitt, M.D., Ph.D.
Director, Research Labs	Head Executive Officer	Distinguished Professor
21 Academic Triangle	Graduate College	21 Research Center
Any University	Any University	Any University
AnyPlace, State, zip	AnyPlace, State, zip	AnyPlace, State, zip
324.432.5678 (Cell)	304.432.5678 (Cell)	384.412.5678 (Cell)
Be-example@univ.edu	Reed-a-lott@univ.edu	Ken-duitt@univ.edu

Always maintain your reference listing throughout your academic career. It's not uncommon nowadays for titles, postal address, and phone numbers to change with little or short notice. Your dissertation advisor may have just been offered a named professorship which bodes well not only for that individual, but for you as well. The stronger your references' credentials, the better the reference.

Why are names of key references not included in the main body of your CV? For several reasons: let's start with job announcements or postings. Nearly all of the advertisements ask that you submit the names of 3 professional references. (They don't want to search through your CV to find the names, phone numbers and emails of the three individuals you have selected for this particular job posting.) Many candidates will ask different references to speak on their behalf depending on the nuances of the academic opening. With that in mind, you want to have a separate reference listing that you can change and submit quickly.

My CV in 3: References

Regardless of where you are in your academic program or professional life, you should have or be able to name at least three people who, at the drop of a hat, could provide a solid and glowing reference on your behalf. As you consider all that is listed and shared in your CV or that you now know to include in your CV, would the three references you provide here be able to adequately speak to different areas of your CV or would they have a major focus in one area only?

For this My CV in 3, take three minutes writing the names of your references and then think for a moment about what that particular reference would say about you. Are they familiar with your scholarly work? Did one of them serve on your dissertation committee? Which one is most familiar with your exceptional teaching abilities or would be able to provide substantial detail about your skill in the lab? Consider why that particular person is an asset to you as a reference. What would they say about you and why is that important?

1	Name: Asset as a reference:
2	Name: Asset as a reference:
3	Name: Asset as a reference:

CV Starter's Guide

The following reflective activity is designed to help you jump start your first CV. Like the volt of electricity that brought Frankenstein to life, hopefully this quick reflective brainstorming activity will get you organized and thinking in the right direction before you turn on your laptop to begin creating your first CV. Follow the directions and pay close attention to the notes sprinkled throughout these pages so that you get the most out of this activity. Directions are given sequentially, don't skip around. Trust us this works.

> *"Sometimes the hardest part of drafting a CV is getting started. Whatever! The hardest part of a CV is accumulating experiences worth writing about. Quit whining and get to work."*
> ~ Grumpy Old Professor, Religious Studies

1. Get a cup of coffee, tea, diet coke, whatever suits your fancy. We firmly believe that a caffeinated vitae is better than an un-caffeinated one. If you don't use caffeine, water will do. Before writing anything, make sure your pencil is sharpened, or that your pen works...nothing can derail good brainstorming faster than a trip to the sharpener.

2. Complete the following activity. Consciously smile a time or two at a stranger. If no-one is around, try to imagine yourself smiling at you. Good vibes positively impact CV writing...we're sure of it. Write the information that will eventually become the first part of your CV.

Contact Information Starter's Guide

NAME	
ADDRESS	
PHONE	
EMAIL	*Remember to use the professional one!*
PROFESSIONAL URL	

3. That was easy, right? If you're still struggling with that one, take 5 and go for a run/walk/stroll, or do some chair yoga if you're feeling lazy.

4. Complete the first section if you haven't yet. Now let's focus on degrees. The CV SAMPLES will provide you with some guidance on the information that's important here in this section.

Education Information Starter's Guide

UNDERGRADUATE COLLEGE	
DEGREE(S)	
MAJOR	
MINOR	
ACCOLADES	
CLUBS/ASSOCIATIONS	
ACADEMICS	
COURSES OF INTEREST	*The ones that really stand out as memorable learning experiences.*

Repeat this if you've had "multiple" undergraduate experiences but only list places where you've received degrees. The only exception to this is applying for work in institutions where past experiences at 'like' institutions is beneficial (community colleges, small liberal arts campus, large public institution).

5. See, this isn't that bad. You definitely need to take a break, though. Some of you may have had flashbacks to your wild undergraduate days, from which you need a moment of silent memorial to commemorate the best years of your life. Some of you just need an antacid as you remember those wild nights in (and out) of the dorms. Once you've collected yourself and given pause, it's time to turn your attention to your graduate programs. Complete the following brainstorming about your graduate degrees:

GRADUATE INSTITUTION	
DEGREE	
THESIS/DISSERTATION	
AREAS OF SPECIALIZATION	
NOTEWORTHY PROFESSORS/MENTORS	
HONORS AND AWARDS	
COURSES OF INTEREST	The ones that really stand out as memorable learning experiences.

6. Many of you will have more than one Master's degree, or additional graduate degrees or certificates that are worth mentioning. Repeat your brainstorming.

7. Once you've completed a thorough analysis of your graduate education, move on to significant research/clinical and teaching experiences. Start off by listing your strengths. This section can easily become your Teaching, Research and/or Clinical Interests section. This is an important area that adds focus to your CV and helps distinguish your accomplishments for your readers.

Areas of Interest Starter's Guide

MY AREAS OF EXPERTISE	
MY SUBSTANTIAL AWARDS/HONORS RELATED TO THIS AREA OF INTEREST	

Once you've established your audience, namely whom you hope to impress with your CV, you can then determine the appropriate categories that should follow. Pick and choose from the following categories which areas you plan to include on your CV. You may want all of them, albeit in a different order, one that accentuates your particular strengths and goals.

Teaching Experience Starter's Guide

INSTITUTION, COURSES TAUGHT, DATES	
ANNOTATIONS, DATES	

INSTITUTION, COURSES TAUGHT, DATES	
ANNOTATIONS, DATES	

INSTITUTION, COURSES TAUGHT, DATES	
ANNOTATIONS, DATES	

Research Experience Starter's Guide

INSTITUTION, RESEARCH TOPIC, DATES	
ANNOTATIONS, DATES	

INSTITUTION, RESEARCH TOPIC, DATES	
ANNOTATIONS, DATES	

INSTITUTION, RESEARCH TOPIC, DATES	
ANNOTATIONS, DATES	

Research Highlights Starter's Guide

PUBLICATIONS (Peer Reviewed, Non-peer Reviewed, National Publications, Books, Reviews, Chapters Contributed, Newsletters, Departmental & University Publications, Reports)	

PRESENTATIONS (National Conferences, State/Regional Conferences, Panel Discussions, Campus Presentations (exclude coursework), Workshops, Trainings, Research Presentations, Teaching/Research Seminars, Invited Presentations)	
PERFORMANCES, EXHIBITS (Recitals, Invited Performances, Roles, Adjudicated Performances, Major Works, Compositions, Galleries, Exhibitions, Guest Appearances, Guest Conducting, Juried Shows, Invitational, Group Shows, Master Classes)	

Service Highlights Starter's Guide

COMMUNITY (Volunteer, Service Projects, Boards, Committees, Foundations)	
PROFESSIONAL & CAMPUS (Departmental Work, Campus Committees, Associations, Conferences, Elected Posts in Profession)	

Now that you've written a killer CV, love it, protect it and use it! Once the initial hard work is done, you can use the CV over and over again, and update it on a regular basis. Don't forget to store it in a secure location (not just your PC hard drive, we recommend Interfolio) and apply to your dream academic job today.

2

CV STYLE GUIDE

A

Action Verbs

Action words are one way to keep the attention of the reader and to present information in an active voice. Represent your work with a variety of action words. Bonus! You'll be surprised how action words help you prepare for that all-important first interview. It's not uncommon for academics to sound like a broken record. Keep your use of language interesting and diversify your word choice.

Action Verbs

Abridged	Allocated	Bolstered	Compiled
Accelerated	Allowed	Boosted	Completed
Accommodated	Analyzed	Brainstormed	Complemented
Accomplished	Apportioned	Briefed	Condensed
Achieved	Appraised	Budgeted	Conducted
Acquired	Arbitrated	Built	Consented
Acted	Argued	Caused	Consolidated
Activated	Arranged	Certified	Constructed
Adapted	Assessed	Chaired	Consulted
Added	Augmented	Changed	Continued
Addressed	Authored	Collaborated	Contracted
Adjudicated	Authorized	Collected	Contributed
Administered	Balanced	Commissioned	Controlled
Advanced	Blogged	Communicated	Convinced
Coordinated	Directed	Empowered	Examined
Corrected	Discovered	Enabled	Exceeded
Correlated	Dispatched	Encouraged	Excelled
Corresponded	Displayed	Endorsed	Expanded
Counseled	Disproved	Engineered	Expedited
Created	Distributed	Enhanced	Explained
Critiqued	Earned	Enlisted	Explored
Customized	Eased	Enriched	Extended
Delegated	Edited	Ensured	Extracted
Delivered	Educated	Enumerated	Fabricated
Designated	Elected	Envisioned	Facilitated
Designed	Elevated	Established	Familiarized
Developed	Elicited	Estimated	Fashioned
Devised	Employed	Evaluated	Figured

Finalized	Graded	Improved	Investigated
Financed	Greeted	Incorporated	Involved
Focused	Grew	Increased	Issued
Forecasted	Grossed	Indexed	Joined
Foresaw	Guaranteed	Inferred	Judged
Formulated	Guided	Informed	Juggled
Forwarded	Handled	Initiated	Justified
Fostered	Heightened	Inspected	Labored
Found	Helped	Instructed	Launched
Founded	Highlighted	Integrated	Lectured
Fulfilled	Hired	Interpreted	Led
Functioned	Identified	Interviewed	Lightened
Gained	Illustrated	Introduced	Linked
Generated	Implemented	Invented	Logged

Maintained	Motivated	Participated	Prevailed
Managed	Multiplied	Performed	Probed
Marketed	Negotiated	Persuaded	Produced
Maximized	Observed	Pioneered	Profited
Mediated	Obtained	Planned	Programmed
Minimized	Officiated	Podcasted	Projected
Mobilized	Operated	Policed	Publicized
Modeled	Optimized	Polished	Purchased
Moderated	Organized	Posted	Quantified
Modernized	Originated	Prepared	Rated
Modified	Overhauled	Prescribed	Reassessed
Monitored	Oversaw	Presented	Recommended

Reconciled	Sanctioned	Supervised	Transacted
Recorded	Saved	Surveyed	Transformed
Reduced	Selected	Sustained	Translated
Refereed	Served	Synthesized	Transmitted
Refined	Settled	Systematized	Turned
Rehabilitated	Shaped	Tabulated	Tutored
Relieved	Simplified	Tailored	Umpired
Remolded	Solicited	Targeted	Uncovered
Reorganized	Solved	Taught	Updated
Reported	Sponsored	Tested	Upgraded
Rescued	Stimulated	Theorized	Validated
Restructured	Streamlined	Tightened	Verified
Returned	Strengthened	Totaled	Visualized
Revamped	Structure	Traced	Volunteered
Reviewed	Substantiated	Tracked	Widened
Revised	Summarized	Trained	Wrote

A

Annotations: Teaching

The following pages represent sample annotations and descriptors that might be beneficial as you consider ways to describe your experiences. Consider your own formatting conventions be it a bulleted list, short descriptive paragraph, or one-liner when you develop your own annotations. Use the following suggestions to think about your teaching, research, and supervisory experience and remember that there is a good chance someone from outside your field will need to get the general gist of what it is you have to describe.

Think about excellence in teaching in your field. What do the best teachers and mentors do? How have your experiences thus far made you the excellent teacher that you are? Don't even think about cutting corners with your annotations. Describe with purpose and be principled in your annotations. Use specific descriptors from your experience that highlight best practices in your field. Teaching is being transformed by 21st century technologies and colleges and universities are looking for individuals with a skill-set to transform learning and appeal to students in the digital age. Write about it – they want to read it.

Teaching Annotation Samples

- *Taught an introductory language course stressing development of oral and written communication skills. Delivered course materials in blended setting: face-to-face and online instruction utilizing social media. Provided lectures and other class discussions via iTunesUniversity™ as podcasts. Shared handouts and written assignments through class website.*

- *Developed new format for online delivery of course material and used distance learning technologies for class interactions and course management; evaluated course materials and assessment tools and provided assistance to students as well as evaluation of research papers and exams. Started an online hotline to help students with content or technology issues.*

- *Improved student lab experiments through implementation of better methods; assisted in the writing and integration of new experimentation methods into curriculum; administered and graded quizzes as a means to provide regular and consistent constructive feedback.*

- *Tutored students from all disciplines and levels in writing by offering individualized strategies; developed student writing and editing skills; fostered self-editing techniques; enhanced confidence in both first- and second-language speaking and writing; aided undergraduate and graduate students with a variety of writing styles from dissertations to creative pieces.*

- *Created a graduate course that examined historical uses of translation to edify or subvert power relations; assigned readings in the translation studies canon, including Walter Benjamin and George Steiner, Sherry Simon and Louise von Flotow, as well as newer voices in the field. Assigned readings in English; held class discussions in both English and Spanish. Created extra study groups and evaluated progress in oral and written examinations.*

- *Designed an entry-level introductory college literature course; imparted a working knowledge of college-level writing skills, from basic organization to elements of personal style; incorporated formal essay assignments, informal written assignments, quizzes, and exams.*

- *Created Mathlab – an online tutorial based skills review and test prep tool for undergraduate non-majors; supervised online Mathlab tutors and honors students working as interns. Managed fleet of iPads.*

My Teaching Annotations

My Courses Taught:

My Duties:

Student Outcomes:

My Reflections:

A

Annotations: Research

What do the best researchers in your field have in common? What are the strengths of their research? Why are they known as the top researchers in your field – did they discover something, did they invent a new research methodology or approach to analyzing a particular issue? Maybe it has something to do with the way they present their research so that someone outside their field can "get it." Many of you are at the beginning of your research careers, but don't be bashful about characterizing all of your research experience in a way that, at a minimum, communicates that you not only get it, but that you're prepared to carry out an active and productive research agenda. Research looks different across disciplines. Make sure you capture what's most important in your field for your particular audience, be it a search committee, funding agency, or your promotion review team.

Sample Research Annotations

- *Conducted applied research in the area of functional communication training and behavioral persistence; assisted in the development of single case designs and interpretation of data; provided supervision and training of junior graduate student team members; conducted sessions with research participants; study included mixed methods research.*

- *Designed implementation of evaluations of educational programs, with emphasis on tasks such as survey/instrument design; collected data using techniques including interviews, focus groups and surveys; edited data analysis and report-writing.*

- *Worked on validity studies for the WTSL including alignment studies, analysis of ESL standards and state standards; assisted in developing listening and speaking modules for several levels of Language Learning tests; developed listening test specifications and multiple-choice items; developed writing test specifications for scoring rubrics.*

- *Participated in data collection, entrance and analysis using SPSS software on a study investigating the relationship between sleep quantity and academic performance in a freshman dorm population.*

- *Consulted with clients in regards to design, data management, statistical analyses, and conclusions and interpretations; taught several sessions on specific statistical software implementation, including an introduction to SAS, and ANOVA in SAS.*

- *Developed and completed research proposal, while securing all necessary funds for project entitled: Biometrics and Lung Performance.*

- *Investigated with cross-disciplinary team underlying causes of math anxiety and working memory deficit; arranged participant screening and data collection; developed online database and survey instrument; received the TRUE Award for innovation in educational research.*

- *Designed and conducted data collection; scheduled research participants for NSF funded research; assisted PI with literature review and proposal.*

- *Conducted formative and summative evaluations of data using visual inspection procedures, descriptive statistics, and inferential statistics; shared experience at three conferences.*

My Research Annotations

My Research Topics:

My Research Duties:

Research Outcomes:

My Reflections:

A

Annotations: Supervision & Leadership

Who was your favorite boss or mentor and why? What characteristics did you find personally- and professionally-relevant and meaningful? In the modern academy, you'll be asked to fill lots of roles: as a supervisor to graduate and undergraduate students, as a committee chair, and other important tasks necessary for department and university function. Be detailed about your supervisory experiences: include relevant budgets; staff and faculty supervision; administration of graduate students; program and department leadership; and include innovative and effective responses to budget crises, student success, and staff support. Include relevant experiences from your life outside the academy if they are significant.

Sample Supervision and Leadership Annotations

- *Supervised staff of nine professionals: responsible for operational management including budgeting and hiring contractors and online instructors; designed distance learning programs; established program goals and course objectives; managed internal and external lecturers; created reports on new course revenue forecast, cost analysis and competitive analysis.*

- *Observed student teachers, provided feedback and support, and conducted formal three-way conferences among student, college supervisor, and cooperating teacher. Organized weekly seminar, monitored portfolio submissions, and evaluated student progress.*

- *Administered and consolidated data management system of Child Welfare Project (cases, activities, tracking, and feedback mechanisms).*

- *Prepared and disseminated educational and promotional program material; edited and wrote articles and reports for publication and distribution; assisted in management of computer databases operated by the Division; supervised work activities of student employees and other assigned support staff; assigned over 450 Clinical Shadowing experiences to participating preceptors.*

- *Conducted business consulting and fund-raising for start-up companies; consulted on operational management, including: strategic planning, international business development, and marketing.*

- *Worked with senior museum administrators in reviewing policies and procedures, budget analysis, and strategic planning; consulted with curators who deal with more than 15,000 objects and numerous collections.*

- *Directed a community service organization providing emergency services to teenagers; recruited, trained, and managed student volunteers.*

- *Supervised and mentored all new TAs for Introduction to Chemistry for undergraduate non-majors; provided training on lab protocol, instructional methods, and assessment for individuals with minimal teaching background; received Outstanding Mentoring Award for efforts.*

- *Developed strategic plans, raised funds, and directed a non-profit organization that trained college students to teach health curriculum in public high schools lacking health education; supervised the development, management, growth, and evaluation of college and high school sites, including training and managing all program staff.*

My Supervision and Leadership Annotations

Supervision Duties:	
Supervision & Leadership Training:	
Unit Outcomes:	
My Reflections:	

A

Alignment

Alignment refers to text position on a page. There are 4 options in Microsoft Word for the alignment of text on a page: left, center, right, and block style.

Most CVs are aligned to the left. Occasionally, centered category headers provide a nice break between sections, though attention should be given that plenty of white space (with no text) needs to be left between sections so that readers can easily scan for those sections that are most relevant (centered text is more difficult to read than text justified to the left.) Rarely, is text on a CV aligned to the right, the exception being when columns have been employed to help organize blocks of lists. Name and page number, where they occur at the top right hand corner of each page after the first, should also be justified to the right, so that they are out of the way, yet visibly apparent.

Block alignment is the style used throughout this book. Block alignment forms two even edges on both the left margin and right margin of the page by uniquely spacing each word. Block alignment can be effectively used in descriptive areas of your CV, though don't over employ this convention. Rarely is it a space saver.

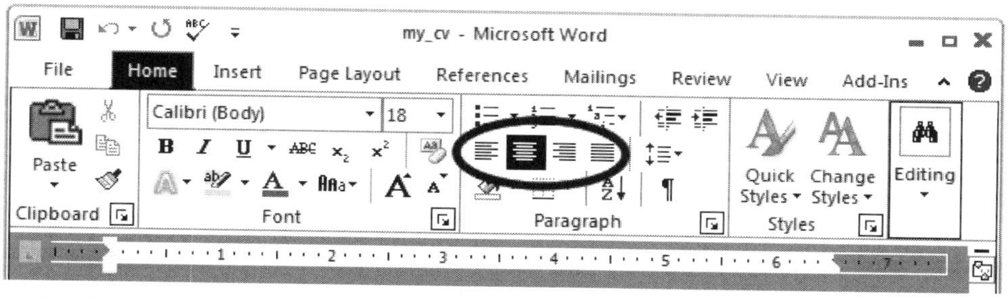

On the home menu, look for the alignment features among the paragraph tools.

B

Borders

Borders add visible horizontal or vertical lines to defined areas of the CV. Borders can also be used to frame entire pages, though we discourage this on your CV. Borders, when used effectively, can create visible breaks between- and within-sections. For example, if you are hoping to highlight coursework in multiple disciplines as a contributing factor in your interdisciplinary work, you might insert a table with visible borders between sections to help your reader understand the multiple departments or areas from which your experience stems.

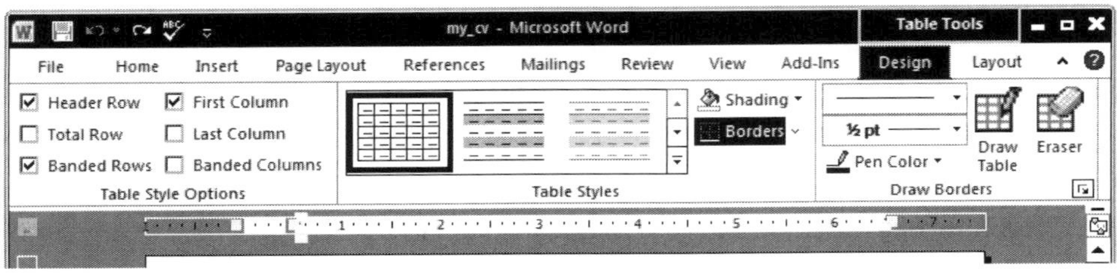

Select the table with borders you'd like to alter. The Table Tools menu appears above Microsoft Word's navigation buttons. Under the Design Tab of Table Tools, you'll find buttons to manipulate borders.

Additionally, the borders shortcut menu, accessible from the Borders button under Table Tools gives users easy access to manipulate elements of the table, including turning borders to non-visible to hide formatting features non-essential to the reader.

In Microsoft Word, the table function allows users to shade and control which borders are visible and the density of the line acting as a border. The term gridlines is also used in Microsoft Word to refer to table borders when set to not visible. Gridlines for formatting are not visible when a PDF is created, though they are still visible when viewing the document in Word. Turn "view gridlines" off when asked to share your Word document. This feature should be skillfully and sporadically employed only when visible breaks positively contribute to the look and feel of your CV. Too many lines and borders can give your CV a busy and unprofessional look.

B

Bullets

Many CVs use bullets to introduce descriptive text and information within a subcategory, but don't be misled that all CVs must contain endless bulleted lists. Indeed, there are multiple ways to organize information and you'll find that many of the CVs and samples within this book don't use bullets at all. One thing we tell our students with great regularity is your CV needs to look like scholar practice, not target practice. Overuse of bullets is counterproductive. Equally counterproductive are CVs that implement non-standard bullets: checkmarks, wingdings graphics or even small pictures. The best bullets are the simplest ones: dots, dashes, or boxes.

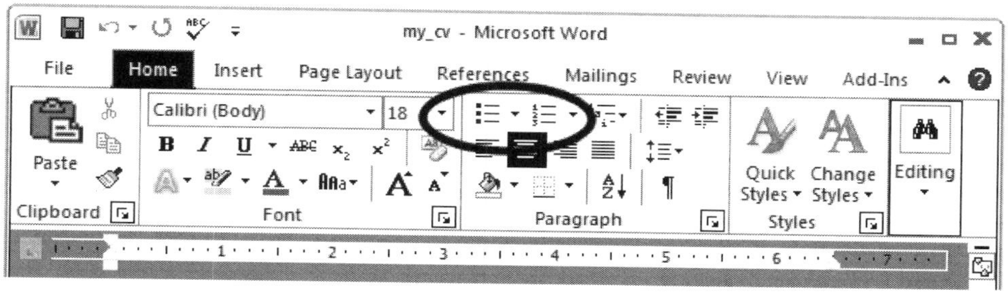

C

Category Headings

CV material is organized under category headings. As we detailed earlier, there are any number of words and phrases that can be used to introduce key CV material. Category headings focus the reader's attention on your qualifications, accomplishments, and productivity. Look at the category headings and find the ones that best fit your information. As you edit and update your CV in future years, your category headings may need revising as well. Remember, the category headings you select for your CV identify and arrange items of importance to potential employers. Category headers can also change over the course of a career so don't feel locked into the original selections.

Category Headings

No two CVs should look alike, but there are a number of categories that disciplines share, and a number that are unique to specialized fields. Find categories that you might have not even considered but might set you apart from the rest of the pack.

Academic Background
Academic Overview
Academic Preparation
Academic Training
Degrees
Education
Educational Background
Educational Overview
Formal Education
Professional Studies
Academic Interests
Administrative Experience
Areas of Concentration
Areas of Expertise
Areas of Knowledge
Areas of Special Interest

Clinical Experiences
Clinical Training
Course Highlights
Educational Highlights
Graduate Fieldwork
Graduate Practica
Residency
Internships

Academic Accomplishments
Academic Service
Administrative Experience
Background
Career Achievements
Career Highlights
Clinical Training
Consultantships
Consulting Experience

Comprehensive Areas
Dissertation
Dissertation Title
Dissertation Topic
Master's Project
Thesis
Academic Appointments
Academic Employment
Academic Overview
Clinical Appointments
Current Projects
Experience
Experience Highlights
Experience Summary
Faculty Appointments
Faculty Development
Fellowships
International Experience
Lectures
Major Teaching & Clinical Appointments
Non-academic Appointments
Overview of Experience
Positions Held
Postdoctoral Appointments

Scholarly Work
Research Areas
Research Interests
Teaching & Research Areas
Teaching Interests
Teaching Strengths

Professional Contributions
Professional Service

Professional Competencies
Professional Development
Professional Interests
Proficiencies
Specialized Training
Scholarship
Technical Applications
Technology Integration
Technology & New Media

Professional Background
Professional Experience
Professional Overview
Professional Summary
Related Experience

Field Research
Research Applications
Research Appointments
Research Experience
Research Responsibilities

Graduate Teaching Appointments
Teaching
Teaching Experience
Teaching Overview
University Instruction

Abstracts
Working Papers
Works in Press
Works in Progress
Works Submitted

Professional Achievements
Professional Development
Related Experience
Research Overview

Reviews
Scholarly Presentations
Scholarly Publications
Scholarly Works
Selected Presentations
Selected Publications
Service
Technical Papers
University Involvement

Workshop Presentations
Arrangements
Exhibits/Exhibitions
Funded Projects
Grants
Grants & Contracts
Grants Held
Group Shows
Patents
Performances
Public Collections
Recitals
Research Awards
Research Grants
Scores
Sponsored Research
Solo & Group Exhibition
Studio Work

Certification
Endorsements
Licensure
Professional Certification
Special Training

Departmental Leadership
Major University Assignment
Mentoring
National Boards
Professional Activities
Advisory Committees
Campus Activities
College Leadership
Committee Leadership
Committees
Conference Leadership

Academic Awards
Activities & Distinctions
Awards
College Activities
College Distinctions
Distinctions
Fellowships
Honors
Honors & Awards
Prizes
Recognition
Scholarships
Special Awards
Honorary Societies

Advisory Boards
Consulting Experience
Convention Addresses
Editorial Appointments
Editorial Boards
Institutional Service
Invited Addresses
Invited Lectures
Lectures and Colloquia
Manuscripts & Research
Multimedia Materials
Patents
Presentations/Publications

Articles/Monographs
Papers in Preparation
Papers Presented
Bibliography
Book Reviews
Books
Chapters
Conference Participation
Programs & Workshops
Publications
Publications in Progress
Refereed Journal Articles
Workshops

Affiliations
Scholarly Societies
Societies
Memberships
Memberships in
  Scientific Societies
Professional Memberships
Professional Organizations

Foreign Study
International Projects
Language Competencies
Language Studies
Languages
Study Abroad
Travel Abroad

Credentials
Dossier
ePortfolio
Letter File
Portfolio
Recommendations
Recordings
References
Writing Samples

C

Color

Never use colored paper or ink colors other than black for your CV. Paper should be standard white and the best ink color is, of course, black. Individuals who attempt to get attention through use of color usually end up getting the wrong kind of attention. As one faculty member recently put it, "Don't they get what we do here?"

Hyperlinks to email addresses, professional web portfolios, or web citations are often defaulted to blue in common web processing software. When documents are submitted online, common sense would seem to dictate that this is a good practice, demonstrating a certain amount of technological acumen, particularly if citations, sample publications, and other relevant information are maintained in a web space that's managed by the candidate. However, these links can be distracting because of the amount of color contrast on a page that continues to be read without intention of leaving the page to view each linked publication, presentation, or past employer. We suggest providing some indication that information is available online if indeed it is and instead use only black on your CV. Even simpler – consider using an online portfolio for links to online information about yourself. Keep your credentials black and white on your CV.

C

Columns

Columns (and rows) in the tables feature of your word processor can be your best friend. You'll find that many of the sample CVs in this book use columns because of the visual way information is organized. In our experience, most readers appreciate an easy-to-read CV, columns help you do just that: create an easy-to-understand visual experience. In Microsoft Word, columns and rows can be inserted via the tables function. Typically, the first column is used for category headers that help orient your reader to the more detailed information in the next column. Usually, just two columns help you create a highly-organized and well-designed CV. Rows needn't be used for each entry within a section.

Within a category, line spacing can help separate individual entries.

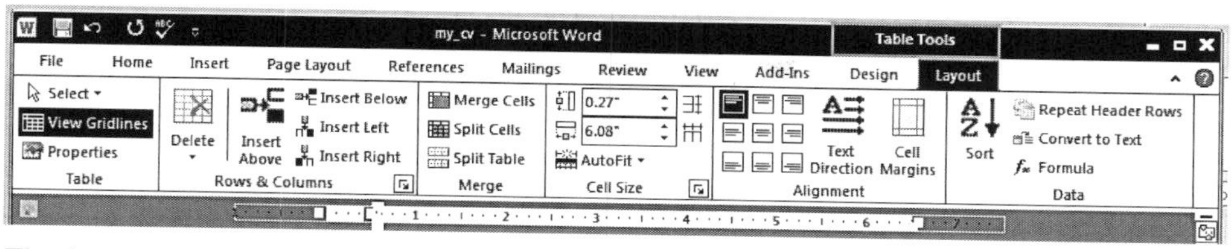

The Layout tab under Table Tools provides quick and easy access to adjust properties of a table, specifically columns and rows.

F

Fonts

Perhaps no other design feature needs as much attention when drafting your CV as does the topic of Font. There are several ways to use font characteristics to effectively highlight and structure information on the CV. Here is a quick look at the many design features you'll find in the samples and the ways fonts were used to create a visually interesting experience on your CV. Which font to choose is probably the most important consideration. You only get one font on your CV – there are lots of ways to play with your singular font to make it look not so singular, but this is one rule of the CV that we won't budge from. You get one font, that's it, you heard us: uno, eins, un. We recommend you pick a relatively standard font, meaning one that you'd recognize from a common list of fonts. Common fonts found in most of today's word processing software (or freeware) come in one of two families: serif fonts, and sans-serif fonts. Serif fonts have additional details at the ends of the letters or characters. Note the difference between the two fonts below. The feet of the Times "A" have much more detail and slope than the bottom of the Gill "A". Likewise, the lowercase letter "b" has greater detail in the Times font than in the Gill font.

Times New Roman (Serif Font)	Gill Sans MT (Sans Serif Font)
Ab	Ab

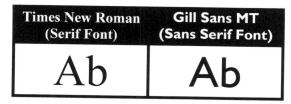

This consideration of fonts is critical to our discussion of CVs because of the way these fonts are read on screens. Modern screens, especially those found in newer eReaders, iPads, and the like seem more forgiving with respect to font choice. Fonts that are Sans Serif (meaning without the extra detail) have traditionally been considered easier to read on screens than are fonts with serif. These fonts also display differently and use line space differently. Carefully selected fonts allow us to make better use of the real estate on our CVs. Additionally, because so much information is shared over the computer these days, one must use fonts that are widely ubiquitous. Not all fonts are installed on all computers and the fonts installed on hand-held devices (iPods, iPads, Cell Phones, eReaders) might be very different than those you used to create your CV. You may spend a great deal of time carefully designing your CV largely focused on layout and effective use of space with your font, but if your reader doesn't have that particular font installed on their machine, there's a good chance your formatting will be lost as the installed software defaults into the next closest font. It's important when saving your document files as PDFs to embed the fonts on the properties menu during the conversion process.

Common Fonts

It's a safe bet that the following fonts will be available on most machines:

Serif Fonts	Sans Serif Fonts
Times New Roman	Calibri
Cambria	Candara
Geneva	Gill Sans MT
Monaco	Tahoma
Georgia	Microsoft Sans Serif
Palatino Linotype	Helvetica
Century Schoolbook	Arial
Bookman	Verdana
Book Antigua	Trebuchet MS
High Tower Text	Lucida Console
Rockwell	Franklin Gothic Book
Garamond	Tw Cen MT Condensed
Bell MT	Segoe UI

While all of the text in the common fonts table was created in font size 10, there are visible differences in how the font uses the space between characters.

The same sized font should be used throughout the CV for both category headings and body text of the individual entries. Minor differences in font size are permissible for stylistic reasons, to bring greater emphasis to category headings, smaller descriptive text, course titles and other citations but, all too often, differences in font size lead to formatting headaches. For this reason, we recommend using different conventions to highlight text: **bold,** *italics,* or different margins to create layers of material that provide for easy scanning of your CV. Take a look at the various ways bolded text has been used in CV SAMPLES to highlight important materials. If you do decide to bold text, make sure you consistently apply the convention throughout your CV, or that particular section, depending on the kind of emphasis you want to make. Italics are a great way to introduce secondary information within a particular entry. Every time there is a change in text type, your brain pays attention to it. This convention is a good technique to differentiate information within singular entries.

Condensing and expanding text provides opportunities to squeeze just a bit more information on a single line, or to space information out a bit more. This convention should only be used when necessary and is available under the Fonts menu on Microsoft Word. Not all browsers will display expanded and condensed text the same way, therefore it's best to use this only with printed materials.

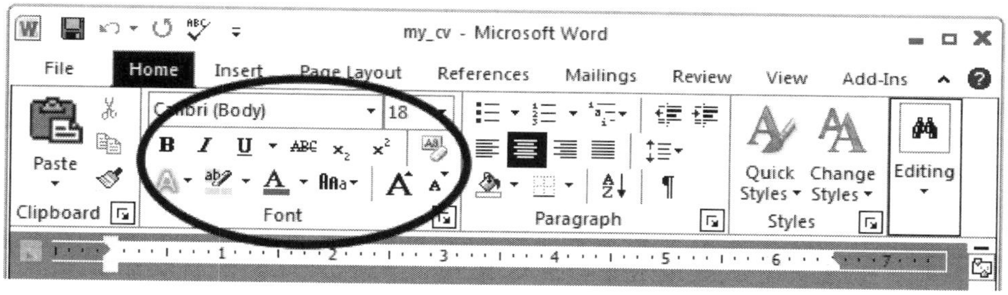

F

Font Size

Standard font size for the main body text of your CV shouldn't be greater than 12, though even that looks big to us. A more common and acceptable size that also provides for better use of space is 10. Smaller fonts typically do better when viewed over electronic media, and don't forget, users can customize and enlarge the size of their view with a few easy user modifications. Fonts that are too big give the appearance of padding. Don't forget that the same folks reviewing your CVs are familiar with all the tricks that undergraduates employ to make a 3 page paper appear like the first chapter of your dissertation. They like adult-sized fonts.

F

Footer (see also Header)

Footers aren't recommended for use on your CV. The best place to list page numbers is in the upper right-hand corner of your CV along with your name. We are accustomed to looking at the top of a page for your name. Forcing committees to look two different places to find your name and page number is just creating more work for them.

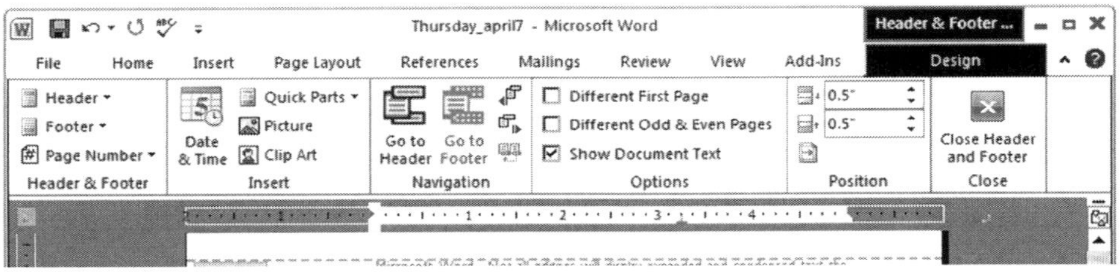

G

Graphics

Save any graphics for the handouts you give your undergraduates or for your PowerPoint, they have absolutely no place on this document and always appear trite. Some candidates think that graphics add to the visual appeal of your page – and certainly they do, when that page is advertising a great talk you're giving or a new seminar you plan to offer, but they are out of place and unappreciated on your CV. Some symbols, like those found on the bullets menu might be used to introduce or break up contact information, lists, or descriptive text and are the only areas where subtle graphic elements are tolerated.

H

Header (see also Footer)

Automating your headers to introduce your name and page number on every page after the first is an excellent way to save you the headache of having to insert them later. To do this, click in the upper area of your page. In Microsoft Word, the Header tab should appear. Carefully select your desired auto numbering location as the upper right hand corner. Also be sure to select the option for a "different first page." The font you select for your header should be no larger, in fact, could be smaller than the body text you use throughout the rest of the document. Make sure the font used for your name and page number is the same as the font you use throughout the rest of the document.

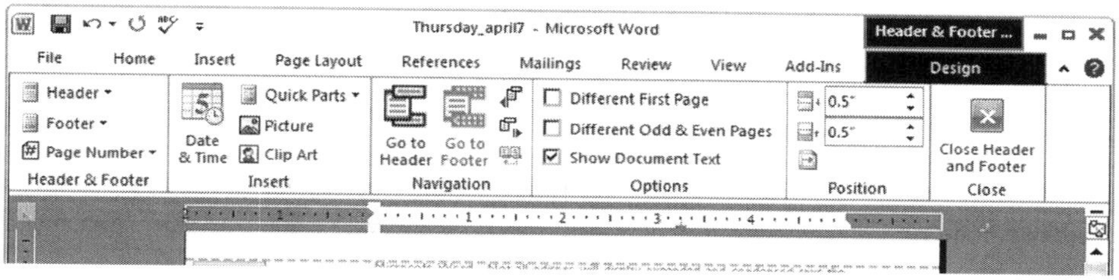

I

Indents

Indents are one way to help differentiate and create information hierarchy within categories to make it easier for readers to quickly scan and understand your information. The easiest way to indent is using the tab key. Indents are often set at the equivalent of about 5 spaces. This is usually a good amount of space. Indents are commonly used to separate degrees from other relevant information like institution, etc. Hanging indents are often used in long lists of publications to separate the first line of a new entry from the other information relevant to that publication. When in a table, hitting the tab key just advances you to the next cell within the table. If you're working in a table and desire an indent, the best way to create indents is on the ruler feature within Microsoft Word.

K

Kern

Kern, otherwise known as character spacing, refers to the amount of space between individual letters. When you open a new Microsoft Word document, the default is normal. Expanded spacing and condensed are the alternates, and as their names imply, one can either expand or shrink the amount of space between letters. While this feature isn't necessarily employed on each CV, it can be hugely beneficial in instances where one needs to sneak a few more words on a single line. Rarely is the expanded text feature necessary on a CV, which is usually already bursting at the seams with information. To adjust the kern of your text, open the font dialog box available from the Home menu. Click on the "Advanced" tab and adjust the Kern by selecting, normal, expanded, or condensed on the spacing pull down.

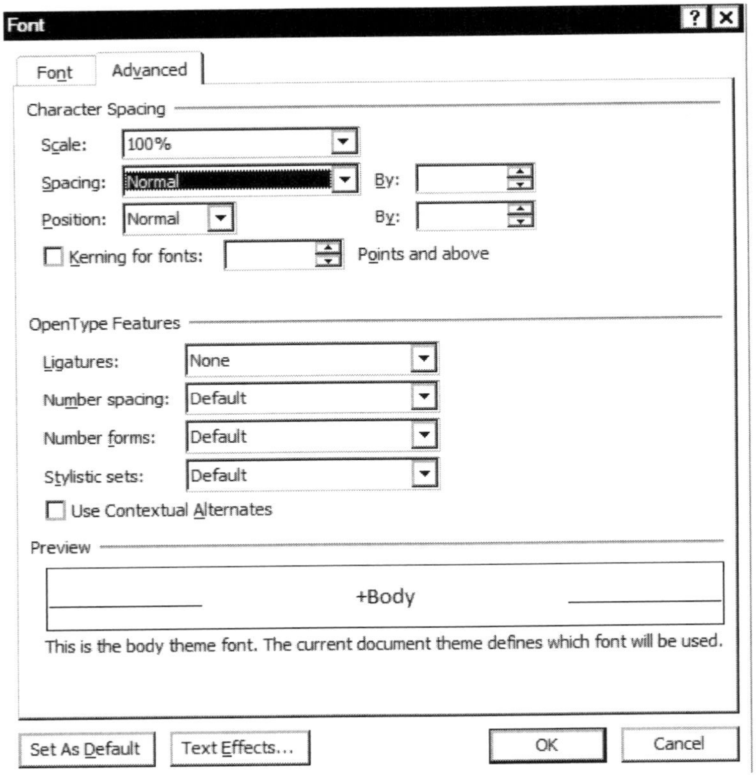

M

Margins

Margins play an important role in the overall look and feel of your CV. Too much extra margin on the top or sides and you give the impression that you're short on valuable experiences, likewise, too little margin and you overwhelm readers with the excessive amount of information on a page. Tools to set and adjust margins are located on the Page Layout Tab. Margins should be set at or near to one inch on all sides. Top/bottom margins and left/right margins should only be slightly different from one another. Balance is an important aesthetic to communicate on your CV.

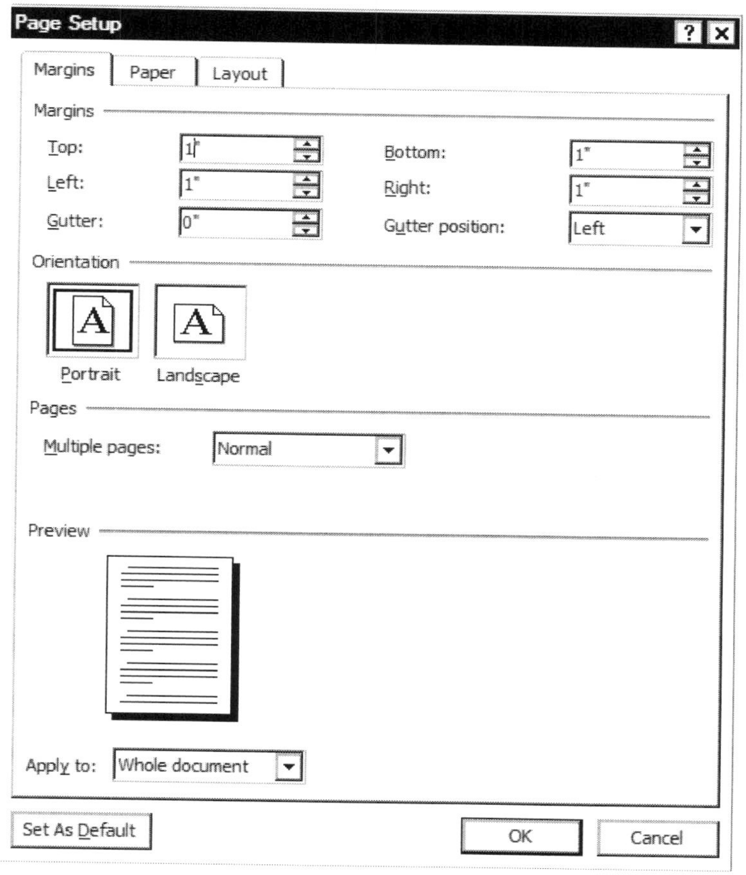

N

Numbering

All pages after the first should be numbered. There's no need to number the first page of a CV. Your name and contact information suffice on the first page. Your name (first and last) should appear somewhere near the page number. It's less difficult for pages to be shuffled digitally (though we have seen this happen), but when faculty reviewers print pages of your CV, it's best to have some tool available (via name and page numbers) should pages of your CV be out of order.

O

Orientation

Rarely do the words "landscape" or "portrait" come up these days when folks talk about orientation, but this is all we're referring to when we talk about this subject. Your CV should never be set using landscape. Use only portrait style, meaning the short side is on the top, with the longer edge being on the sides. Orientation is under the Page Layout Menu in Word.

P

Page Layout

All CVs should be printed and created using a portrait (not landscape) orientation. That means the longest sides of the printed page are the left and right, not top/bottom. Margins should be set to at least .75 inches from all directions (top/bottom & left/right), though we recommend that this be set at one inch. In most instances, your paper size will be the US standard 8.5 x 11 inches.

Again, page numbers should appear in the top right hand corner of all pages after the first. We recommend you include your name alongside the page number so that your page 2 doesn't get confused or mixed up with another individual's second page. It's not uncommon for search committee members to have a hundred or more CVs to review. It's nice to have a reference to your name on each page should pages be mixed up.

Carefully-employed design considerations are imperative. We've heard of the brochure style CV or résumé (Who do these people think we are?), or hanging text boxes all over the place, footers with poems and other quotes…you get the picture. It might be a great quote from Tennessee Williams, but it's just out of place here. Keep your pages clean, aesthetically-pleasing, and well-organized. Categories that extend to another page, need another header or an added "Continued" to orient the reader to your information.

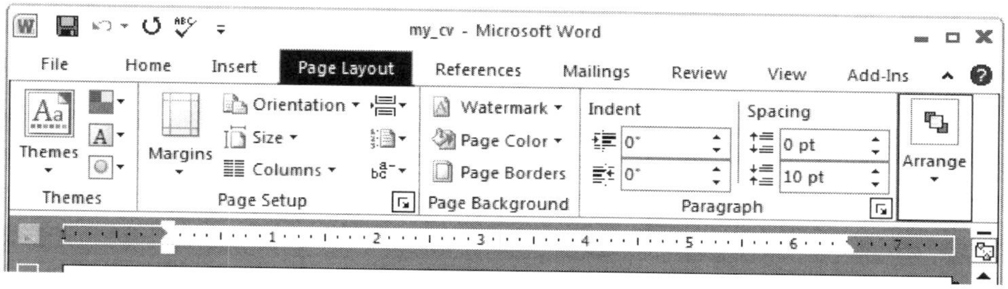

P

Printing, Paper, & PDFs

Probably no other topic related to CV writing is as falsely advertised as the proper paper for CV and résumé writing. Most bookstores have an entire wall devoted to "special" paper that feels more like your shirt than it does the pages of this book. Don't buy into the belief that the heavier your paper the more valuable your CV. Sure, the paper may cost more, but that's not what will get you the job. Your credentials will. Save the few bucks on that paper and instead treat yourself to a nice latte or imported lager after drafting your CV. Our recommendations are easy: go with a simple white paper. You can surely find a standard white 70 lb. at most copy centers.

Printing your CV to mail to search committees or to take along to on campus interviews and conferences is also a topic that should command your attention. Avoid printing on ink-jet printers. The quality is generally not the best and your

CV runs the risk of bleeding should a committee member spill coffee (you know how much coffee we consume here). Ink jets also have a tendency to create visible lines, jagged edges on letters, and long lists sometimes create dust that seems to settle on the paper as a smudge. While a great deal is done online these days, many faculty members still prefer the paper copy to scribble their notes on. Make sure any paper copies you provide are printed on laser printers. If you don't have access to one, visit your local copy center and have them print copies for you.

Many institutions, campus groups, and even private businesses have moved to a completely online application processes, including only accepting electronic documents for academic jobs. Only send PDF versions of your CV and ancillary materials, unless specifically asked for files in different formats. You've spent a great deal of time formatting your CV, don't risk having spent that time in vain when the CV formatting is lost because someone's computer settings are different than yours. By sending your documents as a PDF, you actually provide greater access while not compromising your attention to design. PDFs are also more secure and less vulnerable to accidental changes, deletion, and other mishaps in the same way that other documents types might be.

S

Spacing

Throughout the CV samples, you'll notice instances of line spacing. Frequently a double space is used between various categories and within categories a single space signals the beginning of a new entry. On the Page Layout menu in Microsoft Word, there are all sorts of additional strategies that can be employed, especially to make efficient use of line spacing to maximize the ability of readers to quickly scan your CV for the most important information. For example, readers scan to see if you were the first, second, or last author; what the publication topic was; and journal or publication name. With this information, individuals within a field can assign some sort of relative weight to the publication. This is also true for the Education section of your CV, where readers are primarily interested in knowing where you got your degrees, who your advisors were, and what your cognate area is. With this information they can quickly assess your academic pedigree.

Under the Page Layout menu you'll notice the indent and spacing tools. Indents allow you to create left/right white space and hierarchy, while the line spacing tool allows you to create top/bottom white space. A 3- to 6-point line space is sufficient within a category for adding space without the need to use an full space. This is particularly useful in long lists of performances, publications, or courses taught. An entire line space between each entry seems excessive.

T

Tables

Tables are an absolute lifesaver when it comes to formatting and arranging items on your CV to ensure that all edges line up. Tables are easy to use and, once you get the hang of them, they are fun to manipulate and can actually be used quite intelligently and creatively to capture the perfect formatting or layout of a particular section of your CV. Using a table with several rows and multiple columns gives you versatility later and, when simple formatting is necessary, the tables function has great tools like merge cells, and split cells/table to give you more flexibility. You might use a separate table on each page if you prefer clean breaks or you might insert the entire CV into one table to keep margins, edges and indents consistent.

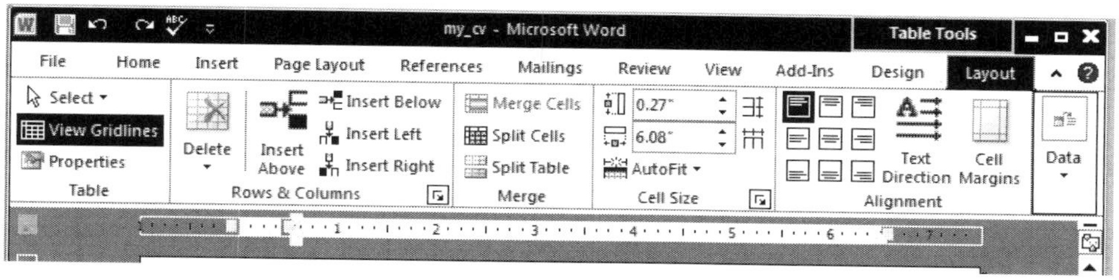

3

CV SAMPLES

Samples

The CV samples were selected to demonstrate multiple disciplines and degrees. Each CV has its own signature or unique qualities: the CV might highlight a special attribute or interest, annotate particular experiences, and/or indicate competencies and expertise that can establish scholarly potential. Inside you'll find CVs for: job seeking, annual reviews, just-in-case scenarios, internships, residency, advanced practica, conference participation, scholarships, speaking engagements, application to graduation programs and tenure review. A *Strategic Features* accompanies each CV. The form outlines key enhancements including layout, design, font, and tips that make that particular CV special.

Many academics find a need to transform a CV into a résumé for opportunities outside of teaching and research positions. Several CVs were selected and transformed so that you can get a good feel of how to take typically large amounts of material and trim it down to one or maybe two pages. If you have decided not to pursue a terminal degree or if you have stepped out of your program, a résumé will be essential for career opportunities. Review the samples provided, along with the corresponding *Strategic Features*, and trust us, you'll know more than most certified résumé writers.

A note of gratitude: A number of graduate students and professionals who we have helped in the past volunteered their CV or résumé to be used as a sample. We all understand how priceless an individual's CV is and we want to say thank you on behalf of all the readers who will benefit from your professional generosity. We dedicate this part of the book to you.

- *R. H. Butler, III*
- *Natalie Ulrich*
- *Anastasia Anthony*
- *Elizabeth Westlake*
- *Evan Meaney*
- *Nirmalla Barros*
- *Leslie Cavendish*
- *Stacey Kerr*
- *Nöel Harmon*
- *LaKaren Rickman*
- *Jess Daley*
- *Florin Opresco*
- *Frank Louis*
- *Stacy Sommerfeld Ross*
- *Anja Apitz*
- *Chris Brus*
- *Colleen Kinder*
- *Aaron Lowen*
- *James J. Jespersen*
- *Meredith Petrie*
- *Zhen Wang*
- *Khadija Bounou*
- *Ekaterina Khmelnitskaya*

How to use these CVs Samples

Make the most of the CV samples in this book by doing these three things:

1 Find the CV from your Field or by Function

- We've tried our hardest to represent the academy to the fullest. You'll find CVs from most major disciplines and academic areas. If you don't see your exact degree program, find a related area and study its contents.
- If you're needing a CV with a special function: for internships; residencies; practica; graduate school admissions; CV to résumé; and a one-page conference CV; locate the CVs by function in the index of CVs.

2 Read the Strategic Features

- Each CV and professional résumé is accompanied by a strategic features page that highlights the specialized design and layout features that accentuate a certain characteristic of the document.
- These design decisions are intentional and geared at helping you more accurately capture and showcase your particular strengths given the goals of the CV.
- Look at multiple CVs to get a sense of various techniques for highlighting specialized skills and talents.

3 Make it your Own and Own it!

- Use the samples in this book to guide the creation of your own CV. We'll be on to you if you start looking too much like Ima Sample or Will B. Goode! Make it your own. You are the only person you can be.
- Understand your CV is just one snapshot of you at any given time, but make it the best you can by carefully implementing our sound advice to make it pop.
- Return to this guide to make additions, alterations, modifications, and to continually adapt to the goals of your CV: be it for job seeking, tenure and promotion, career leadership, funding, professional networking, or other related goals.

We know the work of creating a CV can be time consuming. This document is valuable and worth every second. Don't feel like your time has been spent in vain. You'll be glad you made the investment.

Index of CVs by Discipline

*Represents professional résumés and CVs that have been transformed into résumés.

Index of CVs by Special Use

Admission to graduate school

Condensed versions

Career advancement & promotion

Clinical appointments

Dual programs & interdisciplinary programs

CVs transformed into résumés

CVs for international students/US scholars abroad

Index of Professional Résumés

Résumés by discipline

Résumés by industry & job family

Accounting CV

Strategic Features: Accounting CV

Review this CV if your experience includes assistantships in both teaching and research and you have a successful record of publications and presentations while your dissertation is in progress.

CV BASICS:

Highest Degree:	ABD (all but dissertation)
Experience:	Teaching assistantships Research assistantships
Job Target:	Research universities

CONTENT FEATURES:

- In the *Academic Preparation* section it is clear that the dissertation is in progress, a projected date for completion is anticipated, and a committee established.
- The *Interests* category brings attention to: teaching areas, research competencies and consulting interests. All three areas are requisite for advancement in this field and are included near the top of page one for emphasis. This section says, "I can do it all."
- *Research* is highlighted on page one by employing a unique configuration. The category uses considerable space to combine three essential areas to demonstrate research abilities, publications, and presentations. The same configuration is used in the *Teaching* category on page two.
- Selecting a centered format to highlight category headings draws attention to the content and allows maximum use of the page.

DESIGN FEATURES:

Font:	Arial font, size 11
Margins:	.75" top, bottom, left, right
Layout:	Open new document; use tabs to indent.
Line spacing:	One line space between categories.
Enhancements:	Use of a graphic line to separate categories. Italics and limited bullets are used for emphasis.

Accounting CV

HIREM E. SOON
• 21 University Avenue • Any City, State • 12345 • (201) 565-1111 • hiremesoon@KU.edu

ACADEMIC PREPARATION

Ph.D. **University of Kansas, Lawrence**
Accounting, ABD; Expected completion May 201x
Dissertation Title: Diversity employment trends in international corporations: comparative study of New York and Los Angeles, 1990
Committee: I.M. Riche, PhD (Chair); B.E. Goode, PhD (Co-chair); Will B. Fine, PhD; Kane Howe, PhD; Ken Tanker, PhD

M.A. **Clemson University, Clemson, SC**
Accounting, December 201x

B.B.A. **Clemson University, Clemson, SC**
Professional Program in Accounting, June 200x *with highest honors*
Academic Team: Golf; President's Athletic Award

CPA 201x

INTERESTS

Teaching:
• Auditing • Computer Analysis • Taxation • Financial Accounting • Cost Accounting

Research:
• Political and financial implications of diverse hiring trends in international corporations
• Accounting policies for recession-proof conglomerates
• Bonus mechanisms and salary indices on Wall Street

Consulting:
• Employment laws, trends, and conditions in international corporate environments

RESEARCH

Experience:

Research Assistant, University of Kansas, 201x-present
Responsibilities include conducting research with Dr. Vera E. Goode in two areas: recruitment of minority students into accounting programs (undergraduate and graduate level) and graduate placement rates for women and minorities in public accounting firms. Two publications in press.

Project Assistant, University of Kansas and Governor's Office, Summer 201x
Worked with a team of senior researchers to review auditing procedures used in several state government offices. Prepared a report for the annual legislative session. Met with several elected officials to gather data and to provide on-going reports of the project.

Publications:

Soon, H.E., Swenson, T.T., and Goode, D. (201x) Executive attitudes and hiring procedures. *Journal of Business Education,* 7(5), 38-49.

Mane, W.W., **Soon, H.E.** (201x) An online model for international employment practices. *International Business Journal, 12*(2), 19-24.

Presentations:

"Hiring Practices of the Top 10 International Corporations: A 10 year Analysis." Paper presented at the 21st International Meeting, London, England. November 201x.

"International Students and Corporate Hiring Practices." Invited Address. International Conference, Indiana University, Bloomington, Indiana. May 201x.

Accounting CV, page 2

HIREM E. SOON, PAGE 2

TEACHING

Experience:
Instructor, University of Kansas, Fall 201x; Spring 201x
Responsible for teaching Introductory Financial and Managerial Accounting.
Teaching Assistant, University of Kansas, Fall 201x
Responsible for teaching Introductory Accounting.
Tutor, Business Student Study Lounge, Clemson University, 200x - 200x
Responsible for newly admitted business students with 30 semester hours.

Duties:
Syllabi development, technology integration, course instruction, encouragement of active class participation, individual assessment, student advising, and overall course evaluation.

Recognition:
Of special note: Awarded Outstanding KU Teaching Assistantship Award, 201x
Received outstanding student evaluations in all courses.

SPECIAL RECOGNITION

Faculty Scholar Academic Award in Accounting, University of Kansas, 201x; 201x
University of Kansas Graduate Scholarship Award, Graduate College, 201x
PGA Tour Player, 201x - 201x

CAMPUS SERVICE

Representative, Graduate Student Senate, University of Kansas, 201x - present
Chair, Student & Faculty Roundtable, University of Kansas, 201x
Vice-Chair, Business Student Association, Clemson University, 201x
President, Student Government, Clemson University, 201x - 201x

RELATED EMPLOYMENT

Accountant, Tax Department, State of Nebraska, Omaha, Nebraska, 201x
Responsibilities included the examination of accounts and records and computation of federal and state tax returns. Collected data for analysis of effects of proposed reorganization on taxes.

Programmer, University Campus Center, Clemson University, 201x - 201x (50% appointment)
Responsible for writing application programs in UNIX Operating System. Used technical writing skills, C and shell programming, and relational database programs.

ACADEMIC HONORS

F. Kennedy Scholarship Fund Award, Clemson University, 4 years
B.B.A. with distinction and special honors; Honors Program; Honors Thesis Award
Dean's List and President's List; Convocation Speaker; Phi Eta Sigma

PROFESSIONAL MATERIALS

Philosophy statement, research agenda, teaching evaluations, syllabi, and letters or recommendation available at: www.interfolio.com/portfolio/hiremesoon

Admission CV to Graduate Program

Strategic Features: Graduate Program Application CV or résumé (new degree, no experience)

Review this CV is you are applying to a graduate program. Some applications may request a résumé. If that term is stated, go ahead and use this sample and realize that in this case, the terms "CV" and "résumé" are interchangeable.

CV BASICS:

Highest Degree:	BA Degree
Experience:	Internship experience
Job Target:	Prepared for graduate school applications

CONTENT FEATURES:

- Margin-to-margin layout selected to make best use of space. A second page is not necessary to relay the candidate's strengths and abilities.
- The first category, *Academic Training,* is comprised of four sections: *Degrees, International Study, Language Ability, Honors and Scholarship,* and *Coursework of Interest.* The layout provides the reader with key academic details in one concise category that is easy to read and one that provides a comprehensive picture of the candidate's potential to succeed in a competitive graduate program.
- In the *Coursework of Interest* section courses were selected to demonstrate the candidate's breadth of studies.

DESIGN FEATURES:

Font:	Book Antigua font, size 10
Margins:	.75" top, bottom; 1" left, right
Layout:	Open new document: use tabs to indent.
Line spacing:	One line space between categories.
Enhancements:	Italic and bold fonts used to highlight sub-category headings.

Admission CV to Graduate Program

VERA GOODE

2 The Lodge, City, State 12345 191.567.0321 veragoode@gmail.com

ACADEMIC TRAINING:

Degree:

B.A. Stetson University (Florida), June 201x
Majors: Spanish and International Business Minors: Music and Philosophy

International Study:

University of Alicante, Alicante, Spain, Fall 201x – Spring 201x
College of San Jordi, Barcelona, Spain, Summer 201x
Argentina Center for Language and Culture, Santiago, Fall 200x

Language Ability:

Bilingual – Spanish

Honors and Scholarships:

Norman Wesley Academic Scholarship and Senior Performance Award and Medal
Honors Student and Honors Award, Stetson College of Arts & Sciences
Dean's List, (8 semesters)
Golden Key National Honor Society
University Music Scholarship, 4 years
Cultural Experiences Abroad National Scholarship
Kappa Alpha Theta Regional Scholarship

Coursework of Interest:

Spanish Civilization	Existentialist Philosophy	Statistics
Philosophy of Law	Spanish American Poetry	Computer Analysis
Music Composition I & II	Macro Economics	International Marketing

BUSINESS INTERNSHIP:

Intern, Visual Merchandising; Ralph Lauren, Inc. New York, New York.
September 201x – June 201x (placement in Los Angeles)

HONORS PROJECT AND SENIOR PAPER:

Politics, Family, and Financial Capital in Emerging Economies in Central America-1930's
Supervised by Dr. Red Ponton, DEO, School of Business Administration, 201x
(Publication in press) Presented paper at Campus Scholar's Recognition, May 201x

SERVICE:

Campus

President, Stetson Student Business Council, 201x-201x
Member, Campus Election Committee (201x); Campus Census Surveyor, 201x

Community

Volunteer firefighter, Lone Tree; Bell Ringer, Salvation Army; Red Cross Caller

Admission CV to Graduate Program

Strategic Features: Doctoral Program Application CV or résumé (with experience)

Review this CV is you are applying to an advanced graduate program. Some applications may request a résumé. Multipage CVs and résumés are acceptable for admission to graduate programs.

CV BASICS:

Highest Degree:	MBA
Experience:	International business experience
Job Target:	Prepared for PhD applications

CONTENT FEATURES:

- Margin-to-margin layout selected to make best use of space.
- The first category, *Academic Training,* is comprised of four sections: *Degrees, International Study, Honors and Scholarship, and Coursework of Interest.* The layout provides the reader with key academic details in one concise category that is easy to read and that provides a comprehensive picture of the candidate's potential to succeed in a competitive doctoral program.
- On page two, specific annotations are included about international work experience because the focus of the doctoral program is "international business."

DESIGN FEATURES:

Font:	Book Antigua font, size 10
Margins:	.75" top, bottom; 1" left, right
Layout:	Open new document; use tabs to indent.
Line spacing:	One line space between categories.
Enhancements:	Italic and bold font to highlight sub-category headings. Bullets on page 2 are used for organizational purposes.

Admission CV to Graduate Program

VERA GOODE

2 The Lodge, City, State 12345 191.567.0321 veragoode@gmail.com

ACADEMIC TRAINING:

Degrees:

MBA University of Chicago, May 201x
Emphasis: International Business and Marketing

B.A. Stetson University (DeLand, Florida), June 201x
Majors: Spanish and International Business Minors: Music and Philosophy

International Study:

University of Alicante, Alicante, Spain, Fall 201x – Spring 201x
College of San Jordi, Barcelona, Spain, Summer 201x
Argentina Center for Language and Culture, Santiago, Fall 200x

Honors and Scholarships:

Norman Wesley Academic Scholarship and Senior Performance Award and Medal
Honors Student and Honors Award, Stetson College of Arts & Sciences
Dean's List, (8 semesters)
Golden Key National Honor Society
University Music Scholarship, 4 years
Cultural Experiences Abroad National Scholarship for Language Experience
President, Stetson Student Business Council

Coursework of Interest:

International Marketing	Politics and Marketing	Banking Policies
Finance	Calculus II	Accounting I-III
Marketing & Law	Macro Economics	C++

PROFILE:

Professional Certification: Association of National Advertisers Certification
Language Ability: Bilingual – Spanish
Employment: Global and domestic business experience with expertise in marketing, merchandising, and international business.

INDUSTRY EXPERIENCE:

Advance Holdings, New York and London, January 200x – present
Competitive Intelligence Marketing Manager
New York Corporate Office, 201x – present
London Office, 200x-201x

Designs International & Worldwide, Chicago, January 200x – December 200x
Senior International Marketing Analyst, Latin America, June 200x – May 200x
Volunteer Corporate Spanish Instructor, June 200x – June 200x
Merchandise Distribution Analyst, January 200x – June 200x

Admission CV to Graduate Program, page 2

Vera Goode, page 2

INDUSTRY EXPERIENCE RESPONSIBILITIES:

International Marketing

- Co-manage Sentra and Sentra International advertising agency. Develop and implement creative and media strategies, plans and execution of campaigns, promotions and events.
- Project manager for all promotional development and execution including purchasing, print buying, logistics, customs and budget management.
- Manage integrated customer calendar, tracking seasonal and annual promotional planning and execution. Analyze promotional success including product, media, traffic, ROI and incremental sales.
- Assist Director of International Retail Marketing with annual and seasonal brand and media planning and strategy development, Latin American quarterly marketing board presentations, agency management and evaluation, breast cancer awareness cause marketing program, and grassroots events.
- Travel and work in markets (Guatemala, El Salvador, Honduras, Nicaragua, Costa Rica, Panama, Trinidad, Dominican Republic and Ecuador) to gain greater understanding of the competitive landscape, market trends/opportunities, and customer/associate needs.
- Collaborate with country managers to educate and execute strategies and promotions. Use Spanish to bridge communication gap between markets and US Corporate office.
- Manage $4.3MM budget. Analyze working capital allocation for 8 accounts in 10 countries. Initiated new accounting structure for monthly accruals, domestic and international invoicing and compliance.

Corporate Spanish Instructor

- Created lesson plans and taught beginning and intermediate retail Spanish class.
- Lessons included: survival Spanish, vocabulary, grammar, phonetics, listening comprehension, and cultural observations.
- Taught all levels of professionals from senior vice presidents to entry-level marketing specialists.

BUSINESS INTERNSHIP:

Intern, Ralph Lauren, Inc. New York. October 200x – June 200x
Visual Merchandising; placement in Los Angeles

TECHNOLOGY APPLICATIONS:

Lotus Notes, Adobe InDesign, Photoshop, QuarkXPress, Volo View, Makoro, MicroStrategy, Access, C++

References and research papers are available upon request.

American History CV

Strategic Features: American History CV

Review this CV if you are an experienced academic with teaching appointments, publishing experience, and service accomplishments.

CV BASICS:

Highest Degree:	Ph.D.
Experience:	Tenured
Job Target:	3 page CV (Pages 1 and 2 can be used for grant applications/funding review.)

CONTENT FEATURES:

- The first page presents a comprehensive overview of expertise and progressive experience. Degree information is basic with dissertation and thesis items removed; at this point in career those items are no longer relevant because of scholarly production. To quickly demonstrate career progression, a section in Formal Education and Training was designed and called "Overview." In a few short lines, the reader can quickly see advancement in academe.
- Page two (which is several pages long before condensing) shows considerable scholarly experience. One category is used (*Scholarly Work*) to present the breadth and depth of experience.
- CVs used for funding applications must demonstrate contributions in a consolidated format. Because the RFP requires advanced technology applications, a separate category is designed to demonstrate knowledge and integration of technology. Substantial service is broken into categories for ease of reading and to demonstrate breadth of efforts.

DESIGN FEATURES:

Font:	Tw Cen MT font, size 10
Margins:	.75" top, bottom; .5" left, right
Layout:	Open new document; use tabs to indent.
Line spacing:	One line space between categories.
Enhancements:	Left-justified category headings allow descriptors to extend from margin-to-margin utilizing space wisely.

American History CV

HIREM E. SOON

History Department 321 Center Hall (201)565-2323 hiremesoon@mcc.edu

OVERVIEW

- Professor, History Department, College of Letters, 201x-present
- Gillian Research Award, Society of Historical Antiquities, Mexico City, 201x
- Associate Professor, History Department, College of Letters, 200x-201x
- Director of Technology Center and Assistant Professor, College of Letters, 200x-200x
- Assistant Director of Technology, Learning Systems Lab, Portland, 200x-200x

FORMAL EDUCATION AND TRAINING

UNIVERSITY OF NEW MEXICO, ALBUQUERQUE
Doctor of Philosophy American History. July 201x
Research: Native American Indians: 1800-1815
Master of Arts History. May 200x
Research: Westward Movement, 1820-1890

OREGON STATE UNIVERSITY, PORTLAND
Master of Science Educational Technology. May 200x
Research: Technology Implications in Teaching
Bachelor of Science American History and Computer Science. June 200x
with highest honors
International Study, Mexico City. 200x-200x

CURRENT TEACHING RESPONSIBILITES

Professor, Mesa Community College, Mesa, AR (Maricopa County Community College District) 200x-present. Courses:

- *Volunteerism for History: A Service Learning Experience (1 credit hour)*

Focus: Development of historical research and inquiry skills through on-site volunteer experience with museums, libraries, and volunteer groups.

- *American Indian History (3 credit hours)*

Focus: Survey of American Indian history in relation to cultural, economic, political and social continuity/changes of Sioux, Iroquois, Navajo, and Indians of the Southwest.

- *Southwest History (3 credit hours)*

Focus: Study the peoples (Hispanic, African-American, Anglo, and Native American) who settled the American Southwest. Emphasis on fur trading, cattle, mining, and transportation.

- *Arizona History (2 credit hours)*

Focus: Examine prehistoric/contemporary Native American experience, Spanish Colonial times, the Mexican National period, the US federal territorial years and Arizona's economic development.

FUNDING [current]

Federal Grant: *Federal Policies and Social Changes in the Indians of the Southwest* (3 year grant, 1.5 million) August 201x-present. Principal investigator

Southwest Consortium Grant: *Community Identities of Cherokee and Navajo* (5 year grant, 7.1 million) October 200x-present. Co-Principal investigator

American History CV, page 2

HIREM E. SOON, page 2

SERVICE

Department Coordinator, Fall 201x-present
- Coordinate mentoring program for new faculty
- Develop technology teams for student learning
- Evaluate and assess adjunct faculty with History appointments
- Dean's Administrative Council representative
- Sponsor, History Club

Campus Technology Center, Fall 201x-present
- Departmental Representative, College of Letters
- Team Leader, TILE Learning Centers (technology/multi-space center)
- Co-chair, New Media Committee

Center for Teaching, Fall 201x-present
- Executive Council member
- Seminar and workshop presenter for new faculty on technology integration
- Create new media applications for use by teaching assistants and new faculty
- Work with marketing specialists to create new materials for print and media advertising

SCHOLARLY ACTIVITY [selected list]

Works in Progress:
Soon, H.E., Fine, B.E., and Goode, I.M. Confronting social changes as a result of federal policies (manuscript in progress)
Fine, B.E., and Soon, H.E. Impact of federal policies and community identities of the Navajo (paper in progress)

Works Submitted:
Soon, H.E., Fine, B.E., and Goode, I.M. Federal policies and the political and economic development of Navajo in 1920's (book chapter)
Soon, H.E. Fur trade and social changes for the Indians of the Southwest, 1875-1885 (manuscript)

Publications:
Soon, H.E., and Fine, B.E. The Decade of political and economic change of the Indians of the Southwest, 1880's. Wadsworth Publishing (textbook division), March 201x
Fine, B.E., Soon, H.E. and Goode, I.M. (200x). Social changes and the effect of political decisions, Journal of Social Change and History. 32, 68-127.
Soon, H.E. (200x). Fur trade and social changes for the Indians of the Southwest,1875-1879, Tribal College Journal of American Higher Education. 31, 110-116.

Advisory Boards:
Tribal College Journal of American Indian Higher Education
Native American Public Telecommunications (Lincoln, NE)
Arizona American Indian Higher Education
New Media Consortium for Community Colleges

Book Reviews:
American Historical Review
Los Angeles Times Book Review

American History CV, page 3

HIREM E. SOON, page 3

CONSULTING

Native American Institute, Albuquerque, New Mexico
Center for Cultural Change, Taos, New Mexico and Mexico City, Mexico
Southwest Society for Native American Arts, Phoenix, Arizona
Consulting at the following institutions:

University of Wyoming
Yavapai College
Oglala Lakota College
Eastern Arizona College
Little Big Horn College
Oregon State University

OUTREACH

Speaker, orator, and panel participant for numerous events and organizations at the local, state, regional, and national level. Guest on NPR, CNN, and area TV stations.
Volunteer coordinator for the Navajo state archives and media manager (website, blogs, monthly podcasts and media reviews).

TECHNOLOGY INTERESTS AND INTEGRATION

Using online media tools to enhance students' inquiry and writing skills
Incorporating technologies to augment classroom lectures and activities
Modeling 21st century technologies in speaking, writing and presentation
Integrating Blackboard, podcasts, blogs, wikis, and nings in classroom activities

RECOGNITION

Outstanding Teaching Award, 200x; 201x
National Endowment for the Humanities, Senior nominee, 201x
Governor's Volunteer Award, 201x
Native American Society Summer Fellow, 200x
Summer Research Fellowship, Stanford University, 200x
Ford Foundation Dissertation Fellowship, 200x-200x
Teaching Assistant Award Recognition, 200x
Phi Beta Kappa, inducted 200x
Presidential Scholar, 200x-200x

Complete dossier available at: www.hiremesoon.com/dossier

American Studies CV

Strategic Features: American Studies CV

Review this CV if you are seeking an academic teaching appointment that requires a completed doctorate with evidence of publishing and relevant teaching experiences.

CV BASICS:

Highest Degree:	Ph.D.
Experience:	Adjunct position Instructor Teaching assistantships
Job Target:	College/university teaching at all post-secondary levels including community college positions

CONTENT FEATURES:

- *Degrees* are presented first to emphasize advanced preparation in the content area. Because candidate has teaching experience, dissertation title and cognate areas have been replaced with research focus. This serves a dual role: first, it indicates research concentrations; secondly, it takes the place of a new category typically called *Research and Teaching Interests.*
- *Post-Secondary Teaching Responsibilities* list the courses taught to demonstrate wide-ranging skills; listed on page one to highlight.
- *Awards and Recognition* are included on page one to reveal the ability to be recognized for abilities by university faculty and administrators.
- Page two lists *Technology Integration*, *Scholarly Activity* (including new media and funding), and *Service* with descriptive phrases to highlight diverse responsibilities.

DESIGN FEATURES:

Font:	Tw Cen MT font, size 10
Margins:	.75" top, bottom; 1" left, right
Layout:	Open new document; use tabs to indent.
Line spacing:	One line space between categories.
Enhancements:	Use of bullets in two categories to draw attention to descriptive phrases.

American Studies CV

REED A. LOTT

English Department, 21 Able Hall, University, City, State Zip (201)565-2323 reedalott@riu.edu

FORMAL EDUCATION AND TRAINING

UNIVERSITY OF CALIFORNIA LOS ANGELES
Doctor of Philosophy in English. June 201x
Research Focus: American Literature 1945-1995
Master of Arts Degree in Literature. May 201x
Research Focus: British and American Literature 1914-1945

COLLEGE OF WILLIAM AND MARY (WILLIAMSBURG) AND UNIVERSITY OF ST ANDREWS (SCOTLAND)
Bachelor of Arts, International Honours. June 200x
Focus of Study: English and Economics

AWARDS AND RECOGNITION

Research Award for New Publication, American Literature Society, Los Angeles, May 201x
Outstanding Teaching Assistant Award, UCLA Department of English, Spring 201x
Winchester Dorrington-Niles Dissertation Award, UCLA Department of English, June 201x
International Letters Prize, University of St Andrews, October 200x

POST-SECONDARY TEACHING RESPONSIBILITES

Instructor, College of Liberal Arts and Human Sciences, Virginia Tech, Fall 201x-present

- *Introduction to Critical Reading: (3 credit hours)*
  Focus: Emphasizes the analytical skills, basic critical terminology, and conventions of literary criticism essential to advanced English studies.
- *The English Studies ePortfolio: (1 credit hour)*
  Focus: Lecture/lab course where students learn the technology skills necessary to create an entry-level ePortfolio used during the course of their undergraduate study.
- *Survey of American Literature: (3 credit hours)*
  Focus: Survey of the literary, historical and social contexts of major writers of the American literary tradition. Includes developments in poetry, drama, prose fiction, and criticism.

Adjunct Professor, Tidewater Community College, Virginia Beach, VA. 200x-201x.
Teaching duties in the Associate of Arts (A.A.) degree program. Designed for students who plan to transfer to university programs. Focus on literature and analytical and critical thinking skills.

- *College Composition I and II: (3 credit hours each)*
  Focus: Training in writing analytical and critical essays. Practice in addressing a range of audiences and in using varied styles and organizational patterns. Workshop approach used in course.
- *Business Writing: (2 credit hours)*
  Focus: Stresses practice in forms of persuasive and informative writing such as case analyses, reports, abstracts, and letters. Designed for students in all curricula.

Teaching Assistant, UCLA Department of English, September 200x-June 200x

- *Modernist American Literature: (3 credit hours)*
  Focus: Presents Modernist American literature from 1918 to 1945 in its representative modes and defining contexts, including World Wars I and II, the Great Depression.
- *Modern British Literature: (3 credit hours)*
  Focus: Presents Modernist British literature from 1918-1945 including World Wars I and II, the collapse of the British empire, and literary movements of Modernism and Realism.

American Studies CV, page 2

Reed A. Lott, page 2

TECHNOLOGY INTEGRATION

Incorporate technologies to augment classroom activities (SmartBoard, Google Docs, Blogs)
Upload lectures and class materials to iTunesUniversity for universal access to students 24/7
Modeling 21st century technologies to enhance student's inquiry, writing and presentation skills
Deliver course resources using online management systems
Coach students in technology applications for ePortfolio development

SERVICE

Course Technology Integration Committee, Virginia Tech, Fall 201x-present
- Work with new and senior faculty to examine current uses of technology in teaching
- Evaluate current accessibility issues of campus technology and support staff

Campus Technology Committee, Virginia Tech, Fall 201x-present
- Departmental Representative, College of Liberal Arts and Human Sciences
- ePortfolio team leader and workshop presenter (technology coaching and workshops)

Student Success Center, Tidewater Community College, Spring 201x-201x
- Seminar and workshop presenter for transfer students regarding technology integration
- Create new media applications for use by teaching assistants and peer student assistants

SCHOLARLY ACTIVITY

New Media:
Blog: http://writingandwarblog.com/reed (co-creator with B. Fine)
Reed, A. L. (201x, June 24) Re: ePortfolios raise the bar for outcome-based reviews [Video file]. http://www.youtube.com/Vpo980kl8
Reed, A. L. (Producer). (201x, May 21). *New wave radio* [Audio podcast]. Retrieved from http://www.newwaveradio.com/

Works in Progress:
Reed, A.L., Fine, B.E., and Goode, I.M. Political implications of the literary movements of Modernism (paper in progress)
Fine, B.E., Reed, A.L. Modernism and cultural movement in early 20th century (book chapter in progress)

Works Submitted:
Reed, A.L., Fine, B.E., and Goode, I.M. Modernism, complexity and the notion of final authorities (book chapter)

Publications:
Reed, A.L. (201x). Modernism and postmodernism: extremism or early radical movements, Journal of Literary Works. 12, 18-21.
Soon, H.E. and Reed, A.L. (200x). Examining existence-the impact of the Modernism movement, Journal of American Higher Education. 41, 19-26.

Grant Activity:
Truman Foundation Grant: "American literature and war-time writing," August 201x-present
Coastal States Consortium Literature Grant, October 201x-present. Co-Principal investigator

Complete dossier and teaching portfolio at: www.hiremesoon.com/dossier

Architecture Résumé

Strategic Features: Architecture Résumé

Review this résumé if you want to emphasize specific accomplishments in your field for introductions, speaking engagements and award applications.

RÉSUMÉ BASICS:

Highest Degree:	Master's degree
Experience:	Experienced in field
Job Target:	Speaking engagements, award applications, and new customer relations

CONTENT FEATURES:

- An *Overview* category leads off this résumé to immediately identify work, awards, inventions, and degrees. This is a compact way of providing the reader with the basic and the most significant information about you in one continuous section. If this was divided into 5 different categories, it would lose its impact and would require additional pages.
- Because of the intended use of this résumé, only three categories were included: *Overview, Experience,* and *Service*. This format is quick and easy to read and imparts the most critical information to the person who is introducing you at a speaking engagement or to a committee reviewing material for award nominations.
- Annotations in the *Experience* category accentuate a broad base of skills and achievements from both international employment to stateside positions. Combining all work into one category makes it possible to save space and create a one-page résumé.

DESIGN FEATURES:

Font:	Candara font, size 11
Margins:	1" top, bottom; 1" left, right
Layout:	Open new document; use tabs to indent.
Line spacing:	One line space between categories.
Enhancements:	Graphic line to highlight category headings.

Architecture Résumé

DREW A. PLANN

P.O. Box 45899 Any City, Country 011.10155.50101
www.DrewPlannPortfolio.org
drewplann@gmail.com

OVERVIEW

Architect: • Project Manager for design projects totaling over 277 million dollar over a four-year period • Proficient in Microstation, AutoCAD, Photoshop, Adobe Illustrator, all Microsoft Applications

Inventor: • Board game designed to facilitate master planning and building design

Awards: • Several prestigious awards: *201x Engineering Society of Detroit Awards,* 201x ASID Design Excellence Award; Outstanding Achievement in Design and Construction

Lecturer: • Invited speaker to professional meetings, conferences & seminars.
Graduate Teaching Assistant; College of Architecture, 201x – 201x
(*Modern Architecture* and *Renaissance and Baroque Architecture)*

Degrees: • MA (201x) and BA (200x) in Architectural Studies, University of Kansas
International Studies-201x; Siena, Italy; Berlin, Germany
Studio804 Executive Board (managed finances and client relations)
Won NCARB and SECCA design competitions as member of Studio804

EXPERIENCE

International: **International Inc.**, Qatar, *Project Director, 201x - current*

Stateside: **Building Associates, Inc.**, Chicago, IL. *Project Manager, 201x-201x*
Wesley Architects, Inc., Chicago, IL. *Project Manager, 200x-200x*

Projects and Accomplishments:

- Selected to design and direct a multi-million dollar project for the Qatar Morris Bank; collaborated with a team of consultants and interviewed executive board for input.
- Managed internal teams and coordinated external cross-functional team of consultants; mechanical, electrical, and structural engineers; built design packages for presentations.
- Formulated building scope, building size, room requirements, occupant use and preliminary cost of construction, through analysis of client interviews.
- Provided a $120K return of construction contingency to client, no return expected at beginning of project; reduced typical project duration five months through investigation of project schedule and standard design/construction operations, allowing team to meet aggressive client schedule; devised innovative dimensioning system allowing general contractor to erect a geometrically complex façade.

SERVICE

- Junior Board Member - City of Hope • Associate Member American Institute of Architects
- Young Architects Forum • International Association of Architects

Art CV

Strategic Features: Art CV
(Art History and Printmaking)

Review this CV if you are seeking an academic or professional appointment that requires accomplishment in academic preparation, teaching experience, and artistic recognition in various venues.

CV BASICS:

Highest Degree:	MFAs
Experience:	Teaching assistant Adjunct positions Independent artist
Job Target:	College/university studio positions; Teaching at all post-secondary levels

CONTENT FEATURES:

- *Degrees* are presented first to emphasize advanced preparation in the specific career field and to highlight the dual areas of specialization—printmaking and art history.
- Courses taught are listed under *Teaching Experience: College and University* to demonstrate wide-ranging instructional skills and extensive knowledge base.
- *Languages and International Residences* are included on page one to reveal additional talents and multi-cultural and international awareness.
- Page two lists artistic merits and accomplishments. The first page could be a one-page condensed CV for speaking or conference activities.

DESIGN FEATURES:

Font:	Calibri font, size 10
Margins:	.75" top, bottom; 1" left, right
Layout:	Open new document; set tabs to indent.
Line spacing:	One line space between categories.
Enhancements:	Use of a small bullet in place of a comma in the first four categories.

Art CV

ALEC SAMPLE

#5 Academic Hall • Any City • State 12345 • (101) 555-1110 • a-sample@uxy.edu • www.asample.com

EDUCATION

MFA–Printmaking, Minor–*Photography* • The University of Iowa • Iowa City, Iowa • 201x
Center for the Book • The University of Iowa • Iowa City, Iowa • 201x–201x
MA–Printmaking, Minor–*Drawing* • The University of Iowa • Iowa City, Iowa • 200x
MFA–Art History • Ohio University • Athens, Ohio • 200x
BGS–General Studies • Indiana University • Bloomington, Indiana • 200x
Carolyn Manosevitz Studio • Drawing & Painting Studies • Austin, Texas • 199x–9x
Fulbright Scholar Dependent's Grant [Latvia]

TEACHING EXPERIENCE: COLLEGE & UNIVERSITY

Austin Community College • Adjunct Professor • Department of Art • Austin, Texas • 201x–201x
Course: *Art History I, Asian Art, Art Appreciation*
The University of Iowa • Adjunct Assistant Professor • School of Art & Art History • 201x–201x
Courses: *Digital Imaging, Portfolios in the Arts, Digital Imaging: Materials & Technique*
Kirkwood Community College • Adjunct Professor • Arts & Humanities Department • 201x–201x
Courses: *Beginning Photography, Intermediate Photography, Digital Photography, History of Photography, Art Appreciation, Drawing I, Printmaking I & II*
University of Latvia • Visiting Lecturer • School of Communication • Riga, Latvia • 200x
Courses: *Digital Imaging, Digital Imaging Topics, Visual Perceptions, 2-D Concepts*

TEACHING EXPERIENCE: TEACHING ASSISTANT

The University of Iowa • Graduate Teaching Assistant • School of Art & Art History • 200x
Courses: *Digital Imaging* [Instructor of Record], *Digital Imaging: Materials & Techniques* [Instructor of Record] 200x; *Technology in the Classroom* [Instructor of Record], 200x
Ohio University • Teaching Associate • School of Art & Art History • 199x–200x
Courses: *History of Photography, History of Non-Western Art*

RELATED PROFESSIONAL EXPERIENCE

Interim Fine Arts Coordinator, Arts & Humanities, Kirkwood Community College • 200x
(Exhibition Organizer • Photography Workshop & Exhibition Juror • Gallery Lecture)
Visiting Scholar • *Latvian Center* • Contemporary Art • Riga, Latvia • 200x
Design, Editorial & Marketing Assistant • Ohio University Press • 19xx–20xx
Digital Imaging, Design & Prepress Iowa State University • Printing Services • 19xx-19xx
Freelance Graphic Artist • Cool-Breeze Graphics • Austin • 19xx-19xx

FUNDING AND GRANTS

Arts & Humanities Departmental Technology Grant, Kirkwood Community College, 201x
Exhibition Grant, Iowa Foil Printer Foundation, Iowa City, 201x
Travel Grant, Iowa Fine Arts Council, The University of Iowa, 200x

ORGANIZATIONS [Current & Former]

Chicano Humanities & Arts Council, Association of Hispanic Arts Women Printmakers of Austin, Southern Graphics Council, College Art Association Midwestern Printmakers Association, Friends of Dard Hunter, International Digital Image Exchange

LANGUAGES & INTERNATIONAL RESIDENCE

Fluency in Spanish, and study of French, German, Chinese, Japanese & Latvian
Archival research & residence in Riga, Latvia, 20xx; London, England, 20xx
Residence & secondary education in Nürnberg, West Germany, 198x–198x

Art CV, page 2

Sample, page 2

EXHIBITIONS
"30 Dies de Gravat a Olot," Group Digital Print Exhibition, Galeria el Cailu, Olot, Spain
"Pink Amour" Group Mixed Media Exhibition, Tiru Gallery, Austin, Texas
Naestved International Exhibition, Group Print Exhibition, Copenhagen, Denmark
XII Bienal Guadalupana, Group Small Format Print Exhibition, La Universidad Iberoamericana, San Angel Culture Center, Mexico City, Mexico
4th International Experimental Film Festival Carbunari 200x, Florian Museum, Maramures, Romania
"Daily Palette" Digital On-line Exhibition, The University of Iowa, Iowa City, Iowa
Cascade Print Exchange, Oregon State University, Corvallis, Oregon. [Traveling]
6th Triennial Kyoto International Woodcut Exhibition, Juried Woodcut Print Exhibition, Japan
VIII° International Engraving Biennial: Premio Acqui, Juried Printmaking Exhibition, Acqui Terme, Monferrato, Italy
2nd International Mini Print of Sarajevo, Euro Art Centre, Vaxjo, Sweden [Traveling]
Invitation to 4th Biennale Internazionale Dell'Arte Contemporanea, Fortezza da Bazzo, Florence, Italy

BIBLIOGRAPHY & PUBLICATIONS
The Americas Biennial Exhibition, by A. Sterly, *Printmaking Today,* Issue 1, Spring 201x. [Forthcoming]
The Americas Biennial Exhibition of Contemporary Prints: 200x, exhibition catalogue, Edited by A. Sample, phatpress (Austin, Texas), 201x. [Forthcoming]
Contemporary Art of Latvia: War, Waiting, Inflammation & Pomegranates, exhibition catalogue, Edited by A. Sample, nonphatpress (Iowa City, Iowa), 200x.
The World in a Grain of Sand: Prints by A. Sample, by S Kakarla, in *Frontline,* August 26, 200x.

AWARDS
Arts & Humanities Exhibition Purchase Award, Kirkwood Community College, 201x
1st Place Printmaking Award, *Content Magazine,* Iowa City, 201x
Exhibition Grant, Iowa Foil Printer Foundation, Iowa City, 201x
Dard Hunter Conference Scholarship, Friends of Dard Hunter, Minneapolis, 201x
Commodore of the Texas Navy, Governor of State of Texas [Ann Richards], 199x

SERVICE
Survey of Contemporary Digital Images: The 201x International Digital Image Exchange, International Digital Image Exchange, Austin, Texas, Coordinator, 201x
Americas Biennial Exhibition of Contemporary Prints, Austin, Texas, Organizer, 201x
Americas Biennial Exhibition Archive, Austin, Texas, Curator, 201x
Arts Iowa City, Iowa City, Iowa, Web Manager and member of Board of Directors, 201x
Adjunct Faculty Advisory Committee, Arts & Humanities Representative, Kirkwood College, 201x
Mexic Arte, Volunteer, Austin Texas, 199x–199x
The Council on the Status of Latinos, Graduation Speaker, The University of Iowa, 199x

PUBLIC COLLECTIONS
Universidad Iberoamericana, Departamento de Arte, Diseño y Arquitectura, Ermita, Mexico
Grafisk Vaerksted, Naestved, Denmark
Oregon State University, Department of Art, Corvallis, Oregon
Museum of Engraving, Castello dei Paleologi, Acqui Terme, Moferrato, Italy
American Print Alliance, Peachtree City, Georgia
Florean Museum, Maramures, Romania
Graphium Biennial Contemporary Engraving Collection, Timisoara, Romania
Stockholm School of Economics, Riga, Latvia
Russian State Pedagogical University, St. Petersburg, Russia

Art CV: Condensed

Strategic Features: Art CV
(Condensed CV for experienced academic and artist)

Review this CV if you need to take a multi-page CV and reconfigure it to a one page CV for exhibits and shows, speaking engagements, grant submissions or funding applications.

CV BASICS:

Highest Degree:	Several MFA degrees and specialized training
Experience:	Experience in art-related fields Adjunct teaching experience
Job Target:	Prepared for applications to exhibits and shows, speaking engagements and/or grants

CONTENT FEATURES:

- Full-page layout selected to provide more space because of the density of the information and multiple categories. This one-page transformed CV was redesigned from a 20 page CV.
- *Education* is presented first to stress the extensive academic preparation and training acquired by this candidate.
- Putting the *Funding and Awards* near the top of the page immediately suggests that this person is fully aware of the nuances of applying for and completing competitive projects.
- The last three categories on the page, *Exhibitions, Bibliography and Publications,* and *Public Collections,* indicate that only a "selected list" is presented for the reader. On condensed CVs, this is important so that readers understand that you are highly accomplished.

DESIGN FEATURES:

Font:	Calibri font, size 10
Margins:	.75" top, bottom; .75" left, right
Layout:	Open new document; use tabs to indent.
Line spacing:	One line space between categories.
Enhancements:	Uppercase font for category headings.

Art CV (condensed)

ALEC SAMPLE

#5 Academic Hall, Any College, City, State 12345 (101) 555-1110 sample@uxy.edu www.asample.com

EDUCATION

MFA, Printmaking, *Photography* Minor, The University of Iowa, Iowa City, 201x
Center for the Book, The University of Iowa, Iowa City, 201x–201x
MA, Printmaking, *Drawing* Minor, The University of Iowa, Iowa City, 200x
MFA, Art History, Ohio University, Athens, Ohio, 200x
BGS, General Studies, Indiana University, Bloomington, Indiana, 200x
Carolyn Manosevitz Studio, Drawing & Painting Studies, Austin, Texas, 199x–200x
Fulbright Scholar Dependent's Grant [Latvia]

CURRENT TEACHING EXPERIENCES

Austin Community College, Adjunct Professor, Department of Art, Austin, Texas, 201x–201x
The University of Iowa, Adjunct Assistant Professor, School of Art & Art History, 201x–201x
Courses taught: Art History I, Asian Art, Art Appreciation, Digital Imaging, 2-D Concepts, Portfolios in the Arts, History of Photography, Art Appreciation, Drawing I, Printmaking I

FUNDING AND AWARDS

3-year Humanities Grant, "Art Crosses Borders & Boundaries," New Art Foundation, 201x
Exhibition Grant, Iowa Foil Printer Foundation, Iowa City, 201x
Dard Hunter Conference Scholarship, Friends of Dard Hunter, Minneapolis, 201x
Commodore of the Texas Navy, Governor of State of Texas [Ann Richards], 199x

LANGUAGES, INTERNATIONAL RESIDENCE & ORGANIZATIONS

Fluency in Spanish, and study of French, German, Chinese, Japanese & Latvian
Archival research & residence—Latvia 20xx; England 20xx; Nürnberg 198x–198x
Chicano Humanities & Arts Council, Association of Hispanic Arts, Association for Art History

EXHIBITIONS (selected list—over 50 exhibits)

"30 Dies de Gravat a Olot," Group Digital Print Exhibition, Galeria el Cailu, Olot, Spain
"Pink Amour" Group Mixed Media Exhibition, Tiru Gallery, Austin, Texas
Naestved International Exhibition of Contemporary Prints, Group Print Exhibition, Denmark
XII Bienal Guadalupana, Group Small Format Print Exhibition, La Universidad Iberoamericana, San Angel Culture Center, Mexico City, Mexico
2nd International Mini Print of Sarajevo, Euro Art Centre, Vaxjo, Sweden [Traveling]

BIBLIOGRAPHY & PUBLICATIONS (selected list—over 20 publications)

The Americas Biennial Exhibition, by A. Sterly, *Printmaking Today,* Issue 1, Spring 201x [Forthcoming]
The Americas Biennial Exhibition of Contemporary Prints: 200x, exhibition catalogue. Edited by A. Sample, ArtsPress (Austin, Texas), 201x [Forthcoming]
Contemporary Art of Latvia: War, Waiting, Inflammation & Pomegranates, exhibition catalogue. Edited by A. Sample, Riverpress (Iowa City, Iowa), 200x
The World in a Grain of Sand: Prints by A. Sample, by S. Kakarla, in *Frontline,* August 16, 200x

PUBLIC COLLECTIONS (selected list – over 40 public collections)

Universidad Iberoamericana, Departamento de Arte, Diseño y Arquitectura, Ermita, Mexico
Russian State Pedagogical University, St. Petersburg, Russia
Kyoto International Woodcut Association, Kyoto, Japan
Museum of Engraving, Castello dei Paleologi, Acqui Terme, Moferrato, Italy

Biology (Molecular and Cellular) CV

Strategic Features: Biology (Molecular and Cellular) CV

Review this CV if you have had several appointments as a research assistant or as a research fellow and if your goals include working in a research facility.

CV BASICS:

Highest Degree:	Ph.D. in progress
Experience:	Research fellow Research assistantships
Job Target:	Research position in a clinical or university placement; Industry scientist

CONTENT FEATURES:

- Careful placement of several categories on the first page provides an excellent overview of education, research interests/experiences and key faculty who have been involved in the candidate's scholarly work. By placing the *Thesis Overview* in a separate category, more space can be devoted to a description of the work. If it was placed in the *Formal Background* category, it would overwhelm key material. Institution attended then degree is listed because both degrees were earned from the same intuition.
- The *Research Appointments* arrangement draws attention to research strengths and achievements. Brief annotations are presented here with more detailed information available in the teaching portfolio.
- Creating a *Key Faculty* category is an excellent strategy for identifying renowned individuals who have had an impact on your education and training and are recognized by others in the field.

DESIGN FEATURES:

Font:	Tahoma font, size 10
Margins:	.75" top, bottom, left, right
Layout:	Insert table with two columns.
Line spacing:	One line space between categories.
Enhancements:	Bullets used for visual and organizational emphasis.

Biology (Molecular and Cellular) CV

IMA SAMPLE

16 University Avenue Any City, State 12345 ima-sample@niu.edu (101) 555-0009
Teaching portfolio: www.interfolio.com/portfolio/ImaSample

FORMAL BACKGROUND:

Oklahoma State University, Stillwater, OK
- Ph.D. Candidate, Molecular and Cellular Biology Program
  Anticipated completion, June 201x
- Bachelors of Science, (Honors) Biochemistry and Molecular Biology
  May 201x

THESIS OVERVIEW:

Role of emerin and Protein Kinase C delta in Herpes Simplex nuclear egress. Thesis work involved studying both the viral and cellular kinases implicated in the induction of nuclear lamina disruption during herpesvirus replication.

RESEARCH EXPERIENCE:

Research Fellow: Mayo Graduate School, Rochester, MN, May 201x-present
- Identification of novobiocin binding site on HSP90 using recombinant DNA cloning strategies, protein expression vectors, protein solubility assays, Ni-affinity chromatography and hydrogen-deuterium exchange assays.

Research Fellow: Oklahoma State University, June 201x-May 201x
- Characterization of the promoter region of a tumor suppressor gene using recombinant DNA cloning strategies, tissue culture, and luciferase assays.

Research Fellow: University of Rhode Island, Summer 201x
- Creation of a mutant yeast strain defiant of endogenous Calcinurine using PCR technology, promoter design, and cloning troubleshooting.

Research Assistant: Oklahoma State University, June 201x-May 201x
- Evaluation of EGFR expression in cancer cell lines using immuno-chemistry.

KEY FACULTY:

University of Rhode Island: Stan Talle, M.D., Ph.D., Summer Mentor
Mayo Graduate School: David Kane, M.D., Ph.D., Supervisor & Mentor
Oklahoma State: Will B. Fine, Ph.D., Department Head; Thesis Advisor
Bea Goode, Ph.D., Program Coordinator, Mentor
Phyllis Sea, Ph.D., Lab Director and Research Mentor

AWARDS & FUNDING

Molecular and Cellular Biology Retreat, Best Poster Travel Award, 201x
Symposium Award: Molecular and Cellular Biology, November 201x
Advanced Virology Training Grant, 201x-201x
Virology Training Grant, 201x-201x
State Department of Public Health Grant, 201x

Biology (Molecular and Cellular) CV

Sample, page 2

PUBLICATIONS:

1. **Fine, B., Goode, B., Sample, I., Sea, P.** (201x). Novobiocin induces a distinct conformation of Hsp90 and alters Hsp90-cochaperone client interactions. *Biochemistry*, 40(25): 8217-29.

2. **Sample, I., Fine, B., Goode, B., Sea, P.** (201x). Emerin is hyperphosphorylated and redistributed in herpes simplex virus type 1-infected cells in a manner dependent on both UL34 and US3. *J Virology*. 81:10792-803.

3. **Sample, I., Fine, B.** (201x). Inhibition of PKC isoforms blocks efficient replication and nuclear egress of herpes simplex virus type 1. Submitted.

ABSTRACTS:

Smith, K., Sample, I., and Munch, D. (201x). HSV-1 INFECTION ALTERS THE LOCALIZATION AND MODIFICATION OF LAMIN-ASSOCIATED PROTEINS EMERIN AND LAP2 IN A UL34 AND US3-DEPENDENT MANNER. Poster presentation. International Herpes Workshop. Seattle, WA.

Sample, I., and T.J. Wolfe. (201x). HSV-1 INFECTION ALTERS THE MODIFICATION OF THE LAMIN-ASSOCIATED PROTEIN EMERIN in an U_L34, U_S3, AND PKC-DEPENDENT MANNER. Poster presentation. International Herpes Workshop. Asheville, NC.

Sample, I., and T.J. Wolfe. (201x). INHIBITION OF PROTEIN KINASE C DELTA SUGGESTS ROLE IN HSV-1 NUCLEAR EGRESS AND LAMIN ASSOCIATED PROTEIN DISRUPTION. Poster presentation. FASEB Virus Structure and Assembly. Saxtons River, VT.

Smith, K., Sample, I., and Munch, D. (201x). Role of Emerin and Protein Kinase C delta (PRKCD) in HSV-1 Nuclear Egress. Poster presentation. American Society for Cell Biology. San Diego, CA.

SERVICE:

Departmental:
Undergraduate Accreditation Review Committee Member, 201x -201x
Course Review Committee, Biology Department, 201x-201x
Scholarship Selection and Interview Team Member, 201x
Student Board President, Biology Forum, 201x-present
Volunteer, Departmental Lab Tutor, 201x-201x

Community Service:
AmeriCorps Volunteer, Houston, TX, September 201x-August 201x
Facilitated after-school, classroom, and SAT tutoring programs at Southwestern Tech Magnet High School.

Affiliation:
American Society for Cell Biology

DOSSIER:

References, research papers, presentations, posters, and publications available online at: www.interfolio.com/portfolio/ImaSample

Chemistry CV

Strategic Features: Chemistry CV

Review this CV if your background includes research experiences and training. This science CV has a heavy emphasis on one's identity as a productive researcher. Post-docs, research scientists, and junior faculty in the sciences will find success with this model.

CV BASICS:

Highest Degree:	Ph.D. in progress
Experience:	Fellowships Graduate assistantships
Job Target:	Post doc position, research or faculty line

CONTENT FEATURES:

- In *Education and Training*, graduate study that was halted is listed because related experiences are included in other sections and because of the quantity of research programs at the university.
- Research categories (activities and applications) draw attention to specialized skills. Abilities can be quickly noted by the reader.
- *Honors and Awards* are listed on page one to complement the degree program and emphasize the candidate's academic achievements.
- The *Scholarship* category on page two is divided by types of publications and presentations. Creating one category for all scholarly work can eliminate categories with just one entry.

DESIGN FEATURES:

Font:	Perpetua font, size 11
Margins:	1" top, bottom, left, right
Layout:	Open new document; set tab.
Line spacing:	One line space between categories.
Enhancements:	Left-justified category headings allowing descriptors to extend from margin-to-margin. This is the most basic of all designs—no bullets or italics.

Chemistry CV

IMA EXAMPLE **21 College Street, City, State, Zip (c) 211.509.6789**
www.interfolio.com/portfolio/imaexample
i-example@gmail.com

EDUCATION AND TRAINING
University of Texas-Austin, Department of Chemistry
PhD candidate in Chemistry, January 201x-present

Iowa State University, Department of Chemistry
PhD student in Chemistry, August-December 201x

Nanjing University (China), Department of Chemistry
Diploma in Chemistry, July 200x

CERTIFICATES AWARDED
Graduate Certificate in College Teaching, UT-Austin, 201x
International Communication Skills Certificate, Iowa State University, 200x
Intel® Certificate of Project-based Technology, Beijing, 200x

RESEARCH ACTIVITIES
Enzyme Kinetics
Kinetic Isotope Effects
Protein Expression and Purification
Organic and Enzymatic Synthesis (micro scale)

RESEARCH APPLICATIONS
HPLC; FPLC; Cell Culture; LSC (Liquid Scintillation Counting); UV-Vis spectrometer; NMR; IR; Mass spectrometry; Multivariate analysis (PCA, PLS, and NAS); MATLAB; MiniTab; Sigma Plot; RefWorks; Mathematica; Adobe; Dreamweaver; SharePoint (for website management).

FELLOWSHIPS
Center for Biocatalysis and Bioprocessing Fellowship (UT-Austin), July 201x-present
Graduate College Summer Fellowship (UT-Austin), June-July 201x

GRADUATE TEACHING APPOINTMENTS
Graduate Research Assistant, Department of Chemistry, UT-Austin, January 201x-present
Graduate Teaching Assistant, Chemistry Department, Iowa State University, Fall 200x

HONORS AND AWARDS
Graduate Science Stipend, (UT-Austin), 4 years
Distinction in Sciences Scholarship, (UT-Austin), 2 years
Outstanding Teaching Award (Department of Chemistry, UT-Austin), 1 year
Travel Award, Graduate Student Senate, (Iowa State University), 1 year
Future Scientists Scholarship, Nanjing Scientists Society, 4 years
National People's Scholarship (Nanjing University), 2 years

Chemistry CV, page 2

Ima Example, page 2

SCHOLARSHIP

Publications

Thymidylate Synthase catalyzed H-transfers: Two Chapters in One Tale, Alex Sample. Submitted.

Sample, I., Mousee, N.N., Example, A.E. *The Inhibition of Oxidase Activity of Flavin-Dependent Thymidylate Synthase.* [Journal of Physical Chemistry], 59(14), 687 – 871, 201x.

Recent Presentations

Ima Example and Mousee, N.N. *Kinetic Isotope Effects on H-transfers Catalyzed by Thymidylate Synthase*, 201x Gordon Research Conference: Isotopic Probes For Mechanisms In The Chemical and Life Sciences, Galveston, TX, February 201x.

N.N Mousee and Example, I. *Probing the Dynamics-Kinetics Relationship: Kinetic Isotope Effect Studies of E. coli Thymidylate Synthase*, Midwest Enzyme Chemistry Conference, Chicago, IL, May 201x.

Posters

Kinetic Isotope Effects on H-transfers Catalyzed by Thymidylate Synthase. Poster session, 69th National Conference, Boston, MA (March 201x)

Oxidase Activity of Flavin-Dependent Thymidylate Synthase. Poster session, Chemistry Symposium, San Diego, CA (October 201x)

Contributed Talks

Ima Example, *Exploring the Role of Dynamics in Enzymatic Catalysis: Kinetic Isotope Effect Studies of E. coli Thymidylate Synthase*, 44th ACS Midwest Regional Meeting, Chicago, IL (October 201x)

SERVICE

Professional

Presider of Biochemistry General Session II in 44th ACS Midwest Regional Conference and Meeting, October 201x

Reviewer for the University Executive Council of Graduate and Professional Student Professional Advancement Grants, Fall 201x

Moderator of "Developments in Analytical Chemistry" Session, Annual Graduate Conference, February 201x

Community

Volunteer, Red Cross Disaster Team, Austin area, 201x-present

Tutor, America Reads, Houston Public Schools, 201x-present

Park Zoo Guide (large animal quarters), Houston, 201x

AFFILIATIONS

American Chemical Society

Center for Biocatalysis and Bioprocessing

Medical Portfolio: www.interfolio.com/portfolio/imaexample

Chemistry CV

Strategic Features: Chemistry CV
(One-page condensed CV for experienced academic)

Review this CV is you need to take a multi-page CV and reconfigure it to a one page CV for speaking engagements, consulting, and conference networking.

CV BASICS:

Highest Degree:	Ph.D. with experience
Experience:	Teaching and industry experience
Job Target:	Prepared for grants or speaking engagements

CONTENT FEATURES:

- *University Appointments* are presented first to stress current tenured appointment; customary to introduce the speaker by indicating current employment. *Areas of Expertise* presents the individual's research and teaching expertise with just a phrase or two. For use in speaking introductions, it's advantageous to use terms and phrases that a lay person could easily pronounce.
- *Selected Recent Publications* immediately suggests that there are additional publications; most recent and those in the most prestigious publications are listed.
- Industry positions as well as university appointments are presented without amplification for space reasons.

DESIGN FEATURES:

Font:	Franklin Gothic Book font, size 10
Margins:	.75" top, bottom; .75" left, right
Layout:	Insert table with two columns.
Line spacing:	1.5 line spaces between categories.
Enhancements:	Bold font to highlight category heading.

Chemistry CV

IMA SAMPLE
#5 Academic Hall ▪ Any City, State ▪ 12345 ▪ 101.555.1111 ▪ ima-sample@AU.edu

UNIVERSITY APPOINTMENTS:
Associate Professor, University of Arizona, Tucson, 201x – present
Assistant Professor, University of Arizona, Tucson, 201x – 201x
Chemistry Post-doc, Johns Hopkins University, Baltimore, 200x – 201x

DEGREES:

201x	Ph.D.	Chemistry, Washington University in St. Louis
200x	M.A.	Chemistry, University of Minnesota, Twin Cities
200x	B.A.	Chemistry, Gustavus Adolphus College, St. Peter, MN

AREAS OF EXPERTISE:
Research:
Fiber-optic chemical sensors and biosensors
Microscopic evaluation of acid etched optical fiber

Teaching:
Undergraduate courses in physical and organic chemistry
Graduate courses in diffraction analysis

HONORS:
National Science Foundation Fellow, Washington University
Cargill Fellowship, University of Minnesota
Phi Beta Kappa; Phi Lambda Upsilon
Martin-Merriwether Scholarship, Gustavus Adolphus College

SELECTED RECENT PUBLICATIONS:
"Biosensors and optical fiber," Newsletter of Chemical Scientists, (vol 10) pp 12-16. June 201x.
"Anion selectivity of polymer membrane electrodes," Journal of Chemistry, (vol 7) pp 135-140. March 201x.
"Polymer membrane electrodes: Today's analysis," Newsletter of Chemical Scientists, (vol 6) pp 24- 26. December 201x.

INDUSTRY EXPERIENCE:
Industrial Researcher, Monsanto Company, St. Louis, MO. 201x – 201x
Technical Assistant, 3M Company, St. Paul, MN. 200x – 200x

ACADEMIC SERVICE:
Council President, Faculty Advisory Council, 201x – present
Chair, Departmental Curriculum Committee, 201x – 201x
Member, Search Committee, Graduate School Dean, 201x
Representative, Provosts Committee on Graduate Education, 200x
Co-chair, Campus Space Utilization Committee, 200x

AFFILIATIONS:
Alpha Chi Sigma
American Chemical Society

Cinema & Film Video Production CV

Strategic Features: Cinema & Film Video Production CV

Review this CV if you are in an area that requires evidence of continuous and regular creativity as well as academic accomplishment in your field.

CV BASICS:

Highest Degree:	MFA expected
Experience:	Independent film experience Teaching assistantship
Job Target:	Production studio Teaching at all post-secondary levels

CONTENT FEATURES:

- The overall style/format of the CV denotes creativity and imagination. The name is set off in brackets followed by four areas of expertise.
- After *Education*, the format of the next six categories is arranged by year. This style is only appropriate if productivity can be viewed each successive year. If there is a non-productive year, this style is not advantageous.
- For advancement in this field, it is imperative to show contributions to a myriad of venues—exhibitions, screenings, lectures, residences, curatorial and collections. With a quick glance, all of these competencies are highlighted.
- Two categories on page two demonstrate course knowledge, technology, and new media skills requisite in this area.

DESIGN FEATURES:

Font:	Century Gothic font, size 10
Margins:	.75" top, bottom; 1"left, right
Layout:	Open new document; use tabs to indent.
Line spacing:	One line space between categories.
Enhancements:	Use of a graphic line to separate categories. Spaces used for organizational emphasis.

Cinema & Film Video Production CV

[ima sample]
cinema : emerging media : sound : education

(917)881.6331
imasample@gmail.com
www.imasample.com

EDUCATION

Master of Fine Arts Candidate – Film & Video Production — *New York University*
Department of Cinema and Comparative Literature — (expected May 201x)
NYU Arts Fellow

Bachelor of Science – Cinema & Photography — *University of Oregon*
Department of Cinema, Photography, and Media Arts — (awarded May 201x)
Magna Cum Laude

EXHIBITION / SCREENINGS / LECTURES

201x
Ann Arbor Film Festival Ambient Media Curated Show, *Ann Arbor, MI*
PBS: Independent Lens. Public Broadcasting Service. *New York, NY* (Colorist)
92Y Tribeca Gallery Space, *New York, NY*
Deconstruction Tutorial Lecture. Department of Intermedia, NYU

201x
ArtGrease Television Broadcast. Squeaky Wheel, *Buffalo, NY*
INCITE! Journal of Experimental Media & Radical Aesthetics supplemental DVD
Glitch: Investigations. The School of the Art Institute of Chicago, *Chicago, IL*
Semana del Cine Experimental de Madrid. *Madrid, Spain* (As Land Camera Collective)

200x
Chicago Underground Film Festival, *Chicago, IL*
Videologia. *Volgograd, Russia*
Eight Films International Artist Collective. www.eightfilms.com
Hollis Frampton's 'A Lecture.' New York State Summer School of the Arts, *Ithaca, NY*

AWARDS / RESIDENCIES

201x
NYU Graduate College Thesis Completion Grant
Princess Grace Grant Nominee, *New York, NY*
Pacific Research and Production Grant, *Eugene, OR*

201x
Telluride Film Festival Student Symposium, *Telluride, CO*
Residency at the Experimental Television Studio, *Oswego, NY*
Susan Royal Memorial Grant, *Chicago, IL*

200x
New York Arts Fellowship, *New York, NY*
Verizon Foundation Work Scholarship, *Eugene, OR*
College Presidential Scholarship, *Eugene, OR*

CURATORIAL

201x
Executive Director – Exi Theater, NYU
Director – International Documentary Festival

201x
Board of Directors – Experimental Film Festival
Staff Coordinator – Siren Film and Video Festival

200x
Intern – Finger Lakes Environmental Film Festival
Founder/Director – Couch Physics Microcinema

Cinema & Film Video Production CV, page 2

[ima sample, page 2]

TEACHING EXPERIENCE

201x Teaching Assistantship – Alternate Forms of Distribution, NYU
Responsible for writing an original syllabus, conducting class twice a week, grading papers and other assignments including exhibiting a film festival as a hands-on practicum with 16 students. Of note: festival in conjunction with a plan of study focusing on the history and application of non-commercial distribution in America and abroad.

201x Teaching Assistantship – Modes Film & Video Production, NYU
Responsible for teaching the basics of image, audio, and post-production as well as cinema production theory. Placed emphasis on exceeding the technical aspects of filmmaking to the ideology of creating one's first film or video and the possibilities open to the maker therein. Led discussion section and often addressed class of 67.

PROFESSIONAL / SERVICE EXPERIENCE

201x Editing Consultant – *Getting Accepted,* Rossie Press, *Nashville, TN*
Director/Editor – *Pink Cities music video*, Western Vinyl Records, *Austin, TX*
Technical Consultant – Norman Foundation Web Promotion, *Chicago, IL*

201x Program Coordinator – New York State Summer School for the Arts, *Oswego, NY*
Visiting Artist Coordinator – George Simon Summer Festival, *Taos, NM*
DVD Author – *Selected Works, Oswego, NY*

200x Assistant to the Director – New York State Summer School for the Arts, *Ithaca, NY*
Web & Identity Design / Basic Coding <www.imasample.com> *Eugene, OR*
Faculty Search Committee – Cinema Production, *Eugene, OR*

PUBLICATIONS / COLLECTIONS

Sample, Ima. *Hooliganship: Playtime for the Rest of Us. (Under Review)*
Sample, Ima. (201x) "The Ceibas Cycle – A Nodal Map." *INCITE! Journal of Experimental Media & Radical Aesthetics*. Ed: B.K. Mer
"Ceibas – Sigma Fugue" (200x) available at Rocky Coast Media Library, Eugene, OR

SELECTED GRADUATE COURSEWORK

Post-Structuralist Media Theory	Experimental Film/Video	Reflexive Documentary
Emerging Practices	New Media Philosophies	Locative Media
Informatics	Documentary Ethics	Intermediation

PROFESSIONAL SKILLS

[demo reel available at www.imasample.com]

POST PRODUCTION:

Apple Final Cut	DigiDesign ProTools HD	Adobe After Effects	Apple Color
DVD Studio Pro	Cinema Tools	Apple Soundtrack Pro	Adobe Flash
Audacity	Adobe Media Encoder	Roxio Toast Titanium	FTP Clients

AUDIO PRODUCTION:
Field & Studio Recording Systems (Tascam, Marantz, Fostex, Zoom, M. Audio); 5.1 Mixing & Assignment

IMAGE PRODUCTION:
SD and HD Video Cameras (Panasonic HVX, Panasonic DVX, Canon XL series)
Location Data Collection (P2 card, FireStore Hardware, Line In)

Collegiate Athletic Coaching Résumé

Strategic Features: Collegiate Athletic Coaching Résumé (Accounting CV to Coaching Résumé)

Review this résumé if you are considering a career change and applying for positions that require emphasis on skills and accomplishments that were not highlighted or even included in a CV.

RÉSUMÉ BASICS:

Highest Degree:	ABD (all but dissertation)
Experience:	Tutor, instructor, research assistant
Job Target:	College-level golf coach

CONTENT FEATURES:

- *Interests and Skills,* the first category on page one, outlines job objective and the essential skills required to succeed in this job. By carefully crafting this category, the candidate is prepared to answer all-important interview questions—What can you bring to this position? How does your skillset align with the job objective?
- To complement the *Interests* category, the *Golf Accolades* category demonstrates achievement in career-field.
- Items desired by athletic directors and search teams, e.g. golf accomplishments, recruiting skills, motivation and communication abilities, are carefully stated and positioned throughout the résumé.
- Degrees are presented in chronological order de-emphasizing the level of education obtained.
- Creating one category for a variety of positions, *University Experience,* saves valuable space so that all material fits on one page.

DESIGN FEATURES:

Font:	Candara font, size 10
Margins:	.75" top, bottom; 1" left, right
Layout:	Open new document.
Line spacing:	One line space between categories.
Enhancements:	Select use of bullets for emphasis.

Collegiate Athletic Coaching Résumé

HIREM E. SOON
21 University Avenue, Any City, State 12345
(201) 565-1111 hiremesoon@KU.edu

INTERESTS AND SKILLS

Goal:
- College Golf Coach

Skills:
- Accomplished golfer—success at collegiate level and PGA
- Excellent teacher and coach who can motivate, manage and inspire
- Comfortable interacting with players, parents, adults, and donors in academic, social, and golf settings; facilitate recruitment and retention of student athletes
- Highly skilled in teaching golf fundamentals, strategies, rules, course management, swing mechanics and video analysis

GOLF ACCOLADES

PGA Tour Player, 201x-201x
Four-year letter winner, Clemson University; Captain, two years
Awarded the Smitty Dane Endowed Golf Scholarship, three years; President's Athletic Award
Voted Athlete of the Year, Clemson University, 200x; Academic Team Captain
Minnesota Masters Champion (Amateur Title), 200x

ACADEMIC PREPARATION

Clemson University, Clemson, South Carolina
B.B.A. Professional Program in Accounting, June 200x *with highest honors*
M.A. Accounting, December 201x
CPA 201x
University of Kansas, Lawrence, Kansas
ABD Accounting; expected degree completion May 201x

UNIVERSITY EXPERIENCE

Assistant Volunteer Golf Coach, University of Kansas, 201x-present.
- Assist with budget management, fundraising, marketing and promotions, and working with student golfers on fundamentals and strategies.

Research Assistant, University of Kansas, 201x-present.
- Topic: recruitment of minority students into accounting programs and graduate placement rates for women and minorities in public accounting firms.

Instructor, University of Kansas, Fall 201x; Spring 201x.
- Responsible for teaching Introductory Financial and Managerial Accounting.

Teaching Assistant, University of Kansas, Fall 201x.
- Responsible for teaching Introductory Accounting.

Tutor, Business Student Study Lounge, Clemson University, 200x -200x.
- Responsible for newly admitted business students with 30 semester hours.

Of special note: Awarded Outstanding Teaching Assistantship Award, 201x
Received outstanding student evaluations in all courses

SERVICE, PUBLICATIONS, PRESENTATIONS, AND CAMPUS ACTIVITIES
- View at: www.hiremesoonportfolio.com

Community Development Résumé

Strategic Features: Community Development Résumé

Review this résumé if you want to highlight a number of strengths that can be applied in a variety of professional settings where tasks and dispositions are perhaps more valued than degrees.

RÉSUMÉ BASICS:

Highest Degree:	Master's degree
Experience:	Agency experience Teaching assistantship
Job Target:	Agency, political or governmental organization

CONTENT FEATURES:

- Margin-to-margin layout selected to utilize space; one-page résumé is preferred. Careful selection of material is paramount because of the limited space available in a one-page format.
- *Skills* are presented first to stress employment interests. This is a good option to an "objective" statement.
- Under *Education* high school diploma is included to demonstrate both study and residence in an international setting.
- *University Experience* and *Professional Experience* are briefly described by using bulleted phrases starting with an action word. The bulleted phrases support the *Skills* category by carefully describing skills used in these positions.
- Grants as well as languages are presented to amplify unique strengths and talents.

DESIGN FEATURES:

Font:	Garamond font, size 11
Margins:	1" top, bottom; .75" left, right
Layout:	Open new document; use tabs to indent.
Line spacing:	1.5 lines between categories.
Enhancements:	Use of bullets to draw attention to descriptive statements.

Community Development Résumé

IMA SAMPLE
16 University Avenue, Any City, State 12345   101.555.0101   i-sample@gmail.com

SKILLS
• Legislative Advocate • Family Relocation • Job Placement • Grant Writing

EDUCATION

MA Lehigh University, Bethlehem, Pennsylvania, May 201x
Geography *International Borders Fellow*

BS The University of Vermont, Burlington, Vermont, December 201x
Global Studies and Political Science *with high distinction and honors*

The American School, Larnaca, Cyprus, June 201x
Diploma

UNIVERSITY EXPERIENCE
Instructor, Department of Geography, Lehigh University, Summers 201x, 201x
African Development
- Course focused on the geography of development in Africa
- Designed online course content; created syllabi, assessed exams and final project

PROFESSIONAL EXPERIENCE
Rhode Island Legislative Coordinator, Amnesty International USA, Providence, 201x –
- Mobilized Rhode Island constituent congressional visits to advocate for Amnesty International legislative priorities
- Organized refugee protection conferences to draw attention to legislative issues; participated in strategic planning process with local partner organizations; chaired meetings and prepared reports for committee

Outreach Coordinator, Coalition of Immigrants Rights, Providence, 201x – 201x
- Prepared grant applications to sustain organization's funding
- Designed service learning coursework to further organization's operational needs and provide applied learning opportunities to college students
- Researched country conditions for asylum proceedings (37 cases)

GRANTS
Office of Refugee Resettlement, $200,000, two-year funding
Rhode Island State Department of Economic Development, $130,000, one-year grant
NE Region for Refugee Resettlement Collaboration, $75,000, one-year grant

LANGUAGES
Greek, Spanish, French, English

Comparative Literature CV

Strategic Features: Comparative Literature CV

Review this CV if you have yet to complete your doctoral studies and are still in the process of selecting the title of your dissertation and/or your committee. This CV shows active engagement in the doctoral program.

CV BASICS:

Highest Degree:	Doctoral degree in progress
Experience:	Research and teaching assistantships Instructor
Job Target:	Post-secondary teaching—any setting

CONTENT FEATURES:

- Dissertation topic is identified as "projected," indicating probable areas of research. Projected completion date indicates program towards dissertation completion.
- Page one is primarily focused on teaching responsibilities and abilities. Categories identify teaching appointments, research interests, and technology integration in teaching college courses. The content of this page leaves no question about the professional goals of this candidate.
- Short descriptive annotations use action phrases and specific details to describe teaching, campus involvement, and related activities. Languages, special recognition and professional materials appear near the end of the CV.

DESIGN FEATURES:

Font:	Calibri font, size 10
Margins:	.75" top, bottom, left, right
Layout:	Insert table with two columns.
Line spacing:	.5 line space between categories.
Enhancements:	Use of a bold font for selected words; use of italics for emphasis.

Comparative Literature CV

ALEC SAMPLE

16 University Avenue, Any City, State 12345 (101) 555-0101 a-sample@IU.edu

ACADEMIC BACKGROUND

Ph.D. Comparative Literature
Indiana University, Bloomington
August 201x – present Projected completion date: May 201x
Projected dissertation topic: *Revolutionary poets: 1920's*

M.A. Comparative Literature
Purdue University, June 201x
Thesis: *Eduardo Pinero: An Analysis of Early Writings*

B.A. Spanish and Global Studies *magna cum laude*
Butler University, Indianapolis, June 201x

TEACHING INTERESTS

Narrative Literature
Interpretation of Literature
American Lives
Lyric Poetry

RESEARCH APPOINTMENTS

Research Assistant, Comparative Literature, Indiana University, Fall 201x to present (faculty supervisor, Paul Profff, Ph.D.)

TEACHING APPOINTMENTS

English Department, Teaching Assistant, Indiana University, Fall 201x
Courses: American Lives; Lyric Poetry
Duties: Designed lectures, small group work, weekly readings as well as exams. Used a variety of multimedia resources to enhance teaching. Maintained and uploaded all teaching materials to iTunesUniversity for easy access for on-campus and on-line students.

Department of Spanish and Portuguese, Teaching Assistant, Indiana University, Summer 201x and Spring 201x
Courses: Spanish I; Spanish II (total of 6 sections)
Duties: Created syllabus, designed lectures and exams, and worked closely with other TAs teaching concurrent sections. Primarily upper class students enrolled in course.

INSTRUCTOR

English Department, Instructor, Distance Education Division, Indiana University, Fall 201x. Taught two online sections of Narrative Literature.

Community College of SW Indiana, Summer Sessions, 201x; 201x
Taught Spanish I to freshman/sophomore students and Conversational Spanish to adult learners.

TECHNOLOGY INTEGRATION

Online/distance education teaching:
Online class management software, blogs, nings, Elluminate *Live!*
Started an online hotline to help students with questions regarding course content and technology issues.
Website design and management:
Flash, SharePoint, Adobe Suite, HTML5

Comparative Literature CV, page 2

Sample, page 2

PRESENTATIONS

"Tomorrow's Poets." Paper presented at the 21st International Meeting, Chicago, Illinois. November 201x.

"International Students React to Campus Life." International Education Conference, Indiana University, Bloomington, Indiana. May 201x.

PUBLICATIONS

Sample, A. (201x). *Freshman studies and intercultural expectations.* Manuscript submitted for publication.

Sample, A. (in press). *Learning styles and international students.* International Magazine.

Alot, R., Sample, A., & Fine, B.E. (201x). *International students and poetry: an analysis of affinity*. Journal of Poetry. 36, 122-130.

CAMPUS INVOLVEMENT

Co-chair, Course Review Committee for the course, American Lives. *Recommendations accepted by the General Education Program, 201x.*

Student member, Search Committee for the Vice President—Academic Affairs. *Reviewed application materials; participated in screening and selection process, 201x.*

Member, University Music and Lecture Series Committee. *Responsible for reviewing credentials of proposed lecturers, for securing bids and booking contracts for campus lecturers, 201x-201x.*

RELATED EXPERIENCE

Tutor, Hispanic Learning Center, summers, 201x-201x. *Taught English to non-English speaking immigrants in the evening program. Worked with adults and children in small group settings and one-on-one.*

Peace Corps Volunteer, Kingston, Jamaica, 200x-200x. *Duties included teaching English as a second language in Kingston and mountain towns and villages in community center or churches. Taught all ages.*

PROFESSIONAL AFFILIATIONS

Modern Language Association
Society for Spanish & Portuguese Historical Studies

LANGUAGES

Languages: Spanish, Portuguese, French

RECOGNITION

Kinseth Senior Fellowship for International Dissertation Research
Murray International Scholarship
University Award for Outstanding Conference Paper

PROFESSIONAL MATERIALS

Portfolio available at: www.interfolio.com/portfolio/alexsample
(View: syllabi, student evaluations, research papers, dissertation abstract, conference presentations, video of classroom teaching, campus activities, and community service)

References available upon request

Computer Science, Law/MBA CV

Strategic Features: Computer Science, Law/MBA CV (dual degree program)

Review this CV if you have several degrees and substantial pre-doctoral experience in research, teaching and related areas including professional career experiences.

CV BASICS:

Highest Degree:	Ph.D. in progress; JD and MBA awarded
Experience:	Practicing professional Teaching assistantships Internships
Job Target:	Small liberal arts college to mid-size university. Teaching is top priority.

CONTENT FEATURES:

- Careful placement of several categories on the first page provides a good overview of interests, education and theoretical and practical orientation. By placing the *Teaching Interests* first, search committees can view versatility and interdisciplinary focus. Institution attended then degree is listed to highlight the institution and show breadth of institution type.
- The *Teaching Appointments* category presents duties and responsibilities first and then lists the types of courses taught and location. This arrangement draws attention to teaching strengths.
- Creating a *Principal Teachers* category is an excellent strategy for identifying recognized individuals who have had an impact on your education and training and are recognized by others in the field.

DESIGN FEATURES:

Font:	Century font, size 10
Margins:	.75" top, bottom, left, right
Layout:	Insert table with two columns.
Line spacing:	One line space between categories.
Enhancements:	Bold and italic font used for visual and organizational emphasis.

Computer Science, Law CV

ALEC SAMPLE

16 University Ave Any City, State 12345 (101) 555-0009 alecsample@gmail.com
Teaching portfolio: www.interfolio.com/portfolio/alecsample

TEACHING INTERESTS

Computer Science	Law History	Finance
Management	Economics	Statistics
Law and Ethics	Accounting	Operations Research

EDUCATION

University of Massachusetts Ph.D.
Computer Science, August 201x-present Expected June 201x
Dissertation Topic: Wall Street Economics & Ethics: 1919

Harvard University J.D.
Juris Doctorate, May 201x

Boston College MBA
Business Administration, May 201x

University of Louisville M.S.
Computer Science, June 201x
Thesis: Development of a Digital Circuit Simulator

Berea College B.S.
Accounting/Finance, May 200x
Undergraduate Fulbright Scholar, Summa cum laude

OVERVIEW

Theoretical Background:
Data Structures, Computer Architecture, Operating Systems, Concurrent Programming, Formal Specification of Programming Languages, Data Abstraction, Hardware Description Languages, Distributed Databases

Systems Used:
VAX (Unix), IBM 360/370 (MVS), Prime (Primos)

Languages:
PL/1, Fortran, Pascal, IBM Assembly, COBOL, C, C++

TEACHING APPOINTMENTS

Teaching responsibilities included lecturing for two classes six times per week, designing of tests and programs, and assigning grades. Supervised graduate level students who acted as graders. Complete responsibility for all aspects of Fortran and COBOL courses. Held extra help sessions to assist students who were experiencing difficulties and to help those who had accelerated skills and desired more stimulation/feedback.

COBOL: (University of Massachusetts)
Evening course instructor in programming-level I, fall 201x
Teaching programming course, fall 201x, spring 201x

Fortran: (Boston College and University of Louisville)
Teaching introductory course, fall 201x, spring 201x

Pascal: (University of Louisville)
Teaching assistant in introductory course, summer 200x, fall 200x

Note: Awarded U-Mass Outstanding Teaching Prize, 201x

Computer Science, Law CV, page 2

Alec Sample, page 2

PRINCIPAL TEACHERS

Teachers and Mentors
Honorable Justice Ken Smith, J.D., Ph.D.
Ken Tankerus, Ph.D.
Molly Moreno, J.D., Ph.D.
Winston Kings, Ph.D.

INTERNSHIPS

Legal Research Intern, College of Law, Harvard University, 201x-201x
Worked under the supervision of Dr. M. Moreno. Researched case law and academic journals regarding civil forfeiture and its legality considering the implications of the Double Jeopardy Clause. Assisted Dr. Moreno in drafting and editing manuscript materials for various articles. (Two articles under review; one in press.)

Computer Analysis Intern, Market Research Associates of Greater Boston, Boston, Massachusetts, January-May, 201x. Responsibilities included collecting, processing and analyzing market research data. Prepared summations of the findings for management meetings and for quarterly reports. Observed planning and development meetings dealing with market research and small business concerns.

LECTURES

"Ethics, Recession, and Executive Trusts," Legal Rights Seminar, Boston Student Legal Association, Boston, October 12, 201x.

"Trading Activity and Ethics," Senior Law Seminar, Northeastern University, Boston, November 5, 201x.

BRIEFS

Executive Trusts—a review of 201x. Prepared for American Association of Lawyers Review, vol (2), 123-121, June 201x. Washington, DC

Ethics Research and Implications, 201x-201x. Legal Forum and Journal, vol (8), 28-34, September 10, 201x.

BUSINESS EXPERIENCE

Lawyer, Business Trust Corporation, Boston, 201x-present. Work primarily with small business accounts and executive trusts. Provide pro-bono services to neighborhood businesses struggling in today's recession.

Network Specialist, Louisville County School District, Louisville, 200x. Responsibilities included maintaining and upgrading electronic communication and access to information. Trained professional staff in network usage to ensure access and protect confidential records.

Computer Programmer, First Bank, Inc., Cambridge, 200x-200x. Responsibilities included data analysis, database programming and design of computer programs.

SERVICE

President, NE Boston Crisis and Emergency Center, 201x-present
Speaker, Rotary Club of Boston, December 201x
Volunteer, Good Samaritan Hospital Pediatrics Center, 201x
Member, Massachusetts Legal Society (Board Member and Chair), 201x
Contributor to NoreasternLawBlawgs.com (law ethics legal blog), 201x

Consulting/Design/New Media Résumé

Strategic Features: Consulting/Design/New Media Résumé (Art CV to résumé)

Review this résumé if you are applying for positions that value specific competencies, technology applications and experiences over the type/level of degrees earned.

RÉSUMÉ BASICS:

Highest Degree:	MFA
Experience:	Teaching and studio experience
Job Target:	Creative or consulting position

CONTENT FEATURES:

- Résumé material was tailored from a 20 page CV focusing on client-based skills, languages and new media for a non-academic career.
- *Professional Competencies and Career Overview* is listed early to demonstrate wide-ranging creative background and related employment.
- The layout of page one was a deliberate design—from competences to languages, the six key categories were carefully selected and placed on page one, and could stand alone as a one-page résumé.
- Annotations are included in just one category—*Professional Employment* and the four bullets represent highlights of seven different jobs. This design saves space and eliminates redundancy.
- Under *Professional Materials* four links are included for portfolio materials, ning, and podcasts.

DESIGN FEATURES:

Font:	Calibri font, size 10
Margins:	.75" top, bottom; .75" left, right
Layout:	Open new document.
Line spacing:	1.5 line spaces between categories.
Enhancements:	All-caps to highlight category heading; left-justified category headings allowing descriptors to extend from margin-to-margin utilizing space judiciously.

Consulting/Design/New Media Résumé

ALEC SAMPLE

21 Long Street, Any City, State 12345 (101)555-1110 a-sample@uxy.edu www.asample.com

PROFESSIONAL COMPETENCIES

Collaboration with multi-lingual clients and partners
Consulting and teaching experiences in public and private settings
Oversight of collections: curator, exhibition organizer, gallery lecturer, exhibition juror
Design, editorial and marketing background in new media and traditional art
Digital imaging, design and prepress experience

CAREER OVERVIEW

College-level Instructor .... 4 years
Fine Arts Coordinator .... 3 years
Marketing and Design .... 5 years
Independent Artist .... 10 years

TECHNOLOGY AND NEW MEDIA SKILLS

Course/Content Management Systems [Desire2Learn, Blackboard, Moodle, Sakai]
Video Conferencing Systems [Elluminate Live! Plan/Publish, Echo 360, Polycom]
Microsoft Office Professional applications [Access, Publisher, SharePoint Designer]
Open Office Productivity Suite [Writer, Impress, Base, Draw]; Parallels
Apple applications [Aperture, Final Cut Studio, iLife, iWork]; Pinnacle Studio; FileMaker Pro
Digital prepress workflow systems [trap, impose, OPI]; digital image and video editing
Color separations/proofing for direct to plate, direct to press, and analog printing systems

EDUCATION

MFA, Printmaking, *Photography* Minor, The University of Iowa, Iowa City, 201x
Center for the Book, The University of Iowa, Iowa City, 201x–0x
MA, Printmaking, *Drawing* Minor, The University of Iowa, Iowa City, 200x
MFA, Art History, Ohio University, Athens, Ohio, 200x
BGS, General Studies, Indiana University, Bloomington, Indiana, 200x
Carolyn Manosevitz Studio, Drawing & Painting Studies, Austin, Texas, 199x–9x
Fulbright Scholar Dependent's Grant [Latvia]

FUNDING AND AWARDS

3-year Humanities Grant, "Art Crosses Borders & Boundaries," New Art Foundation, 201x
Exhibition Grant, Iowa Foil Printer Foundation, Iowa City, 201x
Dard Hunter Conference Scholarship, Friends of Dard Hunter, Minneapolis, 201x
Commodore of the Texas Navy, Governor of State of Texas [Ann Richards], 199x

LANGUAGES, INTERNATIONAL RESIDENCE & ORGANIZATIONS

Fluency in Spanish, and study of French, German, Chinese, Japanese & Latvian
Archival research & residence—Latvia 20xx; England 20xx; Nürnberg 198x–198x
Chicano Humanities & Arts Council, Association of Hispanic Arts, Association for Art History

Consulting/Design/New Media résumé, page2

Alec Sample, page 2

PROFESSIONAL EMPLOYMENT

Austin Community College, Adjunct Professor, Department of Art, 201x–201x
The University of Iowa, Adjunct Assistant Professor, School of Art, 201x–201x
Interim Fine Arts Coordinator, Arts & Humanities, Kirkwood Community College, 200x
Visiting Scholar, Latvian Center, 200x; Visiting Artist, Latvian Academy of Art, Riga, 200x
Design, Editorial & Marketing Assistant, Ohio University Press, 19xx–20xx
Digital Imaging, Design & Prepress Iowa State University, Printing Services, 19xx-19xx
Freelance Graphic Artist, Cool-Breeze Graphics, Austin, 19xx-19xx

Key highlights of above positions:

- Used creative skills to design materials for private and public venues
- Communicated with grant agencies, private patrons and board of directors
- Managed and monitored six-figure budgets and expense accounts
- Created curricula and engaged students in intellectual discussions

EXHIBITIONS (selected list—over 60 exhibits)

"30 Dies de Gravat a Olot," Group Digital Print Exhibition, Galeria el Cailu, Olot, Spain
"Pink Amour" Group Mixed Media Exhibition, Tiru Gallery, Austin, Texas
Naestved International Exhibition of Contemporary Prints, Group Print Exhibition, Naestved, Denmark
XII Bienal Guadalupana, Group Small Format Print Exhibition, La Universidad Iberoamericana, San Angel Culture Center, Mexico City, Mexico
2nd International Mini Print of Sarajevo, Euro Art Centre, Vaxjo, Sweden [Traveling]
Invitation to 4th Biennale Internazionale Dell'Arte Contemporanea, Fortezza da Bazzo, Florence, Italy

BIBLIOGRAPHY & PUBLICATIONS (selected list – over 20 publications)

The Americas Biennial Exhibition, by A. Sterly, *Printmaking Today,* Issue 1, Spring 201x. [Forthcoming]
The Americas Biennial Exhibition of Contemporary Prints: 200x, exhibition catalogue, Edited by A. Sample, phatpress (Austin, Texas), 201x [Forthcoming]
Contemporary Art of Latvia: War, Waiting, Inflammation & Pomegranates, exhibition catalogue, Edited by A. Sample, RiverPress (Iowa City, Iowa), 200x
The World in a Grain of Sand: Prints by A. Sample, by S. Kakarla, in *Frontline,* August 16, 200x

PUBLIC COLLECTIONS (selected list – over 30 public collections)

Universidad Iberoamericana, Departamento de Arte, Diseño y Arquitectura, Ermita, Mexico
Grafisk Vaerksted, Naestved, Denmark
Oregon State University, Department of Art, Corvallis, Oregon
Museum of Engraving, Castello dei Paleologi, Acqui Terme, Moferrato, Italy
Florean Museum, Maramures, Romania
Russian State Pedagogical University, St. Petersburg, Russia
Kyoto International Woodcut Association, Kyoto, Japan

PROFESSIONAL MATERIALS

Teaching portfolio materials available at: www.alecsample.com
Teaching ning: www.arthistory.com/university/prints
Podcasts: iTunesUniversity (alecsample course material)
Art portfolio available at: www.samplearts.com

Creative Writing CV

Strategic Features: Creative Writing CV

Review this CV if you want to strongly emphasize teaching abilities, writing strengths, and the ability to publish. Useful in institutions where instructors have broad teaching responsibilities.

CV BASICS:

Highest Degree:	MFA in progress
Experience:	Instructor and adjunct positions
Job Target:	Teaching all post-secondary levels Writing labs or writing centers

CONTENT FEATURES:

- *Teaching Interests* are listed to emphasize breadth of background, preparation, pedagogy, and ability to work with both upper level grad students and Gen Ed students.
- Creating a *Principal Teachers* section allows the reader to quickly see the reputation and quality of instruction; useful with disciplines that value key players and are small academic or professional communities. Using bullets before principal teachers' names saves space yet creates clean breaks for easy scanning.
- *Awards* category immediately follows the principal teacher section on page one because it recognizes significant achievement.
- Page two could easily contain additional publications and readings; only a few are listed on the sample.

DESIGN FEATURES:

Font:	Arial font, size 11
Margins:	.75" top, bottom; 1" left, right
Layout:	Open new document; use tabs to indent.
Line spacing:	Two line spaces between categories.
Enhancements:	Use of a graphic line to separate address from basic CV content; use of limited bullets in *Teaching Interests* to draw attention to courses and pedagogy.

Creative Writing CV

REED A. LOT

21 University Avenue, Any City, State 12345
(c) 201.565.1111 (o) 201.564.1911
Reed-a-lot@fiu.edu Blog: readingmatters.com

TEACHING INTERESTS

Courses:
- Modern Poetry and Poetics – from Stein to Pound, Bernstein and Collins
- Creative Nonfiction – the personal essay
- Creative Writing – exploring genre and genre transformation
- Poetry Writing – emphasis on the poem as an experience

Pedagogy:
- Foster literary exposure by providing varied texts and readings
- Promote in-class writing, peer workshops, and study of the canon
- Use extensive montage of literary terms and vocabulary
- Cultivate curiosity and employ motivation techniques to write articulately

ACADEMIC BACKGROUND

Florida International University Miami, FL	MFA Creative Writing	May 201x – present
Brown University Providence, R.I.	MS Biochemistry BA English *with distinction*	August 201x May 200x

PRINCIPAL TEACHERS

• Binder Tapeé • Ed. U. Cator • Bea Fine • Margarida Swey • U. R. Rite

AWARDS

American Academy Poetry Prize, 201x
Florida Artist Assistance Fellowship, 201x
Jasper Aye Poetry Prize (Chicago), 201x
FIU Poetry Prize Finalist, 201x
National Library of Poetry Award, 201x
College Essay Contest, First, 201x

PUBLICATIONS

Seeing Mountains, Ben and Smother Publishing, (forthcoming)
Thoughts and Lines, Leonardo Press, 201x
Mountain tales – featured writer: www.mtales.com/poems/vol2/reedalot

Poems have appeared in:

Poetry Southeast
The Florida Review
Ironwood
South Florida Poetry Review
Gulf Coast
Antaeus

Creative Writing CV, page 2

Reed A. Lot
page 2

READINGS

Young Poets Series, University of Florida, Gainesville, Florida, October 201x
The Writer's Voice, Orlando Arts Council, Orlando, Florida, December 201x
Live from Prairie Lights, poetry reading and live broadcast, (WSUI Radio), Iowa City, Iowa, March 201x
Voices, reading series for Art Share, Palm Beach Gardens, Florida, May 201x
Cyber-lyrics, Taos Summer Poetry Fair, Taos, New Mexico, July 201x

EXPERIENCES

Teaching Assistant, English Department, Florida International University, Fall semester, 201x – present

Writing Tutor, College of Public Health, Florida International University, 201x

Reviewer, *South Florida Poetry Review,* Florida Poetry Institute, Miami, Florida, 201x – 201x

Blog editor, *readingmatters.com,* 201x – present

Contributing Editor, *New Poems Review,* Albany, New York, 201x

Assistant Editor, *Providence Poetry Series,* Providence, Rhode Island, 200x

SERVICE & COMMUNITY ENGAGEMENT

Volunteer Tutor /Adult Mentor, Miami Community Center, May 201x – present
Health Assistant, Community Health Free Clinic, North Miami, Fall 201x – present
Fundraiser, Habitat for Humanity Bicycle Challenge, Key West, Summer 201x
Translator, Providence Hospice Services, Providence, 200x – 200x

SCHOLARSHIP

Distinguished Scholar Prize, Florida International University, 201x
Phi Beta Kappa
State of Rhode Island President's Scholarship Award, 200x

LANGUAGES

Proficient Spanish
Conversational German
Read Latin

PORTFOLIO

www.interfolio.com/portfolio/reedlot
letters of recommendation available

Dental Science CV

Strategic Features: Dental Science CV

Review this CV if you are seeking a residency or externship-type position. In addition, this CV demonstrates how to represent military service and training. Because of the singular purpose and use of this CV, an "objective" is included.

CV BASICS:

Highest Degree:	DDS with additional specialized training
Experience:	Military Service Clinical/professional experience
Job Target:	Residency

CONTENT FEATURES:

- First four categories (*Objective, Academic Preparation, License,* and *Recognition*) present a clear picture of the candidate's immediate career intention and states appropriate training and qualifications required for the competitive residency.
- *Research Interests* and *Professional Qualifications* are presented on page one to demonstrate scholarly interests and to highlight training and skills to this point in career.
- The *Employment* and *Professional Service* categories demonstrate critical areas of productivity and practice and professional involvement: table clinics, conferences and memberships. To keep CV to two pages as required in the application directions, not all "professional involvement" or undergraduate honors were included.

DESIGN FEATURES:

Font:	Calibri font, size 10
Margins:	1" top, bottom, left, right
Layout:	Insert table with two columns.
Line spacing:	One line space between categories.
Enhancements:	Bold font to highlight material at the beginning of each category.

Dental Science CV

HIREM E. SOON
21 College Street, City, State, Zip
(c) 211.509.6789 hireme-soon@university.edu

OBJECTIVE

Endodontic residency

ACADEMIC PREPARATION

AGED-1 Eglin Air Force Base,
Fort Walton Beach, FL, 200x-200x

DDS The Ohio State University,
Columbus, OH
College of Dentistry, 200x-200x

B.A. Luther College, Decorah, Iowa
Chemistry and Biology majors, 199x-200x

LICENSE

Current license
Ohio State Dental License, 201x-present

RECOGNITION

The Ohio State University College of Dentistry
USAF Health Profession Scholarship Program
Thomas Ruan Fixed Prosthodontics Award

Luther College
Suma Cum Laude
Dean's List, 8 semesters
Phi Beta Kappa
Regents & Presidential Scholarships

RESEARCH INTERESTS

Areas of research interest
new file technologies
anesthetic research
obturation techniques
new irrigation techniques
cone beam CT scans and their use in endodontic procedures

PROFESSIONAL QUALIFICATIONS

Trained in and credentialed to perform independently by USAF:
Initial endodontic treatment and retreatment
Posterior implant placement and restoration
Periodontal surgery including hard tissue recontouring and grafting, connective and free soft tissue autografting
Surgical removal of impacted third molars and biopsy procedures
Prosthodontic single and multi unit fixed as well as removable intravenous, nitrous oxide, and oral sedation techniques
Limited orthodontics

TEACHING EXPERIENCE

Teaching Assistant, General Chemistry, Luther College, 201x-201x
Teaching Assistant, Organic Chemistry, Luther College, 201x-201x

Dental Science CV, page 2

Hirem E. Soon, page 2

RESEARCH EXPERIENCE

Senior honors research project, Biochemistry, Luther College.
Under the direction of Dr. W.B. Fine. Contributed to work published later as: Fine, W.B., et al. Sterol carrier protein-2 expression alters sphingolipid metabolism in transfected mouse L-cell fibroblasts. *Molecular and Cellular Biochemistry* (201x) 283(1-2): 57-66.

Biochemical research internship, The Ohio State University, summer 201x
Biochemical research investigating thermodynamics of protein denaturation in turkey ovomucoid third domain.

EMPLOYMENT

General Dentist, Minot Air Force Base, Minot, ND, 200x-present
(Clinic: 6 general dentists, no specialists, and limited referral options due to remote location; base population: 7,000+ Air Force members)
Overview of responsibilities: Officer in Charge of Radiology
Oversaw the clinic-wide transition from conventional to digital radiology; helped to expand endodontic capabilities by spearheading the purchase of a dental microscope, obtura systems, ultrasonic irrigation capabilities, and additional endodontic file options for the dental clinic.

AEGD-1 Resident, Eglin Air Force Base, Fort Walton Beach, Fl, 200x-200x
Overview: endodontic treatment, retreatment, post op complications and incision and drainage, trauma management, and external resorbtion repair; implant placement and restoration. Periodontal procedures including hard and soft tissue grafting and recontouring; oral surgery procedures including impacted wisdom teeth removal, and both hard and soft tissue biopsy; and operative and prosthodontic procedures.

Of special note: trained and certified in the use of IV conscious sedation, forensic dentistry; attended courses in oral pathology and oral facial pain.

PROFESSIONAL SERVICE

Table Clinic Presentation
"Ultrasonic Irrigation: Root Canal Therapy at the Speed of Sound."
Table Clinic, Hinnman Meeting, Atlanta, GA. October 201x

Professional Conference
Attended AAE Annual Meeting, San Diego, CA. March 201x

Affiliations
Member, American Association of Endodontists, 201x-present
Member, American Dental Association, 201x-present
Member, Phi Beta Kappa

MILITARY SERVICE

United States Air Force
Captain, 201x-present

DOSSIER

Available upon request:
References • Personal Statement • Writing Samples

Economics CV

Strategic Features: Economics CV

Review this CV if you are approaching tenure review. Note the number of varied categories and sections required of an experienced academic. Especially note the publications and general service areas in this CV.

CV BASICS:

Highest Degree:	Ph.D.
Experience:	Recently tenured
Job Target:	Tenure review (This 3-page CV includes categories typically included for tenure review.)

CONTENT FEATURES:

- The first page presents a comprehensive overview of expertise and progressive experience. Degree information is basic with dissertation and thesis items removed; at this point in career they are no longer relevant because of publications, grants, and other relevant experience.
- Page two (which is several pages long before condensing) shows considerable success and writing experience suitable for a wide range of media and publications.
- CVs used for tenure review must demonstrate "general service" contributed to the campus and the community. Page three lists service contributions with minimal annotations.
- Content determines CV length for tenure just as it does for job seeking.
- Substantial service is broken into categories for ease of reading and to demonstrate breadth of efforts.

DESIGN FEATURES:

Font:	Tahoma font, size 10
Margins:	1" top, bottom, left, right
Layout:	Open new document; use tabs to indent.
Line spacing:	1.5 line space between categories.
Enhancements:	Use of italics used for organizational emphasis.

Economics CV

ALEX EXAMPLE

State University Department of Economics o:287.987.4646

COLLEGIATE EDUCATION

PhD	Economics	University of Notre Dame 201x
MA	Economics	Purdue University 201x
BA	Economics	Virginia Tech 19xx

SPECIAL RECOGNITION

University Pew Teaching Excellence Award (201x) competitive teaching award

FACULTY DEVELOPMENT

Seminar Series

"SU Liberal Education Initiative Scholar" (February - April 201x)

Summit

"Community Sustainability Partnership Summit" (May 201x)

PROFESSIONAL SERVICE

Seminars

"Faculty Inclusion Advocate Training," State University (February 201x)
Trained to serve as an Inclusion Advocate during hiring processes.

"Family-Friendly Fringe Benefits and the Gender Wage Gap," (September 201x)
Presentation of research to the Economics Department Seminar Series.

Workshop

"State University General Education Institute on Themes," (May 201x)

TEACHING POSITIONS

Academic: State University, Smithson College of Business
Associate Professor of Economics, July 201x – Present
Assistant Professor of Economics, August 201x – July 201x

Teaching: other instruction
AP Exam Grader - Economics, External to State University, Educational Testing Service, June 201x; June 201x
Honors Senior Projects, 201x; 201x

RESEARCH IN PROGRESS

Refereed Journal Articles

Example, A., and Sample, I. An Experimental Test of Preemptive Collusion. *European Journal of Political Economy.*

Example, A., and Sample, I. A Note on Bribery and Monitoring Technology. *International Review of Law and Economics.*

Approaching Submission

Example, A., and Sample, I. Hispanic Volunteering and Giving Behaviors.

Example, A., and Sample, I. Efficient Enumerative Approach to Land Allocation Problem.

Economics CV, page 2

Alex Example, page 2

PUBLICATIONS

Refereed Journal Articles

Example, A., Hansen, M. R., and Sample, I. (201x). A Note on Bilateral Trade Agreements in the Presence of Irreversible Investment and Deferred Negotiations. *Economics Bulletin,* Vol. 6 (34), pp. 1-10.

Example, A., and Sample, I. (201x). A Survival Analysis of IJV Dissolution. *Journal of Business and Economic Studies,* Vol. 14 (1), pp. 62-80.

Book Chapters

Example, A., Sample, I., Hand, M., and Hansen, M. R., The "Boy Crisis" and the Socioeconomic Status of Young Adults. *Youth Employment: Poverty Impact, Employability and Paths to Adulthood.* Hauppauge, NY: Nova Science Publishers. Forthcoming.

Example, A., Hand, M., Hansen, M. R., and Sample, I. (201x). The Harris-Westin's Index of General Concern About Privacy. *Privacy, Surveillance and the Globalization of Personal Information.* Kingston, ON: McGill-Queen's University Press.

Conference Proceedings

Example, A., Sample, I., and Hand, M. (201x). *You Wanna Step Outside? Testosterone, Risk-aversion, Sex, and the Decision to Compete*: The Proceedings of the Second Annual Conference of the NorthEastern Evolutionary Psychology Society. Forthcoming.

Example, A. (201x). *Estimating Learning Rules: Strategies versus Actions*: Available online: www.cirano.qc.ca/ee/ESA2005_Tucson/ConferenceSchedule.pdf.

Published Research Note

Example, A., and Sample, I. (201x). *Survival Analysis of Joint Venture Relationships* (114th ed., Vol. 13, pp. 1). St. Louis, MO: International Atlantic Economic Society.

Published Working Papers

Example, A., and Sample, I. (201x). *School Consolidations and Teacher Incentive Contracts* (Working Paper No. 1238586): Social Science Research Network.

Example, A., Sample, I., *Learning and Experiments: The Bootstrap to the Rescue.* At: https://biz.edu/accounting/papers/workingpapers/02-14.pdf

Technical Reports

Example, A., and Sample, I. (201x). *The Economic Impact of Nonprofits in Kent County*: Johnson Center for Philanthropy.

Magazine/Trade Publications

Example, A., and Sample, I. (201x). *Education and the Economy: The Challenge for West Michigan*: Smithson Business Review.

Example, A., and Sample, I. (201x). *Women and the Labor Market: The Trends and Implications*: Rapid City Business Journal.

CONFERENCE PRESENTATIONS

Ludium II, "Delegate", Example, A., Indiana University, The Synthetic Worlds Initiative, Bloomington, IN, Ludium II. (June 22, 201x).

Economic and Business Historical Society Annual Meeting, "Incorporating Economic History into Economics Courses," Sample, I., (Presenter & Author), Example, A. (Author Only), Providence, RI (April 201x).

Economics CV, page 3

Alec Sample, page 3

GENERAL SERVICE

Attendee

Attendee, SU Convocation. (August 201x - Present)

Committee

Committee Member, Smithson Pew Teaching Award Committee. (Fall 201x)
Committee Chair, MBA Committee. (January 201x - May 201x)
Committee Member, College Assessment Committee. (August 200x - Present)

Conference

Conference Session Chair, Midwest Economic Conference. (March 201x)
Conference Paper Reviewer, Midwest Economic Conference. (March 201x)
Conference Session Chair, Western Economic Association International. (July 200x)

Professional Memberships, Licensures, and Certifications

American Economic Association
Association for Research on Nonprofit Organizations and Voluntary Action
Faculty, Beta Gamma Sigma Honor Society
International Atlantic Economic Society
Economic Science Association

Student

Department Representative, Student Visitation Day. (April 3, 201x)

Student Org Advisor (Professional Org), SU Economics Club, appointed. (August 201x - August 201x). Supervise student organization activities, monitor finances.

Student Mentor, Student Scholarship Day. (April 201x - Present)
Mentored student research, and helped students prepare for presentations.

Other

Reviewer, Graduate Student Presidential Research Grant Review, SU. (200x)

Journal Referee: *Journal of Socio-Economics; Journal of Virtual World Research*

Faculty Mentor, Faculty Mentorship Program. (August 200x - Present)
Mentor to Adjunct Faculty, Visiting Faculty, and Mentor to New Faculty

Judge, Best Undergraduate Paper Competition, Sponsored by the International Atlantic Economic Society. (201x - 201x)

Interviewer, Awards of Distinction Scholarship Competition. (201x, 201x)

Mascot Judge, SU Homecoming Celebration. (October 200x)
Selected by students to be a judge of mascots in homecoming celebration.

CONTRACTS, GRANTS AND SPONSORED RESEARCH

Funded

Example, A., (Principal), "Research Team Leader: Hispanic Volunteering and Impact on Giving Behaviors," Community Research Institute, External to State University, Funded. (start: September 201x, end: November 201x)

Example, A., "Family-Friendly Fringe Benefits and the Gender Wage Gap," Smithson College of Business, Funded. (start: May 201x, end: August 201x)

Consulting

Morgan Stanley, Compensated, Detroit, Michigan. (April 201x - May 201x).
Data and analysis services.

Johnson Center for Philanthropy, Compensated, SU. (November 201x - March 201x).
Economic impact of nonprofits. Analysis of four countries nonprofit sectors.

Educational Leadership CV

Strategic Features: Educational Leadership CV

Review this CV if you have spent years in a career with substantial responsibilities outside the halls of academe. Learn how to list four degrees from the same institution.

CV BASICS:

Highest Degree:	Ph.D.
Experience:	20 years of experience in K-12 settings
Job Target:	Post-secondary master's or doctorate level teaching

CONTENT FEATURES:

- *Research Interests* and *Experience Overview* are listed early to give focus to the CV and to highlight the desire to be an active researcher at the collegiate level. (An important feature in a career-change CV is to stress current interests and skills and minimize extensive details of the first career, in this case, K-12 education. *Leadership Experience* is listed but only a brief annotation is provided for the last position.)
- *Funding* opportunities appear on page one to reinforce skills and requisite understanding of the nuances of grant writing and funding agencies.
- For purposes of introduction (not related to employment), the first page of the CV could be used alone.
- Page two provides a comprehensive and useful summary of leadership and professional service that can be expanded easily to accommodate new material.

DESIGN FEATURES:

Font:	Segoe font, size 11
Margins:	1" top, bottom, left, right
Layout:	Open new document; use tabs to indent.
Line spacing:	1.5 line space between categories.
Enhancements:	Selected use of bold font to highlight specific words.

Educational Leadership CV

ED HIGHER 5 College Ave, Any Place, State Zip EDHIGHER@mps.k12.us 301.2234.567

RESEARCH INTERESTS

Contemporary Management Theory
Financial Management
School & Community Relationships
Politics & Economics in Public Education
Administrative Leadership Theory
School Organizational Patterns

EXPERIENCE OVERVIEW

Superintendent	8 years
Fulbright Scholar	1 year
Assistant Superintendent	2 years
Principal	3 years
Teacher	6 years

ACADEMIC BACKGROUND

University of Colorado	Ed.D.	Policy Leadership Studies, 201x
Denver, Colorado	Ed.S.	Educational Administration, 200x
	M.A.	Instructional Design/Technology, 200x
	B.A.	German & History, 200x

FUNDING

Promise Project: Initiated and led the design and development of two new high schools and one middle school that incorporated performance-based learning goals; year-round, evening and flexible hours; integrated coursework; compulsory foreign language; technology infusion; teaching teams and advisory boards (201x-present).

Promise Grant: Proposed and received a State Education Grant ($2m) to develop and initiate the Eclipse Project. Worked in cooperation with state education leaders, teachers, business and community leaders to design a *New Schools Proposal* that prepares today's students for a global community (201x).

LEADERSHIP EXPERIENCE

Superintendent of Schools, Mountain School District, Boulder, 201x-present
Enrollment and staff: 12,000 students, 543 staff, 43 administrators.
Budget: 52.4 million; successful bond referendum: 18.2 million
Fulbright Scholar, Warsaw, Poland, 201x
Superintendent of Schools, Park Public Schools, Park, Montana, 201x-201x
Assistant Superintendent, Park Public Schools, Park, Montana, 201x-201x
High School Principal, Omaha Public Schools, Omaha, Nebraska, 200x-200x
Classroom Teacher, German and History, Omaha Public Schools, 200x-200x

Educational Leadership CV, page 2

Sample, page 2

BRIEFS, REVIEWS AND ABSTRACTS

New Schools Research Institute. (201x, April). *Schools of the Future—Accessibility Matters* (Issue Brief No. 97). Washington, D.C. Ed Higher.

Higher, Ed. (201x). *The empty promise of charter schools* [Peer commentary of the paper, "Charter Schools Are Tomorrow's Examples" by C.B. Gove]. Retrieved from http://www.education.us.charter/research/papers.edu

Higher, Ed. School Vision: A neglected opportunity [abstract]. In: Proceedings of the International Conference of the New Schools Movement; 201x May; Sydney Australia. Promise Press; 201x. p 120.

GRADUATE APPOINTMENTS

Research Award-Fulbright Scholar Program, Warsaw, Poland, 201x. Under the Fulbright Scholar Program for graduate research grants, studied school curricula and the integration of technology and second languages and state-mandated materials with a special emphasis on technology.

Graduate Research Assistant, Policy Leadership Studies, University of Montana, 200x-200x. Under the direction of Professor Ed. U. Cator, collected, reviewed, and analyzed the early school restructuring movement. Developed on-line bibliography for use in the course *School Reformation*; bibliography was later incorporated into the index of the *Policy Leadership Handbook* edited by Dr. R. Lott.

PROFESSIONAL SERVICE (selected list)

Leadership:
Appointed member, Governor's Commission on Schools, 201x-present
Chair, Mountain Regional Association, Denver, October 201x
Co-chair, State Economic Development Commission, 201x-present
President (201x) and charter member, New Schools Coalition, 201x-present

Activities:
Board of Directors, County United Way, 201x-present
President, Mountain Youth Action Committee, 201x
Chair, Chamber of Commerce Futures Committee, Colorado Springs,201x

Presentations:
"Restructuring=Total Commitment," State Governor's Forum, Denver, March 201x
"Involving Parents in School Programs," Montana School Conference, April 201x
"Partnerships with Results, " School Administrators Meeting, San Diego, May 201x

Publications:
Higher, Ed. "Demystifying Reform," *Learning Magazine,* 4, 2 (May 201x): 16-17.
Higher, Ed. "Reform: One Approach," *Idaho Curriculum Bulletin,* XI, 3 (Fall 201x): 7-9.

Memberships:
American Association of School Administrators; New Schools Coalition

Teaching and leadership portfolio available upon request

Engineering CV

Strategic Features: Engineering CV & Scholarship CV

Review this CV if you are seeking a scholarship. For organizations offering competitive scholarships, one-page CVs are often requested. In this case, the application stressed formal education, internships, and leadership. For job seeking, expand the categories and add new ones that could not fit on this scholarship version.

CV BASICS:

Highest Degree:	Early in doctoral program
Experience:	Intern and project experience Research and teaching assistant
Job Target:	Scholarship

CONTENT FEATURES:

- Scholarship version trimmed to one page to meet "application requirements." Categories have been condensed to include basic details of education, experience and leadership.
- *Course Project Experience* is included with *Formal Education and Training* category to provide essential project details.
- Responsibilities of each leadership position are briefly annotated to show breadth of experiences and responsibilities.
- Service to department tucked into more professional categories — strong emphasis in collaboration, student support, and recruiting.
- To condense the CV to one page, some categories have been omitted and some represent only selected or most recent activities.

DESIGN FEATURES:

Font:	Gill Sans MT font, size 10
Margins:	.75" top, bottom, left, right
Layout:	Open new document; use tabs to indent.
Line spacing:	.5 line space between categories.
Enhancements:	Use of a graphic line to separate categories. Italics and bold are used for organizational emphasis.

Engineering CV

HIREM E. SOON 21 University Avenue, Any City, State 12345 (201)565-1111 hiremesoon@uiowa.edu

FORMAL EDUCATION AND TRAINING

The University of Iowa, Iowa City, Iowa

Doctor of Philosophy Civil Engineering, 201x – present
Research Focus: Transportation Logistics

Master of Science Urban and Regional Planning, May 201x
Transportation Studies Certificate

Master of Science Industrial Engineering, December 201x
Research Focus: Teenage Drivers, perceived compared to actual distractions

Bachelor of Science Industrial Engineering, May 200x
Focus Areas: Management, Human Factors & Ergonomics

Napier University Study Abroad – Edinburgh, Scotland, 200x

Course Project Experience

- Ergonomics – Conceptualized better processes/products in teams of 3
- Design for Manufacturing – Designed/built mechanical catapult in team of 6
- Transportation Demand Analysis – Assessed local transit use movement
- Operational Systems Design – Updated physical requirement documents; suggested ergonomic improvements later implemented by Fortune 500 company in team of 3
- Field Problems – Developed a sustainable growth plan for city of 1,500 in team of 7

FIELD ENGINEERING EXPERIENCE

Industrial Engineering Intern, Summer 201x, Loram Maintenance of Way Inc., Denver

- Obtained answers to build questions on railway maintenance equipment
- Accelerated manufacturing drawing revision update process

Engineering Orientation Advisor, Summer 200x, The University of Iowa

- Presented overview of policies and procedures for first year students
- Built class schedules and advised 350 students on course selection

Industrial Engineering Intern, Summer 200x, Sonoscan Incorporated, Chicago

- Wrote procedures for packing main products and international field upgrades
- Revised process for documentation modification

ACADEMIC ENGINEERING EXPERIENCE

Research Assistant Road User Study, 201x – present. Public Policy Center

- Conducted statistical analysis of survey responses
- Assisted in informed consent participant training sessions around the country

Research Assistant Teenage Driver Project, 201x. Human Factors Modeling Lab

- Developed and executed plan for participant recruitment
- Analyzed survey responses to develop theory for master's thesis

Industrial Engineering Teaching Assistant, 200x – 200x. The University of Iowa

- Presented weekly Engineering Problem Solving project sections
- Developed seminar course curriculum, coordinated plant visits

LEADERSHIP

Student Recruiter, The University of Iowa, 201x – present

- Coordinated Engineering Connection Mentoring Program for 300 students

Alpha Phi Omega, 201x – present

- Section 21 Vice Chair/Region 9 Scouting Representative

Professional Memberships, 200x – present

- Institute of Industrial Engineers; American Planning Association (vice chair for UI section)

English Literature/English Education (Interdisciplinary) CV

Strategic Features: English Literature & English Education CV

Review this CV if you need to highlight unique graduate programming that might be beneficial to hiring departments and/or if your interests include teaching at a community college. The inclusion of an AA degree indicates an interest in and an awareness of that level of post-secondary education.

CV BASICS:

Highest Degree:	Doctoral degree in progress
Experience:	Teaching assistantships Research assistantships
Job Target:	Community college; small liberal arts college

CONTENT FEATURES:

- In the *Degree* category, the interdisciplinary doctoral program emphasizes nontraditional preparation and helps the reader to view all experiences from that perspective.
- The *University Experience* category accentuates responsibilities at the post-secondary level; subheads within the category direct attention to both teaching and research strengths.
- To highlight the range of literary works, a distinctive configuration is employed. *Publications* are separated into blogs, articles, fiction and poetry using bold font to emphasize. Addresses changing dynamics of publishing in this discipline.
- The *Professional Activities* category contains an assortment of activities including a paper presentation, panelist, adjudicator, and search committee member. Using one category to list a diverse collection of activities saves space and shows the reader your versatility.

DESIGN FEATURES:

Font:	Bell MT font, size 10
Margins:	.75" top, bottom, left, right
Layout:	Open new document; use tab to indent.
Line spacing:	.5 line space between categories.
Enhancements:	Use of bold font to highlight sub-categories.

English Literature/English Education (Interdisciplinary) CV

IMA SAMPLE

16 University Avenue, Any City, State 12345 101.555.0009
i-sample@gmail.com

DEGREES

Ph.D. University of California-Santa Barbara, June 201x - present
English Education and English
Cognate Areas: Contemporary Letters, Adolescent Writing, Literature
Dissertation Topic: *Cultural Perspectives of the Female Adolescent in American Literature -1950*
Committee Co-chairs: Ed U. Cator, Education; Reed A. Lot, English

Interdisciplinary doctoral program incorporates courses from the Department of English and College of Education to examine and to further the relationship between literature and pedagogy. The committee co-chairs have appointments in both departments.

M.A. American Literature, University of Washington, Seattle, 201x
Thesis: *Writers of New York: the 1930's* Advisor: Ed Penn, Ph.D.

B.A. English Education, Carleton College, Northfield, MN, 200x *with distinction*

A.A. Liberal Arts, Mesa Community College, Mesa, AZ, 200x

UNIVERSITY EXPERIENCE

Teaching Experiences

Instructor, Northern Virginia Community College, Annandale, Fall 201x – 201x. (NVCC is part of the Virginia Community College System) Teaching "Introduction to Adolescent Literature" to undergraduate returning adult students. Responsibilities include planning course content, delivering lectures, and evaluating performance.

Teaching Assistant, UC-Santa Barbara, College of Liberal Arts, English Division, Spring semester 201x – Fall 201x. Responsible for instruction and evaluation of student achievement for two sections of Rhetoric. Maintained office hours to work with students individually.

Research Assistantships

Research Associate, Books for Young Readers Program, UC-Santa Barbara, 201x – 201x. Assisted in the review of new adolescent literature. Evaluated books, wrote reviews and participated in regular discussion sessions with colleagues and area teachers.

Washington Foundation Research Assistant, American Studies Division, University of Washington, Fall 201x. Assisted teaching staff with special projects, coordinated material for course syllabi, and entered research data for grant.

Graduate Research Assistant, Center for Talented, UC-Santa Barbara, Spring 200x. Assisted director with summer programs for gifted junior high age girls, and with special projects to encourage gifted female students to pursue interests in sciences and math.

SCHOLARSHIPS

Mellow Dissertation Award and Special Grant, Graduate College, UC-Santa Barbara, December 201x
Graduate Fellowship in American Literature, University of Washington, Fall 201x – Fall 201x
Community College Language Scholarship, Mesa Community College, Fall 201x – Spring 201x

English Literature/English Education CV, page 2

Sample, page 2

PUBLICATIONS

Poetry Blog:
"Voices Never Heard," *Global Press Blog,* May 21, 201x. <www.gPress.com>
"Silence Heard," *Global Press Blog,* March 18, 201x. <www.gPress.com>

Articles:
"Nostalgic Narrative Voices," *Virginia English Bulletin,* (in press)
"Left, Left and Right," *Press of New England,* (in press)
"Eve(ning) in the Garden," *Monday's Daughters,* October 201x

Fiction:
"The Bees and the Frogs," *GLAD,* June 201x
"After Math," *Kid Trails,* January 201x
"The Readers' Club," *The Wanderer,* October 201x
"Coming to Grips," *Inbound,* Spring 200x

Poetry:
"Penelope," *Kid Trails,* September 201x
"Returning to Mars," *Young American,* August 18, 201x
"Chimera, Charisma, Kerygma and Me," *Inbound,* Spring 201x
"Leading to the Left," *Inbound,* Summer 200x

PROFESSIONAL ACTIVITIES

"Tomorrow's Poets." Paper presented at the Southeast Language Arts Symposium, Richmond, Virginia. October 201x.
Panelist, "The Province of Adolescent Literature," Mid-Atlantic Regional Conference on Gifted Education, Baltimore, Maryland. June 201x.
Member, Search Committee, English, UC-Santa Barbara, Spring 201x.
Committee member, Curriculum Review, English Education, University Washington, Fall and Spring semester, 201x and 201x.
Adjudicator: Seattle Student Poetry Competition, April 201x.
Fall Writing Fair, Atlantic Council, International Reading Association, 201x; 200x.
Judge, Minnesota State High School Poetry Contest, March 200x.

RELATED EXPERIENCE

Editorial Associate, Scholastic Teen Reading Series, Boston, 200x. Prepared review and study guide questions for articles and stories dealing with contemporary teen issues; wrote introductions for features and captions for photographs.

Middle School English Teacher, Boston, 200x-200x. Member of teaching team for middle school language arts and reading with emphasis on integrated language arts and the writing process.

AFFLIATIONS

Modern Language Association; International Reading Council; Poetry Council of Boston & New York

Professional materials available in portfolio including: student evaluations; syllabi; writing samples; conference presentations; teaching philosophy; research agenda at: www.interfolio.com/portfolio/ISample

French and Francophone Studies CV

Strategic Features: French and Francophone Studies CV

Review this CV if you want to strongly emphasize your academic background including degrees, fellowships, research and teaching interests, and language abilities. Note: the entire first page is essentially devoted to teaching talents which is useful at institutions where instructors have broad teaching responsibilities.

CV BASICS:

Highest Degree:	Ph.D. candidate
Experience:	Teaching experience Research experience Fellowships
Job Target:	University teaching and research

CONTENT FEATURES:

- An *Academic Overview* category leads off this CV to immediately call attention to the candidate's "academic identity." This layout provides the reader with significant information about the candidate in one continuous section. If this was divided into 5 different categories, it would lessen the power of the candidate's academic identity.
- The categories on page one were carefully selected to show potential as both a researcher and a teacher. Under *Teaching Experience*, four positions are listed with one set of descriptive bullets. This saves the reader from spending time reviewing redundant material. Technology was purposefully positioned on the first page to highlight new media skills.
- Page two continues to focus on the candidate's professional and academic identity with research, employment, service, and publications.

DESIGN FEATURES:

Font:	Candara font, size 10
Margins:	1" top, bottom; 1" left, right
Layout:	Open new document; use tabs to indent.
Line spacing:	One line space between categories.
Enhancements:	Graphic line to highlight category headings.

French and Francophone Literature CV

BEA FINE P.O. Box 45 Any City, Country 011.10155.50101
www.BeaFinePortfolio.org
beafine@gmail.com

ACADEMIC OVERVIEW

Degrees :

- **Ph.D. French and Francophone Studies, PhD Candidate, Vanderbilt University,** Nashville, TN, degree anticipated June 201x
  Dissertation title: Edmond *Amran El Maleh: l'écriture de la mémoire judéo-maghrébine.*

  M.A. Francophone Studies, University of Louisiana at Lafayette, 200x
  Thesis title: *Identités composites des personnages féminins dans quatre romans beurs.*

  License. Langue et Civilisation Françaises, Université Hassan II, Morocco, 199x
  Thesis title : *La violence du texte dans Les Rues Etroites d'Abdelhak Serhane.*

Fellowships:

- Vanderbilt International Dissertation Fellowship (201x)
  Language Graduate Summer Fellowship (201x)
  L. Ziegler Fellowship, University of Louisiana at Lafayette (200x)

Research:

- Francophone and Arab Cinema   Judeo-Maghrebi Literature
  20th and 21st French Literature   Francophone Literatures   Diaspora Literature

Teaching:

- Folk tales in Maghreb and Louisiana   Business and Conversation French
  Advanced French Grammar   French and Arabic Languages   Maghrebi Literatures
  Francophone/Arab Cinema   20th and 21st French Literature

Languages:

- Native speaker: French; Standard Arabic; Moroccan dialect
  Near native speaker: Egyptian and Lebanese dialect
  Fluent speaker: English

TEACHING EXPERIENCE

Intermediate French I/II; Intensive French. Teaching Assistant, Vanderbilt University, 201x – present
19th century French Literature. Teaching Assistant, Vanderbilt University, 201x – present
Instructor of Record in Arabic. Vanderbilt University, 201x – 201x

Accomplishments:

- Analyzed different genres and texts (novel, theater, poetry, short story), assisted students in developing writing techniques, implemented theory based materials.
- Developed proficiency and communication tactics in: listening, speaking, reading & writing.
- Increased students' conversational proficiency and fluency in Modern Standard Arabic.
- Organized the Arabic program, revived curriculum, & developed online course material.
- Worked with audio and video tapes to increase oral and listening skills.

TECHNOLOGY

- Teaching Tools: WebCT, Blackboard, Elluminate *Live!*
- Application Tools: FrontPage, Adobe Photoshop, PowerPoint, Excel, Flash, HTML5, SmartBoard, Blogs, Wikis, Clickers, Google docs

French and Francophone Literature CV, page 2

Bea Fine, page 2

RESEARCH APPOINTMENTS

Special Research Assistant, French Department, University of Louisiana at Lafayette, 200x – 201x

- Researched North African cinema pre- and post-independence.
- Worked with a team of specialist on an international grant to create an online database.
- Built database of colonial cinema in North Africa and translated literary documents from Arabic to French.

Graduate Research Assistant, French Department, University of Louisiana at Lafayette, 200x

- Interviewed students and entered data for a recorded history of immigration and new settlements in the United States and Canada. Supervised by Dr. Will B. Fine.

RELATED EMPLOYMENT

Tutor of Arabic, National Resource Center, International Programs, Vanderbilt University, 201x
Monitor, Information Technology, Language Media Center, Vanderbilt University, summer 201x
Coordinator, Arabic Summer Camp, Talented and Gifted Center, Nashville, TN, summer 200x
Instructor, Summer Camp, Topic: "Africa is not a country," Vanderbilt University, 200x

SERVICE

Campus:

- President, African Student Association
- Department Liaison, Office of International Students
- Representative, Conseil International d'Etudes Francophones (CIEF), Lafayette
- Director, Campus Cultural Diversity Festival

Community:

- Organized community French language circle
- Guest speaker at elementary and secondary schools
- Tutored students in ELL programs

PUBLICATIONS

Fine, Bea & Sample, Ima. *North African cinema pre and post independence. (Under Review)*
Fine, Bea, Goode, W., & Sample, I. (201x) "The Cinema: Colonial North Africa Landscape." Journal of French & Francophone Cinema. vol. 8, 2, October 201x, pp 67-74. Ed: G.W. Serée
Fine, Bea. (201x) "Online Literature Modules for Foreign Language Achievers." Apprentissage des langues et systèmes d'information et de communication (ALSIC), vol. 5, 10, Novembre 201x, pp. 9-14. http://alsic.revues.org/v05/fine/alsic_v05_1x-rec1v2.htm, mis en ligne le 10/11/201x

PRESENTATIONS

"Africa cinema-pre and post independence." Francophone International Convention, Montreal, Canada, March 2, 201x.
"Judeo-Maghrebi literature via online podcast." International Literature Conference, Paris, France, February 26, 200x.

PORTFOLIO

www.interfolio.com/portfolio/beafine

International Education and Policy Studies CV

Strategic Features: International Education/Policy Studies CV

Review this CV if you have interests in using your academic background for a position in an organization outside academe that requires research, significant professional accomplishments, and international experience.

CV BASICS:

Highest Degree:	ABD (all but dissertation)
Experience:	Fellowship Graduate assistantships Professional positions
Job Target:	Policy think-tank International aid organization

CONTENT FEATURES:

- The first category, *Degrees*, clearly identifies all degrees earned and in progress and presents details about the anticipated dissertation and comprehensive areas. By isolating PhD, MA, BS, RN, it is clear that appropriate degrees are in progress, earned, and in areas relevant to research.
- The *Professional Service* categories are accentuated by creating subheads within the category to direct attention to various leadership, consulting and affiliations.
- A *Publications* category is designed to give the reader a quick review of published and in-progress manuscripts as well as the use of new media in academic publications.
- The *Experience* category summarizes 5 disparate positions with short annotations. Use space that relates to your teaching and research.

DESIGN FEATURES:

Font:	Franklin Gothic Book font, size 10
Margins:	.75" top, bottom; .75" left, right
Layout:	Insert table with two rows.
Line spacing:	1.5 line spaces between categories.
Enhancements:	Use of bold font to draw eye to subheadings.

International Education and Policy Studies CV

Alec Sample	#5 Academic Hall, Any University, Any City, State 12345 alec-sample@UU.edu (101)555-1110	
DEGREES:	**Ph.D.**	*International Education and Policy Studies* University of Hawaii at Manoa, Honolulu, Hawaii PhD Candidate, anticipated completion date, May 201x *Dissertation title: Early childhood accessibility in developing countries, a 10 year analysis* Dr. Ken Tenkerus, Advisor *Comprehensive areas: Early Childhood Education, Global Health, International Health Policy*
	M.A.	*Early Childhood, 201x* Emory University, Atlanta, Georgia *Thesis: Policy decisions in childhood program: 1960's* Dr. Able Persson, Advisor
	B.A.	*Elementary Education & Library Science, 200x* University of Hawaii at Manoa
	RN	*Registered Nurse, 200x* Applied College of Nursing, Spokane, Washington
AREAS OF CONCENTRATION:	**Research Focus:** Early Childhood - Education and Care Global Health Issues: Newborns and Pre-school Children International Health Policy	
INTERNATIONAL FELLOWSHIP:	**Graduate Fellowship for International Research & Fieldwork** Fall 201x. Collected data and conducted extensive fieldwork regarding early childhood programs in southeastern China. Presented seminars for childcare professionals; worked with community teams to establish centers in rural areas and worked with faculty at Nanjing Normal University to develop coursework for future teachers.	
PROFESSIONAL SERVICE:	**Leadership:** President (201x); Executive Officer (201x-201x), Pi Lambda Theta Chair, Hawaii Department of Education Childhood Council, 200x Board Member, President's Council on Head Start Policy, 200x **Consulting:** Institute for China Infant Centers, Beijing (current) Idaho State University Innovative Child Center Aerospace Childcare Center, Seattle, Washington **Affiliations:** National Association for the Education of Young Children Association for Childhood Education International	

International Education and Policy Studies CV, page 2

Alec Sample, page 2

PUBLICATIONS:

Published:

Sample, A., & Goode, B. (201x, November). Developmentally appropriate health precautions. Health Times, pp. 5-17.

Ready, I. R., Sample, A., & Doc, I.M. (201x). Health tools for mothers in developing environments. Journal of Early Childhood. 36, 153-157.

Fine, B.E., & Sample, A. (in press). Learning, living, and life-long health accessibility. International Health Magazine.

In Progress:

Sample, A. (201x). *Intercultural expectations in health-care settings.* Manuscript submitted for publication.

Sample, A., Alot, R., & Fine, B.E. (201x). *Cognitive abilities and caloric intake as infants.* Manuscript in preparation.

Media:

Sample, A. (201x, May 2). Re: Health care and early childhood changes: your mind [Web log post]. Retrieved from http://healthblog.com.education/201x/02/mindwork

Sample, A. (Producer). (201x, June 24). *Simple Ways to a healthy classroom* [Audio podcast]. Retrieved from http://www.healthy.com/

PRESENTATIONS:

International:

"Tools for Health." Early Childhood International Convention, Montreal, Canada, November 21, 201x.

"Prekindergarten readers: Strategies for Health Living." 55th International Reading Conference, London, December 12, 200x.

EXPERIENCES:

Supervisor - Student Teachers, University of Hawaii, 201x-201x
Coordinated overseas student teaching assignments. Initiated contacts with students and international headmasters. Conducted seminars for college supervisors. Manage pre-education practicum assignments. Conducted formal three-way conferences and evaluated student progress.

Research Assistant, Emory University, Public Health, 200x-200x
Researched and collected data for an international project on accessibility of early immunizations in rural China.

Classroom Teacher, Bangkok Patana School, Bangkok, 200x-200x
Prekindergarten teacher (ages 3 to 5) and head teacher.

Classroom Teacher, Department of Education, Honolulu, 200x-200x
Kindergarten (5 years) Developmental Kindergarten (3 years)

Nurse, Children's Hospital, Spokane, Washington, 199x-199x

PORTFOLIO: Writing samples, syllabi, evaluations, and references available for review

Law/MBA/Economics CV

Strategic Features: Law/MBA (dual program) & Economics CV

Review this CV if you are at the final stage of a J.D./M.B.A. dual program. This is a good model for job seekers focused on faculty, consulting, or clinical appointments with ABD status.

CV BASICS:

Highest Degree:	Dual degree program in final stages; doctorate at ABD stage
Experience:	Research/teaching assistantships Law clinics Internship
Job Target:	Clinical faculty, consulting, or entry-level professorial appointment

CONTENT FEATURES:

- The first page presents a comprehensive overview of degrees, honors experience highlights (*Overview*), teaching and research interests and graduate assistantships. Degree information is basic with the dissertation and thesis lines replaced with *Research Focus*. The *PhD* is listed as *ABD (all but dissertation)*. The application cover letter would give more details as to the current progress of the doctorate. A *Special Honors* section was added to the *Degree* category to draw attention to these accolades.
- The *Overview* category brings attention to the breadth of experience and the potential for scholarly productivity. Search committees immediately recognize what this candidate can bring to their department. Both research and teaching are requisite for advancement in this field and are included on page one for emphasis.

DESIGN FEATURES:

Font:	Tw Cen MT font, size 10
Margins:	.75" top, bottom, left, right
Layout:	Open new document; set tab to indent.
Line spacing:	1.5 line space between categories.
Enhancements:	Use of bullets to identify descriptive phrases.

Law/MBA/Economics CV

ABLE PERSSON

16 First Avenue Any City, State 12345 persson@au.edu (c): 101.555.0009 (o): 101.515.9009

DEGREES

THE UNIVERSITY OF ARIZONA, TUCSON
Dual Degree Program: J.D./M.B.A. pending June 201x
Research Focus: Immigration Law; Corporate Law
Ph.D. Economics. August 201x–June 201x (ABD)
Research Focus: Tax Law

UNIVERSITY OF NEVADA-LAS VEGAS
M.A. Economics. May 200x
Research Focus: Tax Stratifications
B.S. Social Work and Computer Science. June 200x
summa cum laude

SPECIAL HONORS:
Graduate Fellow, Arizona Institute of Economics
Hilton Corporation Scholarship
Presidential Fellowship
International Study Award, London

OVERVIEW

- Fellow, Arizona Institute of Policy and Law, Phoenix, September 201x-present
- Research Assistant, James E. Rogers College of Law, The University of Arizona, 201x-201x
- International Research Award, Economic Forum, Mexico City, 201x
- Community College Economics Instructor and Technology Coordinator, 200x-200x
- Peace Corps (Western Samoa), 200x-200x

TEACHING AND RESEARCH INTERESTS

Introduction to law	Immigration law	Introduction to legal process & civil procedure
Law and economics	Managerial economics	

GRADUATE ASSISTANTSHIPS: THE UNIVERSITY OF ARIZONA

Teaching Assistant Supervisor – Introduction to Law, College of Business, Fall 201x-present.
- Meet regularly with faculty to evaluate curricula and performance of graduate teaching assistants.
- Coordinate and direct four graduate-level teaching assistants teaching *Introduction to Law* course.
- Responsible for online content for course management system for *Introduction to Law* course.

Teaching Assistant – Introduction to Law, College of Business, Spring 201x; Summer 201x.
- Presented course material using online course management system and direct classroom instruction.
- Offered extra work sessions for students to discuss legal rules and principles.
- Created new teaching materials to supplement existing course syllabus; designed test items and tracked student and class outcomes for a department-wide study.
- Received student evaluations averaging 4.91/5.00 scale.
- Acknowledged by College of Business students as the "201x outstanding teaching assistant."

Law/MBA/Economics CV, page 2

Able Persson, page 2

RESEARCH APPOINTMENTS

Fellow, Immigration Law Clinic, James E. Rogers College of Law, September 201x-present

- Assist law faculty in coordinating induction programs for first and second-year law students
- Develop seminars and podcasts dealing with the topics of asylum-seekers, permanent residents seeking humanitarian waivers and victims of domestic violence.
- Work with issues of U.S. immigration law and assess caseload evidence.

Legal Research Assistant, James E. Rogers College of Law, Fall 201x-present

- Review case law and provide abstracts for faculty preparing briefs and reports on immigration issues.
- Prepare materials that assist law students in the doctrines, procedures and ethical issues unique to the practice of immigration law (Gonzales v. State; People v. Garcia) and the area of legal practice.
- Coordinated the planning and organization of a regional law conference involving students, scholars, and legal experts in the field of immigration law.

International Research Award, Economic Forum, Mexico City, 201x

- Selected to participate in the Economic Forum with participants from 10 countries.
- Attended seminars and workshops presented by experts in the field of economic policy and reform.

SCHOLARLY ACTIVITY

Works in Progress:

Soon, H.E., Persson, A., and Goode, I.M. State law and immigration policy: A climate of hate. (manuscript in progress)

Persson, A., and Fine, B.E. Indigent refugees and immigrants: No counsel, no hope, no future. (paper in progress)

Publications:

Persson, A., and Fine, B.E. (201x, May) Indigent refugees and adverse immigration consequences of a guilty plea: Reminder of an effective counsel. Legal Times. 13, 29-32.

Fine, B.E., Soon, H.E. and Persson, A. (201x, October) The impact of deportation decisions and the social psyche. Journal of Policy and Social Change. 39, 161-172.

Media:

Persson, A. (201x, December 17). Re: Community support of permanent resident cards. [Web log post]. Retrieved from http://immigrationtodayblog.com.resident/201x/12/residentcards

Persson, A. (Producer). (201x, March 28). *Racial profiling: what is reasonable suspicion?* [Audio podcast]. Retrieved from http://www.immigrationtoday.com/

EMPLOYMENT AND COMMUNITY SERVICE

IT Specialist, Department of Corrections, State of Arizona, Phoenix, AZ, 200x-200x

Responsibilities included: staff supervision for the maintaining, upgrading, and replacing components for over 200+ computers; inventory management of software licenses and equipment, administration user accounts and services; and training seminars for staff on new software and system technologies.

Service Opportunities

Family Services Volunteer and Mentor, Bilingual Community Resource Center, Tucson, 201x-201x
Clinic Board Member, Free Health Clinic and Language Center, Tucson, August 201x-May 201x
Coach, Assistant Club Director and Treasurer, Mustang Youth Soccer Club, Tucson, 200x-201x

Professional materials available upon request.

Literacy Education

Strategic Features: Literacy Education (One-page CV for new PhD)

Review this CV if you need a one-page CV for a proposal or conference where it is stipulated that one-page is the maximum limit. This CV truly offers a brief yet comprehensive overview of the individual's broad accomplishments.

CV BASICS:

Highest Degree:	Ph.D. in progress
Experience:	Fellowship and assistantships
Job Target:	Conference use, proposals

CONTENT FEATURES:

- Careful selection of material presents a clear picture of the candidate's academic training, research interests, publications and international experience. A quick glance at the category headings on the left give the reader a quick overview. That is one of the reasons why it is so important to select category headings that are descriptive and meaningful. (See Category Headings in the STYLE GUIDE.)
- To save space but to demonstrate writing and speaking skills, just the basics are presented in the publications and presentations subcategories.
- The *International Experience* and *Service* categories demonstrate critical areas of skill, study, and professional involvement. To keep CV to one page as required, not all material was listed.

DESIGN FEATURES:

Font:	Garamond font, size 11
Margins:	1" top, bottom, left, right
Layout:	Insert table with two columns.
Line spacing:	One line space between categories.
Enhancements:	Italic font to highlight key material and to introduce sub-categories (see *International Experience* and *Service*).

Literacy Education

WILL B. FINE 21 Book Ave, Any City, State 12345 319. 555.1111 will-b-fine@um.edu

ACADEMIC BACKGROUND:

Ph.D. Literacy Education, University of Maine, Orono, May 201x - present
Dissertation title: *Developmentally Appropriate Learning Styles for Acquisition of English for Chinese-speaking Immigrants.*

M.A. Elementary Education - Bilingual Emphasis, 201x
Lewis and Clark University, Portland, Oregon

B.A. Spanish and Elementary Education, 199x
University of Hawaii at Manoa *cum laude Phi Beta Kappa*

RESEARCH INTERESTS:

Emergent Literacy
Integrated Language Arts
Ethnography
Infant Cognition

FELLOWSHIP & GRADUATE APPOINTMENTS:

Ollie Fellowship for International Research Fieldwork, Fall 201x
Research Assistant, Cross-cultural Literacy Project. Fall 201x
Teaching Assistant, University of Maine, Bilingual Methods, 201x

PUBLICATIONS & PRESENTATIONS:

Publications in process or published including articles in:
Teacher Magazine
Journal of Early Childhood
Preschool Times

Presentations to regional or national groups
Washington State Bilingual Conference, Seattle
International Society for Technology in Education Conference, Vancouver, BC
Western Regional Conference on Educational Technology, Los Angeles

INTERNATIONAL EXPERIENCE:

Languages
Fluent in Spanish; bilingual in Mandarin; read French

Study
Advanced Spanish Language, Mexico City & Madrid Institute
Literature & Language, Nanjing Normal University, China
Foreign Exchange Student Scholarship, Madrid, Spain

Classroom Teaching
Primary teacher, International School of Shanghai, 199x – 201x
Upper elementary teacher, Madrid English School, 199x – 199x

SERVICE:

Leadership:
Executive Officer (200x – present), Pi Lambda Theta
Chair, Region 10 Early Childhood Advisory Council, 200x

Consulting:
Bilingual Learning Centers, Inc., Washington, DC
University Center for Child Development, Idaho State University

Complete CV and dossier at: www.willbfineportfolio.com

Literacy Studies (Education) CV

Strategic Features:
Literacy Studies, Language Arts and Children's Literature

Review this CV if you have substantial pre-doctoral teaching experience in K-12 settings and in collegiate classrooms. This CV demonstrates how to focus on international teaching and service by presenting relevant materials early in the CV.

CV BASICS:

Highest Degree:	Ph.D. in progress
Experience:	Practicing professional, K-12 international classrooms Teaching assistantships Research assistantship
Job Target:	Small liberal arts college to mid-size university. Teaching is top priority.

CONTENT FEATURES:

- Careful placement of several categories on the first page provides a comprehensive overview of degrees, scholarly interests, international experiences, and graduate assistantships. Five of the six categories on page one reflect knowledge and interest in some aspect of international education.
- The *Scholarly Interests* category presents research interests and teaching interests in one category. This arrangement draws attention to both research and teaching strengths.
- Placing the *International Teaching Experiences* category on page one is tactical. The teaching and research interests are linked to cultural competencies and global awareness.

DESIGN FEATURES:

Font:	Cambria font, size 10
Margins:	.75" top, bottom, left, right
Layout:	Open new document; set tab to indent
Line spacing:	One line space between categories.
Enhancements:	Underlining and italic font used for visual and organizational emphasis.

Literacy Studies (Education) CV

Will B. Goode

121 Campus Hall Any Place, State Zip (c):193.876.0034 willbgoode@gmail.com

Teaching statement, research agenda, teaching philosophy, course syllabi at www.interfolio.com/portfolio/WBGoode

DEGREES

University of Florida, Gainesville

Ph.D. Literacy Studies, Language Arts and Children's Literature, anticipated May 201x
Dissertation Title: *Stories from International Teachers: A narrative inquiry about culturally responsive teaching.*
Dr. I. M. Moore, Advisor

M.A. Reading Education, May 200x

Kenyon College, Kenyon, Ohio

B.A. Majors: Elementary Education and Spanish, May 200x Middlebury Arabic Summer Language Session, 200x

SCHOLARY INTERESTS

Research:

• International Teaching • Immigrant Communities/Schools • Culturally Responsive Teachers
• Narrative Inquiry • Struggling Primary Readers • Multicultural children's Literature

Teaching:

• Developing Culturally Responsive Teachers • Methods of Teaching Reading and Language Arts
• Qualitative Research Methods • Children's Literature • Inquiry-based Teaching

RECOGNITION

Ballard Dissertation Fellowship, 201x-201x
Graduate Student Excellence in Teaching Award Spring, 200x
International Dissertation Research Fellowship, 200x
Executive Council of Professional and Graduate Studies Research Grant, 200x

INTERNATIONAL TEACHING EXPERIENCES

Shanghai American School, Shanghai, China, 200x-201x
Mont' Kiara International School, Kuala Lumpur, Malaysia, 200x-200x
Bahrain Bayan School, Isa Town, Bahrain,199x-199x

Grade levels: first grade: third grade; third grade bilingual
Professional development: visiting author committee; developed new school-wide Social Studies curriculum; primary reading and language arts curriculum committee
Leadership: Western Association of Schools and Colleges Accreditation committee; represented school at Near East South Asia conference, Sri Lanka; Southeast Asian Teachers and Counselors Conference representative; achieved certification, International Schools Curriculum Project, Maastricht, The Netherlands (PYP-Primary Years Program of International Baccalaureate)

LANGUAGES & TRAVEL

Languages studied: Spanish, Dutch, Arabic, Bahasa Malayu, Mandarin Chinese
Travel: Extensive travel across Asia, Middle East, Europe and Australia

UNIVERSITY GRADUATE APPOINTMENTS

Research Assistant: Department of Teaching and Learning, College of Education, The University of Florida

Immigrant Families and Preservice Teachers, 200x-200x

Assisted in video and audio data collection of fieldwork sites including the Puertas Abeirtas After School Program, and the Community Center of immigrant family participants; coded written data using QSR (qualitative research software)
Participated in discussion sessions with team regarding data analysis, article contributions and research findings

Ethnographic Independent Research Fieldwork

Interviewed family and children participants
Collected data with program supervisors, instructors, community coordinator and volunteers
Developed ethnographic film with participants and research assistant

Literacy Studies (Education) CV, page 2

Will B. Goode, page 2

University Appointments continued:

Teaching Assistant: Department of Teaching and Learning, College of Education, The University of Florida

Methods of Teaching Reading and Language Arts. Focus of instruction was literacy development, student assessment and effective instructional strategies. Complete responsibility for instruction for both courses for three semesters. Duties included course development, instruction, student assessment, supervising field experiences and course evaluation.

Methods of Teaching Reading and Language Arts: Fall 200x (2 sections), Spring 200x, 200x, 201x
Methods of Teaching Reading: Spring 200x, Fall 200x ,Summer 200x, 200x, 201x
Practicum in College Teaching: Fall 200x (3 sections), Fall 200x

Reading and Responding to Children's Literature. Focus of instruction was developing a critical stance towards children's literature, knowledge of authors, illustrators, poets and use of literature in classroom practices and curriculum. Complete responsibility for course implementation and instruction. Duties included course instruction, student advising and assessment, and course evaluation.

Reading and Responding to Children's Literature: Fall 200x (1 section), Fall 200x (3 sections)
Practicum in college teaching: Spring 200x

Reading and Writing: Processes and Instruction. Focus of instruction was literacy assessment, language development and instructional approaches for K-12 students. Assisted in course responsibility and student evaluation coordinated with education faculty for two semesters. Duties included student advising, assessment, and collaborative teaching.

Reading and Writing: Processes and Instruction. Spring 200x, Fall 200x

Summer Reading Clinic. Focus of instruction was effective instructional practices with struggling elementary readers, literacy development and assessment. Assistant supervisor of master's degree students in clinical practicum literacy program for the College of Education and City Community School District. Duties included observing reading tutors, modeling and assessing reading tutor practices.

Assistant supervisor: Summer 200x
Reading clinician: Summer 200x

PRESENTATIONS & PUBLICATIONS

Fine W. (201x) International teachers: Understanding being a cultural agent through narrative. American Education Research Association. Denver, CO

Moore, I.M., Fine W. & Goode, B. (200x) Read it again! Multiple and critical engagements with books we love. Whole Language Umbrella; a division of the National Council of the Teachers of English. Louisville, KY

Moore, I.M. & Fine W. (200x) "You could be my Spanish teacher!" Cross mediation moments in Literacy teaching apprenticeships. American Education Research Association. Chicago, IL

Fine, W. International jet-setters; Educators around the world. (book in press) World Impact Printers, New York, NY

SERVICE

Malaysia: Orang Asli Taman Negara outreach
Coordinated school-wide medicine drives; delivered donations to orang asli villages through bi annual rainforest trek.

China: Shanghai China Children's Welfare Institute
Volunteered to feed babies at local orphanage and supervised middle-school students' participation in volunteer program.

China: School donation drives
Delivered supplies collected during travels to: Tibet, Myanmar, Laos, Thailand and Vietnam.
Assisted in implementing school wide fundraising for Braille without Borders (Tibetan School for the Blind).

China: 200x T. B. Fox Cancer Run
Assistant director of T.B. Fox Run Committee; Coordinated funding drive with Canadian Consulate.

Florida: Puertas Abiertas
Coordinated volunteer and child participant pairings in immigrant community activity development.

MEMBERSHIPS

American Educational Research Association; International Reading Council; National Council of Teachers of English; Literacy Research Association (National Reading Conference-NRC)

Marketing Résumé

Strategic Features: Marketing Résumé

Review this résumé if you are applying for industry-related (non-academic) positions that request a summary of your qualifications and work experience.

RÉSUMÉ BASICS:

Highest Degree:	MBA
Experience:	Internship Related employment
Job Target:	Industry

CONTENT FEATURES:

- Layout allows for complete use of the page providing maximum space for competencies and employment overviews. Selecting a format that allows use of the entire width of the page provides more space for relevant information.
- Résumé material was tailored for a one-page version focusing on competencies and an overall summary of work highlights. As promotions occur in industry positions, the bulleted lists can expand to a point where the reader can reach "bullet fatigue."
- *Degrees* were included at the top of the page for one reason—the academic reputation of both institutions sends a clear message to the reader about the candidate's academic ability. The second category, *Competencies,* identifies the specialized skill-set and abilities that can be brought to an organization. This list can be altered to meet the advertised requirements of the opening. The same is true for the *Highlights* section. This format is versatile and the focus on the résumé can be altered with little time or extra work

DESIGN FEATURES:

Font:	Palatino Linotype font, size 10
Margins:	.75" top, bottom; 1" left, right
Layout:	Insert table with two columns.
Line spacing:	1.5 line spaces between categories.
Enhancements:	Bold font to highlight category heading; limited use of bullets to draw attention to highlights.

Marketing Résumé

WILL B. FINE PO Box 21101, City, State, Zip (c)123.765.8876 (o)321.8745.0980 willbfine@gmail.com

DEGREES

University of California at Berkeley, Haas School of Business, May 201x
Degree: Master of Business Administration, Marketing Concentration

Stanford University, June 201x
Degree: Bachelor of Arts, Psychology, English and Communication, Triple Major

COMPETENCIES

Proven ability to maintain strong partnerships with marketing groups, production teams and major licensors.
Expertise in prioritizing/supervising multiple projects under time constraints.
Skilled in budget development, execution and competitive analysis.
Experience managing teams of marketing and licensing professionals.
Excellent public speaking, written and interpersonal communication skills.

EXPERIENCE OVERVIEW

National Basketball Association, New York, NY
Director of Entertainment Products, Licensing, 05/201x - present
Sega Corporation, San Francisco, CA
Senior Product Marketing Manager, Sega Sports, 10/201x -08/201x
Panasonic Interactive Media, Santa Clara, CA
Marketing Associate, 08/200x-03/200x
Intel Corporation, Santa Clara, CA
Marketing and Sales Co-op, 01/200x-06/200x
Rolling Stone Magazine, San Francisco, CA
Advertising Intern, 09/200x-03/200x

Key highlights and accomplishments of above positions:

- *Manage budgeting, strategy, P/L and direction of entertainment product business.*
- *Build annual business plans for products complete with forecasts and growth targets.*
- *Oversee licensing support staff to ensure materials are in line with corporate identity assurance guidelines and style guides.*
- *Synergize plans with international licensing organization and present licensing plans at Global Business Development Summit and consistently communicate with regional offices on domestic business activity.*
- *Focus promotions, public relations and events teams to ensure a successful launch of new products.*
- *Direct advertising agency in developing and executing strong television, print and online campaigns.*
- *Work closely with the sales and channel marketing organizations, visiting top eight accounts and developing sales presentations and account-specific retail programs.*
- *Conduct competitive analysis and work with market research departments to identify trends and monitor consumer behavior.*

Of special note: *Awarded Sega's Employee of the Year in 200x for leading the transition to marketing games for non-Sega hardware platform.*

Marriage and Family Therapy Résumé

Strategic Features: Marriage and Family Therapy Résumé (Psychology CV to résumé)

Review this résumé if you are applying for agency or clinical (non-academic) positions where a one page résumé is the norm.

RÉSUMÉ BASICS:

Highest Degree:	Master's degree
Experience:	Assistantships and related employment
Job Target:	Human services position

CONTENT FEATURES:

- Layout allows for complete use of the page providing maximum space for counseling skills, client populations, education and licensure, employment and activities. Selecting a format that uses graphic lines to divide categories clearly delineates each particular section.
- Résumé material was tailored for a one-page version focusing on counseling skills for a non-academic career.
- The top two categories, *Counseling and Therapy Skills and Client Populations Served* quickly identify the abilities you can bring to an organization as well as the wide-range of clients you can serve. Counseling organizations are seeking licensed individuals with very specialized skill-sets and this is an excellent way to demonstrate this to members of a search team.
- Employment titles are descriptive thus no annotations are included. The top two categories (therapy skills and clients served) provide details at a glance.

DESIGN FEATURES:

Font:	Gill Sans MT font, size 9
Margins:	.75" top, bottom; 1" left, right
Layout:	Open new document; use tabs to indent.
Line spacing:	1.5 line spaces between categories.
Enhancements:	Bold font to highlight category heading; limited use of bullets to draw visual attention; graphic line to separate categories.

Marriage and Family Therapy Résumé

IMA SAMPLE

16 University Avenue, Any City, State 12345 (101)555-0101 i-sample@du.edu

COUNSELING AND THERAPY SKILLS

- intake interviews
- neuropsychological testing
- intervention planning
- assessments—diagnostic and psychosocial
- group, individual, and family therapy
- treatment plans and strategies

CLIENT POPULATIONS SERVED

- Children ages 3-10 exhibiting attention and hyperactivity concerns
- Adolescents and children 5-18 years-old with psychosocial mental health concerns
- Youth, ages 12-18 in K-12 school counseling setting
- Adolescents with chronic illnesses

EDUCATION, LICENSURE AND CERTIFICATIONS

Berry College, Mount Berry, Georgia. B.S. Psychology, May 200x *with high distinction*
Valdosta State University, Valdosta, Georgia. M.S. Marriage and Family Therapy, June 201x
Valdosta State University, Valdosta, Georgia. M.A. Psychology, December 201x
Duke University, Durham, North Carolina. Advanced Studies, May 201x – present

Licensed Associate Marriage and Family Therapist
Certified Mental Health Professional
Certified School Guidance Counselor, Georgia

EMPLOYMENT

Director, Psychosocial Day Support Program, Mountain Center, Atlanta, May 200x – June 200x
Child Therapist, Whitecloud Counseling Center, Athens, June 200x – May 200x

PROFESSIONAL ACTIVITIES

Service:
President and Member, Society for Pediatric Psychology Diversity Committee, 201x – 201x
Pediatric Psychology and Diabetes Lecture, University Pediatric Psychology Course, Fall 201x
Staff Therapist, Family Camp for Diabetes, Camp Hertko Hollow, Atlanta, Spring 200x

Grants:
Student Grant Recipient, Society for the Advancement of Behavior Analysis, 201x; 201x

Fundraising:
Chair and Lead Fundraiser, Ronald McDonald House "Reach for the Sky" 201x Campaign

Measurement & Evaluation CV

Strategic Features: Measurement and Evaluation CV

Review this CV if you are at the defense stage of your doctoral program and you are launching a job search for a faculty appointment.

CV BASICS:

Highest Degree:	Ph.D. in final stages
Experience:	Research and teaching assistantships Internships
Job Target:	Faculty appointment in a research institution

CONTENT FEATURES:

- In the *Academic Background* section it is clear that the dissertation is in the final stages and that a projected date for completion is anticipated. Honors received during degree programs have been added thus saving space and further accentuating academic achievement.
- The Research and Teaching *Interests* category brings attention to the breadth and depth of scholarly potential. Search committees immediately recognize what this candidate can bring to their department. Both research and teaching are requisite for advancement in this field and are included near the top of page one for emphasis.
- The category, *University Experiences,* employs a useful configuration when there is a need to annotate different types of experiences. The category uses the space to demonstrate consulting skills, research abilities, and teaching experiences.
- An important category on page two, *Technical Skills,* could be moved to page one if vacancy ad stated that the candidate must have this skill-set.

DESIGN FEATURES:

Font:	Times New Roman font, size 10
Margins:	.75" top, bottom, left, right
Layout:	Open new document; set tab to indent.
Line spacing:	.5 line space between categories.
Enhancements:	Use of bullets to identify descriptive phrases.

Measurement & Evaluation CV

STAN DeVIATE 21 College Street, City, State, Zip (c) 211.509.6789 stan-deviate@gmail.com

ACADEMIC BACKGROUND

Ph.D. Measurement and Evaluation, Teachers College, Columbia University, expected June 201x
Dissertation: Computerized Adaptive Testing Frameworks
Advisor: Dr. Archy Medes Cognate areas: Applied Statistics, Correlation and Regression

M.A. Educational Policy, Teachers College, Columbia University, June 201x
Honors: Graduate Scholarship, Outstanding Teaching Assistant

B.A. Mathematics, Brown University, June 200x
Honors: Dean's List, Academic Achievement Award, Merit Scholarship
State of Rhode Island Teaching License

RESEARCH INTERESTS

Classical test theory, item response theory, vertical scaling, equating/linking, structural equation modeling

TEACHING INTERESTS

Statistical methods, item analysis, test-taking behavior and analysis, educational policy, statistical modeling

UNIVERSITY EXPERIENCES

Consultant, Statistical Outreach Center, Columbia University, 08/201x-08/201x
- Provided guidance to graduate students conducting statistical analysis for thesis-level projects.
- Served as methodology review consultant for advanced-level graduate proposals.
- Developed marketing materials and plan to advertise center services.

Graduate Research Assistant, Measurement and Evaluation, Columbia University, 08/201x-07/201x
- Reviewed research design and conducted literature review for faculty members.
- Prepared manuscript for publication with faculty guidance, sought feedback through various list-serves.
- Supervised new graduate students in research center, and organized new graduate student orientation.

Teaching Assistant, Educational Policy, Teachers College, Columbia University, 08/201x-08/201x
- Collaborated with graduate teaching team in undergraduate level "Issues in American Education."
- Managed online course website for team, provided remote technical assistance for students.

PROFESSIONAL EXPERIENCES

Research Intern, Psychometrics Services, Pearson Educational Measurement, Iowa City, IA, 201x-201x
- Developed test delivery materials and student guidebooks for academic proficiency assessment.
- Validated academic proficiency assessment through comprehensive analyses and literature review.
- Coordinated assessment delivery protocols and procedures with multiple offices and constituents.

Educational Statistics – Asia Program Intern, Woodrow Wilson Policy Center, Washington, DC, 201x
- Conducted policy research in Southeast Asia Unit on economic trends that affect schools.
- Organized multiple center meetings and conferences for national and international dignitaries.
- Co-authored white paper later used to justify programming support for educational outreach.

Actuary, Farmer's State Automobile Insurance, Statistical Modeling Group, Bloomington, IL, 200x
- Extracted data from large databank to perform variable manipulations to assess product costs.
- Tested various rate implementation models to secure higher yields and better returns.
- Coded variables during crossover to upgraded data systems.

Measurement & Evaluation CV, page 2

Stan DeViate, page 2

PUBLICATIONS

DeViate, S. (201x). *Cracking the Code: Computer Aided Testing Security Issues.* Testing, vol. 24, Zeus Press.

DeViate, S. (201x). *Putting the Cart before the Horse: Trends in Computerized Testing.* Annual Review, Testing Association of America, Atlanta, GA, 224-234.

DeViate, S., Pascal, B. (201x). *Computerized Testing: A literature review.* Graduate Student Bulletin, American Association of Test Designers, AATB Press, 345-377.

DeViate, S. & Lorner, M. (201x). *Asian Educational Policies and Economic Factors: a multi-nation approach.* Proceedings of Education in Southeast Asia Summit, Washington, DC, 135-149.

PRESENTATIONS

"Linking Educational Policy to Educational Statistics." Keynote, Midwest Testing Grad Conference, Milwaukee, April, 201x

"Performance Assessments and Computer Aided Testing." Area Educational Research Forum, Chicago, May 201x

"Computerized Adaptive Testing: Then and Now." AERA, San Francisco, March 201x

"Domestic and International Tests: Are we measuring the same traits?" Summit on International Education, Singapore, May 201x

"International Educational Research: Crossing borders, crossing methods." AERA, Detroit, March 201x

TECHNICAL SKILLS

- Command of data management software and analysis using SAS, SPSS, LISREL, R, BILOG, PARSCALE, and DIMTEST.
- Univariate and multivariate statistics and analysis, including: ANOVA, MANOVA, Factor Analysis, Regression, and Profile Analysis.
- Bayesian data analysis, specific languages and applications: SAS, IML.
- Development of computer adaptive test forms.
- Web-based course management and site development software: Flash, Dreamweaver, Contribute, Adobe, Microsoft Suite.

SERVICE & MEMBERSHIPS

Member, Educational Statistics Conference, Advisor, Graduate Student Initiatives, 201x-Present
Co-Chair, New York Testing Consortium, Graduate Student Division, 201x-201x
Reviewer, Journal on Testing in Education, 201x-Present
Editorial Board, Graduate Student Research in Educational Testing Quarterly, 201x
Member, National Leadership Honor Society, 200x-201x
Volunteer Consultant, New York City Schools, Data Integration Initiative, 201x
Member, Partnership Committee, New York City Schools and Columbia University, 201x
Volunteer Saturday Morning Teacher – Advanced Math, New York City Schools for the Gifted, 200x-200x

PROFESSIONAL MATERIALS

ePortfolio: View documentation of research, teaching, service at: www.sdeviateteachingportfolio.com
Blog: testingtoday.com (*Tags:* testing, testing software, testing analysis, testing policies)

Medicine CV

Strategic Features: Medicine (M.D.) CV

Review this CV if you are preparing to apply and interview for select residency programs.

CV BASICS:

Highest Degree:	M.D. nearly finished
Experience:	Intern, research fellowships
Job Target:	Residency

CONTENT FEATURES:

- Careful placement of several categories on the first page provides a good overview of the candidate's academic background and related experiences as well as medical volunteer activities.
- By highlighting key research positions (research fellow, summer externship fellow, and research intern) readers can see versatility and focus in an area of specialty. Descriptions beginning with action words provide the reader with specific details that demonstrate breadth of training.
- Descriptive statements begin with a variety of action verbs including: *performed, collected, served, observed, and evaluated.* Careful selection of action words draws attention to strengths, abilities, and range of experience. (See *Action Words* in the STYLE GUIDE.)
- An *Awards* category includes academic honors as well as athletic recognition and awards. These awards are integrated into the CV because the candidate is seeking a residency in sports medicine and has been a highly competitive collegiate athlete.

DESIGN FEATURES:

Font:	Century Gothic Bold font, size 10
Margins:	.75" top, bottom, left, right
Layout:	Insert table with two columns.
Line spacing:	1.5" line space between categories.
Enhancements:	Selected use of bullets for emphasis.

Medicine CV

BEA FINE — 21 College Street, City, State, Zip (c) 211.509.6789 beafine@nyu.edu

---

DEGREES

New York University School of Medicine, New York, NY
August 201x – Present (Currently MS3)

New York University, College of Arts and Sciences, New York, NY
Bachelor of Arts with Honors: May 200x Major: Psychology, Pre-Medicine
Cum Laude

RESEARCH FELLOW

Laboratory for Minimally-Invasive Surgery, New York University Hospital for Joint Diseases Research Fellow, June 200x – January 201x, New York, NY

- Collected data for a preliminary study involving the design of an early intervention knee implant.
- Assisted in data collection and performed data analysis for a study examining lesion patterns and cartilage thickness in early osteoarthritis of the knee joint.
- Performed data analysis and co-authored paper entitled "Optimization for Head Height, Head Offset, and Canal Fit in a Set of Uncemented Stemmed Femoral Components" published in a peer-reviewed journal (*Hip International*).
- Attended 201x Annual Meeting of American Academy of Orthopaedic Surgeons in Las Vegas, and 201x Institution of Mechanical Engineers Conference in London, UK, where the results of study were presented.
- Served as initial research fellow and project coordinator for clinical study entitled "Progress of Rehabilitation after Total Knee Replacement." Duties included recruiting and testing patients (at doctor's office and bedside), data collection and analysis, and collaborating with senior faculty.

SUMMER EXTERNSHIP FELLOW

Summer Externship Program, New York University Hospital for Joint Diseases Summer Fellow, June 200x – August 200x, New York, NY

- Observed and assisted in a wide variety of orthopedic procedures, including arthroscopies, arthroplasties, and trauma.
- Evaluated patients and assisted with patient care in outpatient setting.
- Attended daily rounds with a team of residents and attending, and participated in educational didactic sessions.
- Conducted research on osteoarthritis of the knee and presented project to fellow peers and NYU-HJD faculty.

RESEARCH INTERN

Medical Center Research Intern, Summer 200x, Chicago, IL

- Assisted with study entitled: Effects of Vertebroplasty and Kyphoplasty on Spinal Alignment. Participated in the analysis of vertebral fractures; assisted with kyphoplasty and vertebroplasty procedures on cadavers.

MEDICAL VOLUNTEER ACTIVITIES

Post-Anesthesia Care Unit, New York University Hospital for Joint Diseases
Summer 200x, New York, NY

Adult Occupational Therapy Department, New York University Hospital for Joint Diseases Volunteer, January 200x – July 200x, New York, NY

Musculoskeletal Biomechanical Research Laboratory, Loyola University, Summer 200x, Chicago, IL

Medicine CV, page 2

Bea Fine, page 2

PAPERS

Fine, B., Soon, H.E., Swenson, T.T., and Goode, D. Optimization for head height, head offset, and canal fit in a set of uncemented stemmed femoral components. *Hip International.* 200x; 18: 286-293.

POSTER PRESENTATIONS

Soon, H.E., Fine, B., Swenson, T.T., and Goode, D. MRI analysis of femoral cartilage thickness in early osteoarthritis knee patients for uni-condylar knee potential. Annual Meeting of American Society of Mechanical Engineers. Lake Tahoe, NV. June 200x.

Fine, B., Soon, H.E., Swenson, T.T., and Goode, D. Optimization for head height, head offset, and canal fit in a set of uncemented stemmed femoral component. Annual Meeting of American Academy of Orthopaedic Surgeons, Las Vegas, NV. February 200x.

Goode, D., Soon, H.E., Fine, B., and Swenson, T.T. Optimization for head height, head offset, and canal fit in a set of uncemented stemmed femoral components. Institution of Mechanical Engineers Conference, London, UK. May 200x.

Sample, A., Kane, D., Soon, H.E., Fine, B., Swenson, T.T., and Goode, D. A Risk of adjacent vertebral body fractures after balloon kyphoplasty: a biomechanical study. 7th International Congress on Spinal Surgery, Antalya, Turkey. April 200x.

AWARDS

New York University Dean's List 200x-200x
NCAA Postgraduate Scholarship Finalist 200x
New York University Student Athlete Academic Achievement Award 200x
New York University Founders Day Award 200x
New York University Student Athlete Honor Roll 200x-200x
AVCA First Team All-America 200x, 200x, 200x
Division III NCAA National All-Tournament Team 200x
UAA First Team All-Conference 200x, 200x, 200x
New York State Player of the Year 200x; Rookie of the Year 200x
Volleyball Team MVP 200x, 200x, 200x; Team Captain 200x

COMMUNITY SERVICE

Vice President, Orthopaedic Surgery Club, New York University School of Medicine, 200x-200x, New York, NY. Established a mentorship program for students interested in orthopaedics. Coordinated with Hospital for Joint Diseases faculty and residents in various events. Organized club activities such as dinner lectures and workshops.

Volleyball Mentor, Get Up and Try Something (G.U.T.S.) Mentor Program Associated with Y.M. Magazine and the Center for Disease Control, August 200x – May 200x, New York, NY

Publications, research papers, & CV at: www.interfolio.com/portfolio/beafine

Medicine CV (M.D. and Ph.D. Program)

Strategic Features: Medicine M.D. and Ph.D. CV

Review this CV if you are selecting CV material that is critical for search teams seeking the "right-fit" for a specialized residency or post-doc.

CV BASICS:

Highest Degree:	M.D. and Ph.D. in process
Experience:	Traineeships Mentoring Teaching assistantships
Job Target:	Post-doc

CONTENT FEATURES:

- Presenting a number of categories on page one highlights essential areas including: degrees, traineeships, research, teaching, mentoring and service.
- Name of advisor is included in research area because of the nature of the advisor's role in medical research. Researchers are generally well-known in their field and including researcher's name provides credence to your tutelage under their supervision.
- *Publications* include five subcategories; this CV tactic saves space, creates an easy-reading experience, and can demonstrate the versatile abilities of the candidate. Numbered publications common in sciences.

DESIGN FEATURES:

Font:	Cambria font, size 10
Margins:	.75" top, bottom, left, right
Layout:	Open new document.
Line spacing:	1.5" line space between categories.
Enhancements:	Left-justified category headings allowing descriptors to extend from margin-to-margin. This is the most basic of all designs—no bullets or italics.

Medicine CV (M.D. and Ph.D. Program)

HIREM E. SOON **21 College Street, City, State, Zip (c) 211.509.6789** **hireme-soon@nu.edu**

EDUCATION

Northwestern University, Evanston
Medical Scientist Training Program, MD and PhD expected, May 201x

Smith College, Northampton
B.A. *magna cum laude* in Neuroscience, 201x

TRAINEESHIPS

Traineeship/Fellowship: Medical Scientist Training Program, NIH and Northwestern University, September 201x-present.

Traineeship: Neuroscience Traineeship, NIH, 201x-201x.

Grantee: New England Consortium for Undergraduate Science, 201x.

Grantee: Kirschstein National Research Service Award, NIH, 201x.

RESEARCH EXPERIENCE

Doctoral Dissertation, June-May 201x; Neuroscience, Northwestern University
Advisor: Bea Goode, MD, PhD
Toxic intermediates and protein quality control in Spinocerebellar Ataxia Type 3

Honors Thesis, August 201x-May 201x; Biology, Smith College
Advisor: Will B. Fine, PhD
Localization of IP receptors in adult mouse skeletal muscle in junctional (motor endplate) and extrajunctional regions

Rotation, May-June 201x; Molecular Ophthalmology, Northwestern University
Advisor: Bea Goode, PhD
Molecular serum biomarkers of age-related macular degeneration

Rotation, July-August 201x; Cognitive Neuroscience, Northwestern University
Advisor: Fine A. Dande, PhD
The role of the basal ganglia in set-shifting tasks

TEACHING AND MENTORSHIP POSITIONS

Tutor, January-May 201x and January-May 201x
Medical Neuroscience, Northwestern University

Mentor, June-July 201x, Northwestern University
MSTP Summer Undergraduate Research Program (SUMR)

Teaching Assistant, June-August 201x , Northwestern University
Analyzing & Presenting Medical Research, Medical Scientist Training Program

SERVICE

Intern, January-March 201x; Department of Mental Health and Substance Abuse, World Health Organization, Geneva, Switzerland

Clinic Coordinator, April 201x-present; Women's Health Clinic, North Chicago

Medicine CV, page 2

Hirem E. Soon, page 2

PUBLICATIONS
Research Articles:

1. Goode B, Dande FA, Fine WB, Soon HE (201x) Live-cell imaging reveals divergent intracellular dynamics of polyglutamine disease proteins and supports a sequestration model of pathogenesis. *Proc Natl Acad Sci USA* 99: 9310-9315.
2. Sample I, Goode B, Dande FA, Soon HE (201x) IP3 receptors and associated Ca2+ signals localize to satellite cells and to components of the neuromuscular junction in skeletal muscle. *J. Neurosci.* 23: 8185-8192.
3. Goode B, Dande FA, Sample I, Fine WB, Soon HE (201x) CHIP suppresses polyglutamine aggregation and toxicity in vitro/in vivo. *J. Neurosci.* 25: 9152-9161.

Book Chapters and Reviews:

1. Goode B, Dande FA, Fine WB, Soon HE (201x) Polyglutamine Repeat Disorders, including Huntington's Disease. Molecular Neurology; 257-76. Academic Press.
2. Soon HE, Goode B (201x) Polyglutamine neurodegeneration: protein refolding revisited. *Trends Neurosci.* 31:521-528.

Abstracts

1. Fine WB, Soon HE (201x) Body Dysmorphic Disorder and Perfectionism in a nonclinical Sample. *Women in Science: 200x Summer Research*. Smith College.
2. Soon HE, Sample I (201x) Ubiquitination of the polyglutamine disease protein ataxin-3 enhances its activity as a deubiquitinating enzyme. *FASEB J* 22:1026.

Poster Presentations

1. Goode B, Dande FA, Fine WB, Soon HE. In vivo suppression of polyglutamine neurotoxicity by C-terminus of Hsp70 interacting protein (CHIP) supports an aggregation model of pathogenesis. Gordon Research Conference on CAG Triplet Repeat Diseases, May 201x, Aussois, France.
2. Goode B, Dande FA, Fine WB, Soon HE. Ataxin-3 controls parkin levels by editing K63-linked ubiquitin chains. 2nd Annual National Ataxia Foundation Ataxia Investigators Meeting, March 201x, Las Vegas, NV.

Committees

201x – 201x	Medical Scientist Training Program Invited Speaker Committee
201x – 201x	Neuroscience Program Admissions Committee
201x – 201x	Office of Student Affairs Advisory Group on Diversity

PROFESSIONAL MEMBERSHIPS
Phi Beta Kappa; Sigma Xi; Society for Neuroscience

ACADEMIC RECOGNITION
Highest Honors in Neuroscience, Smith College, 201x
John and Edith Knowles Memorial Scholarship, Smith College, 201x
Smith College Dean's List, 201x; First Group Scholar, Smith College, 201x-201x

Museum Studies Résumé

Strategic Features: Museum Studies Résumé

Review this résumé if you want to stress certain competencies in a specific area. This sample also demonstrates how to briefly present coursework, both online and campus-based.

RÉSUMÉ BASICS:

Highest Degree:	Master's degree with specialized certificate
Experience:	Museum work
Job Target:	Museum – university, private or non-profit

CONTENT FEATURES:

- *Museum Interests*, followed by *Coursework Highlights*, immediately identify strengths; useful alternative to Job Objective category. By identifying *Interests* for placement on the résumé, it also prepares you to answer the questions: *What are your strengths? What can you do for us?*
- *Course Highlights* category clearly demonstrates extensive range of study. This category can be solely focused on a particular field of study or can demonstrate your wide-range of coursework.
- Museum certificate program is unique; space is made available in *Academic Background* category to list the graduate courses.
- Annotations in *Professional Museum Experience* category accentuate responsibility and skills; annotations use descriptive phrases that are quickly noted by the reader.

DESIGN FEATURES:

Font:	Palatino Linotype font, size 11
Margins:	.75" top, bottom; .75" left, right
Layout:	Open new document; use tabs to indent.
Line spacing:	Two line spaces between categories.
Enhancements:	Limited use of bullets and italics for emphasis.

Museum Studies Résumé

BEA GOODE 16 A Avenue, Any City, State 12345 (101)555-0101 beagoode@gmail.com

MUSEUM INTERESTS

- Collection Management
- Education Outreach and Development
- Exhibit Design

COURSE HIGHLIGHTS

Exhibition Planning and Design	Museum Laboratory Methods	Art, Law, and Ethics
Digital Imaging in Museums	Building Museums	Museum Marketing
Conservation of Museum Objects	Museum Administration	Archival Practices

ACADEMIC BACKGROUND

George Washington University, Washington, D.C.
Graduate Certificate, Museum Collections Management and Care, July 201x
Online Courses - Graduate Certificate:
Collections Management: Legal and Ethical Issues
Collections Management: Practical Applications
Preservation Conservation: Philosophy and Theory
Preservation Conservation: Practical Applications

University of Florida, Gainesville
M.A., August 201x, Philosophy B.A., May 200x, Archaeology *Phi Beta Kappa*

PROFESSIONAL MUSEUM EXPERIENCES

Florida Museum of Natural History, Gainesville
Position: Collections Assistant Archaeology, September 201x – present
Worked with senior museum administrators in strategic planning, exhibit design, budget analysis, policy review and procedures for: Archaeology of Pearls, Grenada; Florida Archaeology Excavations, Fort Lauderdale; Environmental Archaeology, Port Lucie; St Augustine, America's Ancient City-Online Exhibit.

Matheson Museum Inc., Gainesville
Position: Registration Assistant, May 201x – July 201x
Responsible for inventory of postcard collection (20,000+); isolated 500 un-catalogued photographs from the Bone Photograph Collection; assisted Preparator in installation and de-installation of exhibitions.

COMMUNITY SERVICE

Fundraising volunteer, Alachua County Historic Trust, Gainesville
Builder, Habitat of Humanity Project, Gainesville
Youth coach and volunteer commissioner, Gainesville Area Youth Soccer League

PROFESSIONAL MATERIALS

Portfolio of museum internships and coursework available: www.beagoode.com

Music CV

Strategic Features: Music CV

Review this CV if you have an extensive record of exhibits or performances; and if your record of performances/exhibits requires frequent updating.

CV BASICS:

Highest Degree:	DMA
Experience:	Performing experience First tenure-track teaching position
Job Target:	CV used to document teaching and performances for annual reviews leading up to tenure review.

CONTENT FEATURES:

- Page one represents key professional material regarding academic training, awards, expertise and current experience. The first page could be used as a one-page condensed CV for speaking engagements.
- Creating a category for *Principal Teachers* is especially important because of the specialized training opportunities afforded musicians and the guest appearances expected in the performing arts.
- Page two documents performance and conducting experiences. These experiences augment basic information on the first page; this section could extend to several pages. This format allows new works and performances to be added easily and without disturbing the first page.
- Current university experience demonstrates broad range of necessary skills for musicians in academic settings.

DESIGN FEATURES:

Font:	High Tower Text font, size 10
Margins:	1" top, bottom, left, right
Layout:	Insert table with two columns.
Line spacing:	One line space between categories.
Enhancements:	Italics and bold are used for organizational emphasis. Select use of bullets in the *Experience* section clearly aligns the three responsibilities of the position.

Music CV

Lotte Noisse

21 College Street, City, State, Zip (c)211.509.6789 lotte-noisse@tlu.edu

FORMAL TRAINING	**Doctor of Musical Arts, University of Texas, 201x** **Master of Arts in Music, Southern Methodist University, 201x** **Bachelor of Music, Oberlin College & Conservatory, 200x**
PRINCIPAL TEACHERS	**Choral Conducting:** Samuel F. Batonn Mia Elizabeth Lin Harry Thomas Yuciva Jorge Hernadez **Voice:** Daphne Kolter-Smith Maria Kallousious Oliver Vera LanFranco Merendé
AWARDS	Master Prize, International Collegiate Conducting Exposé Top Prize, Original Score, Collegiate Music Society Competition
AREAS OF EXPERTISE	Conducting Accompanying and Coaching Vocal Studies Digital Music Applications
CURRENT UNIVERSTIY EXPERIENCE	**Assistant Professor, School of Music, Texas Lutheran University** August 201x – present Conducting responsibilities: • Texas Lutheran Choir • TLU Women's Chorus • Chapel Choir • Kantorei Chamber Choir Performance responsibilities: • Musical theatre workshops • Annual Christmas Vespers • Solo recitals Teaching responsibilities: • Conducting I & II • Music Appreciation • World Music Culture • Music Theory
SERVICE	**Director of Music, Texas Youth Community Choir, Sequin, TX** Fall 201x – present **Acting Director of Choral Activities, Center for Music Studies, Dallas, TX** January 201x – present **Affiliations:** American Choral Directors Association; College Music Society
PORTFOLIO	**View performances (group and solo) and teaching dossier at:** www.LotteNoisePortfolio.com

Music CV, page 2

Lotte Noisse

Conducting and Performances

MAJOR WORKS CONDUCTED	Bach, J.S.	*Cantata #140* "Wachet Auf" *Cantata #4* "Christ lag in Todesbanden" *Cantata #82* "Ich habe genug"
	Brahms, J.	*Ein Deutsches Requiem*
	Fauré, G.	*Requiem*
	Handel, G.F.	*Messiah* (excerpts)
	Haydn, J.	*Kleine Orgelmesse* "Missa brevis St. Joannis de Deo"
	Mozart, W.A.	*Regina Coeli*, K.276 *Exultate, Jubilate*
	Orff, C.	*Carmina Burana* (excerpts)
	Saint-Saëns, C.	*Christmas Oratorio*
	Schubert, F.	*Mass in G*
	Vivaldi, A.	*Magnificat*

GUEST CONDUCTING

Summer Music Academy, TLU, June-July, 201x
Southwest Community Chorus Festival, Austin, TX, October 201x
Texas All-State Men's Chorus, Houston, TX, January 201x
Texas State High School Music Festival, Grapevine, TX, November 201x
SMU Music Camp, Summers 201x; 201x
Region IX Honors Choir, Oklahoma City, OK, March 201x
Ohio High School Choral Clinic, Cleveland, OH, February 201x; May 201x
Buckeye State Music Clinic for Talented Youth, Oberlin, OH, June 201x
Festival of Lights, Cleveland, OH, December 201x

PERFORMANCES

Representative Vocal Soloist:

Bach, J.S	*B Minor Mass* *St. Matthew Passion*
Handel, G.F.	*Israel in Egypt*
Haydn, J.	*Harmoniemesse*
Mendelssohn, F.	*Elijah*
Mozart, W.A.	*Requiem*
Stravinsky, I.	*Les Noces*
Vivaldi, A.	*Gloria*

Nonfiction Writing CV

Strategic Features: Nonfiction Writing CV

Review this CV if you have an extensive record of publications, teaching experiences, appointments, speaking engagements, unique grants and fellowships.

CV BASICS:

Highest Degree:	MFA
Experience:	Experience in publications/press Teaching assistantships
Job Target:	Academic teaching positions

CONTENT FEATURES:

- The four categories on page one–*Education, Appointments, Publications,* and *Speaking Invitations*, gives the reader a quick overview of this individual's multiple talents and recognition in the field.
- A slightly different approach was taken in this CV to show the many courses taught by this candidate. A list of the courses was inserted in the *Education* category each separated by a semicolon. Listing these courses separately would take key CV space and could become redundant.
- The *Honors* category provides a weighty beginning for page two. Again, take a look at the spacing technique and how this set-up saves space and maintains the style of the CV. The other entries on page two document the unique *International Research and Fellowship* opportunities and the experiences in both professional and community-based services.

DESIGN FEATURES:

Font:	Gill Sans MT font, size 10
Margins:	.75" top, bottom, left, right
Layout:	Open new document; use tabs to indent.
Line spacing:	One line space between categories.
Enhancements:	Italics and bold are used for organizational emphasis. Select use of bullets in sections that detail multifaceted experiences.

Nonfiction Writing CV

IMA SAMPLE

#5 Academic Hall | Any University | Any City, State 12345
c: (101)555-1110 | o: (102)555-1998 | ima-sample@gmail.com

EDUCATION

Master of Fine Arts, Nonfiction Writing Program, The University of Iowa, May 201x
Thesis: "Before There Was After in Havana," a memoir about living in Castro's Cuba.
Bachelor of Arts, English, Writing Concentration, Yale College, May 200x, *magna cum laude*

Courses taught: Rhetoric and Composition (undergraduate introductory course, 4 semesters); Advanced Rhetoric (undergraduate introductory course, 1 semester); Nonfiction Writing Workshop (advanced undergraduate course, 2 semesters); Intermediate Nonfiction Readings (advanced undergraduate course, 1 semester); Travel Writing I (online workshop, 7 classes); Creative Writing 101 (online workshop, 1 class); Teen Creative Writing (summer course for high school students)

APPOINTMENTS

Gotham Writers' Workshop, Instructor, Fall 0x-present
- Taught seven online courses in conjunction with *New York Times* Knowledge Network
- Led an introductory creative writing workshop for nontraditional students
- Created a summer writing workshop for New York City teenagers

The University of Iowa English Department, Teaching Assistant, Fall 0x-Spring 0x
- Taught two undergraduate workshops in creative writing
- Designed curriculum for a new course, "Nonfiction Readings," and taught pilot class
- Nominated for "Outstanding T.A. Award" in Graduate College

The University of Iowa Rhetoric Department, Teaching Assistant, Fall 0x-Spring 0x
- Prepared curriculum for four freshman Rhetoric courses
- Instructed over 100 undergraduates to write college papers and deliver speeches
- Distinguished by the Center for Teaching based on student feedback

PUBLICATIONS

"Surfacing: New Life On an Old Street, Mexico City." *The New York Times,* March 17, 201x.
"Mexico's Copper Canyon Pure Gold." *Chicago Sun Times,* January 201x.
"Havana Holiday," *Prairie Schooner,* Summer, 200x.
"Moderate Pomp," *Witness Magazine,* Fall, 200x (Africa issue)
"Luisito Grau de Armas." *The Gettysburg Review,* Summer, 200x.
"Liberia's Iron Sisterhood." *Ms. Magazine*, Winter, 200x.
"One Bright Case of Idiopathic Craniofacial Erythema," *Readings for Writers* (Kenyon Review, 200x).
Confessions of a High School Word Nerd. Co-editor (Penguin, 200x).
"The Sympathy Test." *Ninth Letter*, Winter, 200x.
"Horns for the Revolution." *A Woman's World Again* (Travelers' Tales, 200x).
"Not a Delay, But a Detour." *Washingtonpost.com*, April 29, 200x.
"Idiot's Guide to Your Palm." *20-Something Essays by 20-Something Writers* (Random House, 200x).
"One Man's Prison." *Salon*, August 200x.
Delaying the Real World: A Twentysomething's Guide to Seeking Adventure (Running Press, 200x).

SPEAKING INVITATIONS

NPR's *On Point* with Tom Ashbrook. June 4, 200x.
ABC News Now *The Influentials.* June 9, 200x.
Sirius Satellite *American Voices* with Bill Bradley. August, 200x.
WCAU TV NBC10 *Philadelphia Morning Show.* February 7, 200x.

Non-Fiction Writing CV

Sample, page 2

HONORS

MacDowell Colony Fellowship (201x) | La Muse Writer Retreat Fellowship, Southern France (201x)
Breadloaf Conference Scholarship (201x) | Nomination for Pushcart Prize (200x)
University of Iowa Art Museum Writer-in-Residence (200x) | Center for Teaching Recognition Award (200x)
Random House 20-By-20 Contest Winner: named one of the "best new voices of 200x"
Yale English Department Henry P. Wright Prize for Journalism (200x) | Yale Herb & Jean Cahoon Public Service Award (200x) | Yale English Department Award for Best Work of Fiction (200x) | Yale English Department Award for Best Freshman Essay (200x)

EDITORIAL EXPERIENCE

Barnes & Nobles, May 200x-June 200x, Freelance Writer of Quamut Charts
- Researched and wrote the mini-guides "How to Go Green" and "Google Guide"

Life Magazine, January 200x-May 200x, Research Assistant
- Fact-checked content of weekly magazine with a circulation of twelve million

Topic Magazine, November 200x-Spring 200x, Contributing Editor
- Copy-edited magazine and collaborated with editors to develop topical story ideas

INTERNATIONAL RESEARCH & FELLOWSHIPS

Mexico, Fall 200x-Spring 201x
- Selected by the Fulbright-Hayes Commission to pursue a creative writing project, "Counter-Migration: Traversing the Border with American Expatriates"
- Profiled U.S. citizens residing in Mexico, as part of a larger nonfiction book project (working title "Americans Elsewhere") about Americans living abroad

Iceland, Summer 200x
- Awarded grant for summer research by the American-Scandinavian Foundation
- Interviewed diverse Americans living in Reykjavik and published two literary essays

Liberia, Summer 200x
- Convened with government leaders in Monrovia to research an article for *Ms. Magazine* about the post-war rise of women in politics
- Won the Kevin Balle Dissertation Research Grant to research an essay about 21st century Liberia

Cuba, Fall 200x-Summer 200x
- Chosen as one of two Samuel Huntington National Public Service Fellows
- Received $10,000 grant to execute my proposed project in Havana nursing homes
- Transcribed oral histories and wrote feature articles about eldercare in Cuba
- Attained high fluency in Spanish

COMMUNITY WORK

Better Brooklyn Community Center, Brooklyn, New York, Spring 200x
- Tutored high school students in reading, language, and mathematics

Patient Voice, Fall 200x, Therapeutic Writing Teacher, Iowa City, Iowa
- Designed and taught a weekly writing course for schizophrenic patients

Presidential Campaign, Fall 200x, Field Organizer
- Managed a campaign office in Little Havana and trained over 500 volunteers

Yale College Dean's Office, Fall 200x-Spring 200x
- Selected by Dean's Office to mentor incoming freshman and advise course selection

Dwight Hall at Yale, Summer 200x, Intern
- Toured and compared 60 nursing homes to write a guide book for consumers

Writing and teaching portfolio at: www.interfolio.com/portfolio/isample

Occupational and Environmental Health CV

Strategic Features: Occupational and Environmental Health CV

Review this CV if you are seeking a research-based fellowship and where application instructions restrict the CV length to one page.

CV BASICS:

Highest Degree:	Mid-point in doctoral program
Experience:	Research assistantships
Job Target:	Fellowship with research emphasis

CONTENT FEATURES:

- The emphasis of the CV is *Research*. The fellowship application allows only a one page CV. Two areas are stressed: research interests/experiences and leadership activities. By briefly describing two specific areas makes the condensing process feasible.
- One category heading is used to illustrate *Relevant Coursework and Software*; this technique allows several line spaces to be saved and removes the "one-line" category which never looks quite right.
- *Research Experience* is the only category on this one-page CV that provides descriptive statements. Again, focusing on the Fellowship Application instructions, the emphasis is on research related experiences. Action statements begin with words like "examine, optimize, evaluate, judge, develop, implement," and allow the reader to get a sense of the significance of the three experiences.
- The *Leadership & Service* category combines a variety of campus and community-based service activities. Entries were limited because of space limitations.

DESIGN FEATURES:

Font:	Perpetua font, size 10
Margins:	.75" top, bottom, left, right
Layout:	Open new document; use tabs to indent.
Line spacing:	.75" line space between categories.
Enhancements:	Use of bold font for visual emphasis.

Occupational and Environmental Health CV

BEA GOODE || 5 College Ave, Any Place, State Zip goode@rutgers.edu (o) 301.223.4567 (c) 301.321.6098

FORMAL BACKGROUND

Ph.D. Occupational and Environmental Health, College of Public Health, Rutgers University, expected May 201x

M.P.H. Quantitative Methods: Biostatistics and Epidemiology, School of Public Health, University of Medicine and Dentistry of New Jersey, August 201x

B.A. Philosophy, Haverford College, Haverford, PA *with high distinction* June 200x

RESEARCH INTERESTS

radon | exposure assessment | gamma spectroscopy | radiological hazard preparedness | radiation toxicity

RELEVANT COURSE WORK & SOFTWARE

Environmental Health	Assessing Physical Hazards	Environmental Toxicology
Industrial Hygiene Fundamentals	Occupational & Environmental Epidemiology	Occupational Health

SOFTWARE: SAS, SPSS, S-PLUS, Perl, MS Excel/Access/PowerPoint

RESEARCH EXPERIENCE

Graduate Research Assistant | Department of Occupational/Environmental Health, Rutgers University | 01/200x-Present

Examine possible links between workplace munitions-related exposures and adverse health outcomes in Congressionally-mandated Department of Defense study.

Intern | Radiochemistry, University Hygienic Lab, Rutgers University | 08/201x-Present

Design apparatus to hold several biological samples for faster throughput using gamma spectroscopy to conduct rapid radionuclide screens; optimize and evaluate effect of relationship of spatial placement of apparatus on gamma detector versus efficiency calibration to obtain maximum design position.

Graduate Research Assistant | Department of Epidemiology, Rutgers University | 09/200x-12/201x

Wrote and implemented statistical programs using SAS; judged validity of data obtained and recommended additional statistical tests and/or modifications; developed study website in 3 languages for international collaborative project to facilitate entry of subject information; constructed course management system.

PUBLICATIONS

In-Preparation Manuscripts

Fine,W.B., Goode, B. The Use of Gamma Spectroscopy to Conduct Rapid Urine Radionuclide Screens in the Event of a Radiological Emergency.

PRESENTATIONS

Poster Presenter - The Use of Gamma Spectroscopy to Conduct Rapid Urine Radionuclide Screens in the Event of a Radiological Emergency, Research Week, Rutgers University | April 201x

Co-Workshop Presenter, Women in Science and Engineering K-12 Outreach, Open Minds Open Doors Conference, College of Saint Elizabeth, Morristown, NJ | October 200x

FELLOWSHIPS & AWARDS

National Institute for Occupational Safety & Health (NIOSH) Fellow Traineeship

Graduate Scholarship and Research Excellence Award, Rutgers University

LEADERSHIP & SERVICE: Rutgers University

Environmental Policy/Action Coordinator, Environmental Coalition | 02/201x-Present

Service Committee Co-Chair, Graduate Student Senate | 01/201x-Present

Women in Science and Engineering K-12 Outreach Ambassador | 09/201x-08/201x

Travel Funds Committee, Graduate Student Senate | 08/201x-12/201x

NIOSH Coastal Center for Occupational Health & Safety Student Representative | 09/200x-08/200x

Pharmacy CV

Strategic Features: Pharmacy CV

Review this CV if you need to accentuate specializations and unique preparation but are restricted to two pages.

CV BASICS:

Highest Degree:	Early in doctoral program
Experience:	Limited research/teaching assistantships
Job Target:	Fellowship with research emphasis

CONTENT FEATURES:

- The emphasis of the first page centers on *Research*. The fellowship application allows only a two page CV and stated: to be considered as serious applicant "research interests, background and skills" must be emphasized. Broad research details help "enhance your identity" as a new researcher.
- To demonstrate wide-ranging experiences, one category is used to present all research-type experiences and abilities (research assistantship; fellow; grants; awards; funded projects; analytical, equipment, and technical skills). Because only one category heading is used, *Research Experience,* several line spaces are saved, thus allowing all relevant material to fit on page one.
- Page two reveals relevant teaching, consulting and service experiences as well as publications, awards, and professional materials. The top category on page two combines four-related categories into one broad category which saves valuable space and makes for easy reading.
- The *Scholarly Work* category combines publications, presentations, and posters. This is a good technique if there are limited entries.

DESIGN FEATURES:

Font:	Rockwell font, size 9
Margins:	.75" top, bottom, left, right
Layout:	Open new document; use tabs to indent.
Line spacing:	.75" line space between categories.
Enhancements:	Use of bold font and bullets for visual emphasis.

Pharmacy CV

ALEC SAMPLE

5 College Ave, Any Place, State Zip sample@uiowa.edu 301.223.4567

EDUCATION

The University of Iowa, Iowa City, Iowa

Doctorate of Philosophy, Pharmaceutical Science, January 201x – Present

Bachelor of Science, Chemical Engineering with Honors, August 201x

RESEARCH EXPERIENCE

Graduate Research Assistant:

Pharmaceutics Laboratory, University of Iowa, January 201x-Present

- Designing a lung-relevant *Pseudomonas aeruginosa* bacteria biofilm *in vitro* model; Optimizing formulation and processing parameters for co-delivery dry powder aerosols

NSF Fellow:

REU Program in Micro/Nano-Structured Materials, Therapeutics, and Devices, Summer 201x, Auburn University, AL

- Investigated a supercritical core-shell coating process by custom design of experiment; compiled and analyzed data for a potential patent application

REU Program with Institute for Cellular Engineering, Summer 201x, Amherst, MA

- Formulated perfluorocarbon microemulsion gels with triblock copolymers; characterized gels by thermal stability and rheological behavior

Grants:

- Keith Guillory Pharmaceutics Fellowship, Spring 201x
- Iowa Center for Research by Undergraduates Assistant Scholar, Fall 201x
- Chemical Engineering Departmental Research Grant, Spring 201x
- University Student Government Scholarly Presentation Grant, Fall 201x

Awards:

- University-wide Excellence Research Award, Spring 201x
- Engineering Excellence in Undergraduate Research Award, Spring 201x
- Distinguished Poster Presentation Award, Spring 201x

Equipment:

- Spray dryer: one-step, easily scaled up process to make dry powder aerosols; supercritical core-shell process; investigated high pressure coating process with supercritical CO_2

Analytical Skills:

- Next Generation Impactor: *in vitro* lung model for aerodynamic diameter and deposition estimate based on material concentration collected
- UV Spec: determined organic material concentration
- Aerodynamic particle sizer: time of flight system for determining diameter
- Laser diffraction: determined geometric particle diameter
- Confocal microscopy: visualized bacterial biofilm growth and death
- Thermogravimetric analysis: quantify water content in aerosols
- Tap density: quantified dry particle density

Computer Skills:

- MATLAB (with COMSTAT biofilm quantification programs)
- Volocity Imaging Software; MiniTab Statistical Software

Affiliation:

- American Association of Pharmaceutical Scientists Student Member

Pharmacy CV, page 2

Sample, page 2

TEACHING, CONSULTING, INTERN AND SERVICE EXPERIENCE

Teaching Assistant, Pharmacy Practice Laboratory, January 201x - Present

- Assisting first-year pharmacist students through pharmaceutical compounding; mentoring a small group to answer questions

Peer Consultant, Hanson Center for Technical Communication, May 201x

- Used writing and communication expertise to critique and hone student lab reports, technical correspondence, and proposals

Process Intern, General Electric Healthcare, Summer 201x

- Developed processes to determine oxidation state and to quantify hydration of raw materials; assisted with validation of equipment and researched improvements for scale-up process

PharmCamp Volunteer, Summer Camp, Summer 201x

- Assisted in activity brainstorming for this new engineering / pharmacy summer camp; led an interactive session on technology

SCHOLARY WORK

Peer-Reviewed Publications:

A. Sample, I. Scriptt, B. Cane. Treating lung biofilm infections: dispersion and eradication via dry powder aerosols, *Respir. Drug Deliv*. 201x. In press.

Presentations:

A. Sample, I. Scriptt, & B. Cane. Treating lung biofilm infections: dispersion and eradication via dry powder aerosols. *2010 Respiratory Drug Delivery*, Orlando, FL, April 25 - 29. (Accepted)

A. Sample, I. Scriptt, & B. Cane. Co-delivery of antibiotic and dispersion compounds to eradicate *pseudomonas aeruginosa* biofilms in the cystic fibrotic lung. *Pharmaceutics Graduate Student Research Meeting*, Purdue University, IN, June 2, 201x.

Poster Presentations:

A. Sample & I. Scriptt. Investigation of polyacrylamide initial size distribution and mass along with sonication method on the supercritical core-shell coating process. *200x NSF REU Program in Micro/Nano-Structured Materials, Therapeutics, and Device Poster Session*, Auburn, AL, July 9, 201x.

A. Sample & I. Scriptt. Formulation and optimization of aerosols containing a bacterial-killing enzyme. *200x Spring Engineering Poster Session, Chemical Engineering*, Iowa City, IA, April 1, 201x.

AWARDS

Outstanding Senior Award at College of Engineering Graduation, Fall 201x
Nominated to give College of Engineering's student commencement speech, 201x
Ray Collins Engineering Communications Scholarship, Fall 201x
Wisconsin Science Talent Search State Winner, Spring 200x

PROFESSIONAL MATERAILS

Portfolio: www.alexsample.com Review publications, abstracts, syllabi, philosophy

References: Available upon request from faculty, supervisors, employers

Physical Therapy & Rehabilitative Sciences CV

Strategic Features: Physical Therapy CV

Review this CV if you are applying for clinical practica positions in health fields that require licensure and/or certification.

CV BASICS:

Highest Degree:	Ph.D. in progress
Experience:	Clinical internships
Job Target:	Clinical placement appointment for finishing degree requirements

CONTENT FEATURES:

- First category states appropriate training and qualifications required for the clinical placement appointment.
- *Clinical Experience* includes two major components of physical therapy training: *Clinical Internships* and *Integrated Clinical Education.* To keep CV to one page in length, four internships are described with one comprehensive annotation. This technique helps to reduce repetitive phrases.
- The *Service* category again saves space by listing several key areas of service (presentations, memberships, volunteer) in one space. Make it clear to the search team that only "selected" presentations have been included.

DESIGN FEATURES:

Font:	Calibri font, size 11
Margins:	.75" top, bottom, left, right
Layout:	Insert table with two columns.
Line spacing:	One line space between categories.
Enhancements:	Italic font to highlight key material and to introduce sub-categories (see *Clinical Experience* and *Service*).

Physical Therapy CV

Hirem E. Soon
University Hill, Any City, State 12345
(office: 101.444.3456) (cell: 198.621.4089) hireme-soon@iu.edu

DEGREES

Indiana University, Bloomington
DPT, Physical Therapy and Rehabilitation Science, December 201x

Valparaiso University, Valparaiso, Indiana
B.S. Degree, *with distinction,* May 200x
Majors: Computer Science and Psychology

HONORS

Phi Beta Kappa; Outstanding Section Award, 201x
Department of Mathematics and Computer Science Outstanding Student Award, 201x

CLINICAL EXPERIENCE

Clinical Internships:

Mayo Clinic and St. Mary's Hospital, Rochester, MN, October – December 201x
OrthoWest, Omaha, NE, August – October 201x
University of Chicago Hospitals, Chicago, IL, May – August 200x
Vail Valley Medical Center, Vail, CO, July – August, 200x

- Internship responsibilities: evaluation and treatment of patients with varied diagnoses, discharge planning, documentation, consultation, and supervision of supportive personnel. Contributed to program development, quality improvement, problem solving, and productivity enhancement.

Integrated Clinical Education:

Outpatient Rehabilitation, Washington, IN, January 201x
Rotations (half-day) in multiple clinics in eastern Indiana, 201x – 201x

- Worked under the supervision of physical therapists in various environments. Observed and assisted with patient treatment in the area of orthopedics, burns, cardiopulmonary, sports medicine, geriatrics, pediatrics, neurology rehabilitation.

PREVIOUS WORK

Computer Programmer, Comsat Laboratories, Clarksburg, MD, July 201x – May 201x

- Member of the satellite telecommunications research and development team. Contract focused on subsystems and technologies testing, data analysis, and report writing.

SERVICE

Presentations: (selected)
Poster Session, "Technology and Physical Therapy," Physical Therapy Research Symposium, Indiana University, April 201x; Purdue University, May 201x
Workshop Leader, "Advising the New PT Student," Physical Therapy as your Future, Graduate Recruitment Day, Indiana University, October 201x
Co-chair, Wheelchair Challenge, PT Student Organization, IU v. Purdue, May 201x; May 201x

Memberships:
American Physical Therapy Association, student member
Indiana University Physical Therapy Student Organization, member and officer

Volunteer:
Physical therapy aide, Iowa Musculoskeletal Center, Bloomington, 201x – present

Professional Writing/Translating Résumé

Strategic Features: Professional Writing/Translating Résumé

Review this résumé if you are seeking opportunities that do not require a particular degree or academic discipline.

RÉSUMÉ BASICS:

Highest Degree:	Ph.D.
Experience:	Teaching assistantship Peace Corps Professional position
Job Target:	Setting is open: government, corporate, non-profit Focus on writing, editing, translating

CONTENT FEATURES:

- Focus is on *Competencies* not on degree attainment. To support and strengthen the *Competencies* category, identifying accomplishments is key. The second category, *Accomplishments*, quickly demonstrates skills and abilities. All entries are stated in phrases (remember—no complete sentences are ever included in a résumé).
- *Experiences* are listed but without annotation. The *Education* section is placed in the middle of the document because the emphasis is on what the person can do, not on the degree level.
- *Writing and Speaking Experiences* are grouped together and summarized. This format allows the résumé to be one page in length.
- Items listed in the *Service* category are presented to counter the academic image.

DESIGN FEATURES:

Font:	Bookman Old Style font, size 11
Margins:	.75" top, bottom; .75" left, right
Layout:	Insert table with two columns.
Line spacing:	Two line spaces between categories.
Enhancements:	Spaces used for emphasis.

Professional Writing/Translating Résumé

Alec Example
16 University Avenue, Any City, State 12345 (101) 555-0101 a-sample@gmail.com

---

COMPENTENCIES

Translating Writing Editing New Media

ACCOMPLISHMENTS

Proficient in Spanish, Portuguese, Swahili
Translated from Spanish to English and English to Spanish
Prepared reports for U.S. Department of Education
Created new media applications for communication
Selected as outstanding graduate teaching assistant
Awarded four-year graduate fellowship

EXPERIENCE

Language Specialist, U.S. Department of Education, 201x-present, Washington, DC

Teaching Assistant, Spanish and Portuguese Department, 201x-201x, Syracuse University

Peace Corps, Teacher Trainer and Environmental Specialist, 201x-201x, Uganda

EDUCATION

BA Biology; Spanish *with honors,* May 201x
Pacific Lutheran, Seattle, WA

MA Spanish, June 201x
University of Oregon, Portland

PhD Second Language Acquisition, August 201x-May 201x
University of Maryland, College Park

SERVICE

Volunteer Housing Coordinator, DC Refugee Center, 201x-
Hospital Volunteer Translator, St. Mary's Hospital, 201x-
Amnesty International Board Member, 201x-201x
Animal Rescue Society (Rat Terrier), 201x

WRITING/ SPEAKING EXPERIENCES

Writing: articles published in newsletters (*Refugee Center News, Animal Rescue Read!,* and *Saving our Creatures*); managed a blog; designed brochures; developed logos; and created a nonprofit website (www.refugee_center_news.org)

Presentations: speaking engagements with local volunteer groups interested in Amnesty International projects; invited lecturer at George Washington International Center, the Peace Corps Recruitment Center, and Global Initiatives, Inc.

Writing samples available: www.alecsampleportfolio.org

Psychology CV

Strategic Features: Psychology CV

Review this CV if you have a clinical background with a number of supervised practica and internships.

CV BASICS:

Highest Degree:	Doctoral studies near completion Licensed professional
Experience:	Teaching assistantship Clinical experience
Job Target:	Teaching position at small liberal arts college or a community college Clinical appointment at a teaching hospital

CONTENT FEATURES:

- Page one clearly highlights *Licensure and Certifications* and *Clinical Training* experiences. Note in the *Academic Background* category that five degrees are stated, two being earned from the same institution. An AA degree was earned by attending an online college. For clarity sake, accreditation status is included: regionally accredited by North Central Association (Higher Learning Commission).
- *Clinical Training* and *Supervision* categories include the following: Supervisor; Site Description; Responsibilities; and Client Population. This style is the convention in this specialty and should be used for primary clinical placements.
- The *Professional Activities* category presents several critical areas of productivity and professional involvement: posters, case presentations, papers, service and memberships.

DESIGN FEATURES:

Font:	Gill Sans MT font, size 10
Margins:	.75" top, bottom, left, right
Layout:	Open new document; use tab to indent.
Line spacing:	One line space between categories.
Enhancements:	Use of a graphic line to separate categories. Italics and bold are used for organizational emphasis.

Psychology CV

IMA SAMPLE

16 University Avenue, Any City, State 12345 101.555.0101 i-sample@du.edu

ACADEMIC BACKGROUND

Psychology Doctoral Candidate, Degree expected May 201x
Duke University, Durham, North Carolina Advisor: Dr. Bea Fine

Master of Science Degree, Marriage and Family Therapy, June 201x
Masters of Science Degree, Psychology, December 201x
Valdosta State University, Valdosta, Georgia Advisors: Will Gab, PhD; Sam Hoppin, PhD

Bachelor of Science Degree, Psychology, May 200x *with high distinction*
Berry College, Mount Berry, Georgia

Associate's Degree in Medical Administration, June 200x *President's Scholar Recognition*
Rasmussen College Online (regionally accredited by NCA)

LICENSURE AND CERTIFICATIONS

Licensed Associate Marriage and Family Therapist, North Carolina and Georgia, 201x – present
Certified Mental Health Professional, Georgia and North Carolina, 201x – 201x
Certified School Guidance Counselor, Georgia, 200x – 200x

RESEARCH ACTIVITIES

Increasing Adherence to Diabetic Regimen in Adolescents, August 201x – present
Dissertation research examining increasing adherence to medical regiments in chronically non-adherent adolescents diagnosed with Type I Diabetes Mellitus.

Developing Inpatient Consult and Liaison Services, June 201x – present
Conducted research surrounding the development of the new consult-liaison service. Examined the use of technology and telehealth in increasing adherence to medical regimens in adolescents with chronic illnesses.

Brief Treatment Probes for Elopement, January 201x – present
Examining the development of a protocol for rapidly identifying a treatment for elopement in an outpatient setting through the use of treatment analyses.

CLINICAL TRAINING

Carolina Children's Hospital, Chapel Hill, North Carolina, August 201x – May 201x
Attention-Deficit Hyperactivity Disorder Clinic, Department of Pediatric Psychology

Supervisor: Karen B. Norse, Ph.D.
Site Description: Multi-disciplinary outpatient medical clinic. Staffed by a pediatric psychologist, pediatric nurse practitioner and pediatrician.
Responsibilities: Provided assessment of ADHD. Conducted intake interviews, structured observation of academic performance, neuropsychological testing and intervention planning with parents and medical staff.
Client Population: Children ages 3-10 exhibiting attention and hyperactivity concerns

GRANTS

Student Grant Recipient, Society for the Advancement of Behavior Analysis, 201x; 201x

Psychology CV, page 2

Sample, page 2

PROVISION OF SUPERVISION

Carolina Children's Hospital, Chapel Hill, North Carolina, June 201x – June 201x
Pediatric Psychology Consult-Liaison Service, Department of Pediatric Psychology

Site Description: Inpatient medical setting. Consult-based service with patients from inpatient hospital unit staffed by a pediatric psychologist, pediatric nurse practitioner and pediatrician.

Responsibilities: Provided weekly individual supervision to first-year psychology doctoral students in a practicum setting. Provided on-site observation and mid-term and final reviews with site supervisors.

Client Population: Children in inpatient pediatric unit

EMPLOYMENT

Mountain River Center, Atlanta, Georgia, May 200x – September 200x
Director, Psychosocial Day Support Program

Responsibilities: Supervised staff of five para-professionals providing psychosocial mental health services to children 5-18 years-old. Designed, implemented, and directed psychosocial day support treatment and services. Collaborated with parents, psychiatrists, schools, and case managers to meet the needs of patients. Provided diagnostic assessments and therapy.

Whitecloud Counseling Center, Athens, Georgia, June 200x – May 200x
Child Therapist

Responsibilities: Provided group, individual, and family therapy to children and adolescents in the partial hospitalization program. Wrote treatment plans, facilitated treatment team meetings, conducted psychosocial assessments. Monitored progress and conducted discharge planning.

PROFESSIONAL ACTIVITIES

Poster Presentations:

Sample, I., and Fine, B. (May 201x). A Model for Brief Outpatient Evaluation of Problem Behaviors. Poster presentation at the 35th Annual Convention for Association of Behavior Analysis.

Sample, I. (May 201x). Brief Treatment Evaluation of Elopement. Poster presentation at the Holmes Fellowship Annual Conference.

Case Presentation:

Fine, B., and Sample I. (April 201x). Inpatient Consult-Liaison Case Study of a Hematology-Oncology patient. Case presentation at Children's Hospital Grand Rounds.

Paper Presentations:

Sample, I. (February 201x). Brief Treatment Approaches of Elopement: Closing the Achievement Gap Through Applied Research Methods. Paper Presentation at the Southeast Society of Pediatric Psychology Regional Conference.

Service:

President and member, Society for Pediatric Psychology Diversity Committee, 201x – 201x
Pediatric Psychology and Diabetes Lecture, University Pediatric Psychology Course, Fall 201x
Staff Therapist, Family Camp for Diabetes, Camp Hertko Hollow, Spring 200x

Memberships:

Association of Behavior Analysis International
Psychological Association of Graduate Students
American Psychological Association
Society for Pediatric Psychology

Public Health CV

Strategic Features: Public Health CV

Review this CV if your experience includes specialized research, consulting, funding opportunities, and professional experience.

CV BASICS:

Highest Degree:	Ph.D. in progress; MBA and M.D.
Experience:	Research and teaching assistantships Professional medical practice
Job Target:	Global health organizations Government policy position

CONTENT FEATURES:

- Placing *Research Interests* first emphasizes the importance of research in your career and alludes to your ability to succeed in an organization that values research strengths.
- *Funded Projects and Consulting* are carefully placed on page one because of the importance of these two skills in an international aid/policy position or in a nonprofit setting.
- Short descriptive annotations use action words and specific details to describe teaching, research and service responsibilities.
- Page two provides relevant teaching and research appointments as well as comprehensive categories outlining invited lectures, publications and professional service. To demonstrate technical competence, a special category is designed to list software and new media applications.

DESIGN FEATURES:

Font:	Bookman Old Style font, size 10
Margins:	.75" top, bottom, left, right
Layout:	Open new document; use tab to indent.
Line spacing:	.5 line space between categories.
Enhancements:	Left-justified category headings allowing descriptors to extend from margin-to-margin utilizing space wisely.

Public Health CV

HIREM E. SOON
21 College Street, City, State, Zip (c) 211.509.6789 hireme-soon@university.edu

GLOBAL HEALTH RESEARCH INTERESTS:

- Global needs assessment for providers in developing countries
- Global health and knowledge sharing
- Innovations in injury control and prevention
- Development of new format for online delivery of course material
- Capacity building: utilization of practitioners in data retrieval

FORMAL EDUCATION

PhD Division of Public Health, University of Utah School of Medicine
Candidate in Public Health, Global Health Track
Expected completion August 201x
Thesis: Data management and digital recordings of newborn birth defects in developing countries: a 10 year analysis
Advisor: H.E. Proffe, M.D., Ph.D.

MBA School of Management, University of Missouri-KC
Marketing, Strategic Management and Consulting, June 201x
GMAT: 730 (95th percentile) GPA: 4.00/4.00

MD College of Medicine, University of Missouri-KC, July 201x
Class rank: top 5%

BS Computer Science, University of Wyoming
May 200x high distinction
Study projects in Haiti, Colombia, Finland

RECOGNITION

Fellowship for International Research, Oxford University, 201x
Thomas & Thomas Trainee, Research Award in Occupational Health, 201x
University Award for Distinguished Student Leadership, 201x

FELLOWSHIP

Health Organization of the Americas, Mexico City
Fellow: Prevention, Research and Knowledge Management Division, 201x
Provided strategic consulting for development of the digital retrieval system initiative; participated in the establishment of an international working group, introduced new communication technologies and strategic recommendations.

FUNDED PROJECTS

Principal Investigator, International Collaborative Trauma and Injury Training Program, University of Utah (award $200,000)
Co-Investigator, Newborn Safety and Attitudes Study, funded by University of Utah and BYU College of Public Health, (Output – 3 peer reviewed papers) (award $94,500)
Co-Investigator/Coordinator, Rural Risk Assessment of Environmental Factors in rural Mexico, funded by Health Organization of the Americas (award $100,000)

CONSULTING

Telemedicine: Evaluation of information technology for transnational collaborations, International Data Group, London, 201x – 201x
Digital retrieval systems, World Health Systems and Innovations, Los Angeles, 201x

Public Health CV, page 2

Hirem E. Soon, page 2

RESEARCH APPOINTMENTS

University of Utah: Graduate Research Assistant, Environmental Health Center, Fall 201x – Summer 201x, Dr. H.E. Proff, supervisor

Graduate Research Assistant, Center for Evaluation & Research, Spring 201x, Dr. Bea Fine, graduate supervisor

TEACHING APPOINTMENTS

University of Utah: Teaching Assistant, Qualitative Research for Public Health, Spring 200x; Introduction to Disease Prevention, Fall 201x; Spring 201x

PUBLICATIONS

Journals:

Soon, H.E., Smith, T.T., Proff, H., and Goode, D. (201x) Community attitudes and disease prevention. *Journal of Disease Prevention,* 5(5), 28-39.

Kane, W.W., **Soon, H.E.**, (201x) An online model for newborn safety. *Safety Medicine: Occupational and Health Education Journal, 12*(2), 19-24.

Media:

Soon, H.E., and Goode D. (201x) Community responses to disease prevention. View at: *www.doctortalks/response221/vol3.com*

Soon, H.E. (201x) Talking to your kids about diseases. DoctorsBlog Contributor. View at: *www.doctorsblog.talkabout diseases/paper376.com*

PROFESSIONAL EXPERIENCE

Food Bank Consultant and Relief Coordinator, Haiti, February – May 201x
Researcher, Center for Public Health, Dominican Republic, July 201x – present
Principal Investigator, Injury Prevention Research Project, Haiti, 200x

SERVICE & AFFILIATIONS

Academic service:
Awards Committee Student Representative, College of Medicine, 201x
Board of Advisors, Division of Public Health Student Association, 201x

United States affiliations:
Beta Gamma Sigma International Honor Society in Business
Alpha Phi chapter of Delta Omega Honorary Society in Public Health
Global Health Council
American Public Health Association

International affiliations:
World Health Organization
Worldvision

TECHNICAL APPLICATIONS & LANGUAGES

SAS, SPSS, AMOS (Confirmatory Factor Analysis, Structural Equation Modeling)
Elluminate *Live!,* WebCT, Blackboard, Desire2Learn; MySQL (basic)
Bilingual in English and French: advanced level; Spanish; laughter yoga

PROFESSIONAL MATERIALS

For evidence of scholarly work/professional projects, visit: www.hiremesoon.com

Religious Studies/Library and Information Science CV

Strategic Features: Religious Studies/ Library and Information Science CV

Review this CV if you are an established academic or professional and are using your CV for annual reviews, promotions, or for leadership positions.

CV BASICS:

Highest Degree:	Ph.D.
Experience:	Professional experience Consulting Invited workshop presentations
Job Target:	Leadership and professional use

CONTENT FEATURES:

- Page one clearly highlights a strong professional identity. *Degrees* begin the CV followed by *Languages*. The academic training is rich and diverse; the range of languages impressive.
- The third category, *Current Professional Appointment* on page one, provides an overview of the responsibilities and specialties of this appointment. It was kept brief so that the other considerable talents and abilities could be highlighted. The *Professional/Scholarly Activities* category demonstrates the wide-ranging talents and professional contributions of the individual.
- Because of the nature of the career and the specialized languages involved in the career, Chinese transliterations are presented in the publications category. Chinese characters are intentionally not used to prevent formatting issues if the Chinese fonts aren't installed on the recipient's computer. Individuals perusing the CV will most likely be conversant in the language as well.

DESIGN FEATURES:

Font:	Gill Sans MT font, size 10
Margins:	.75" top, bottom, left, right
Layout:	Open new document; use tab to indent.
Line spacing:	One line space between categories.
Enhancements:	Use of a graphic line to separate categories. Italics and bold are used for organizational emphasis.

Religious Studies/Library and Information Science CV

REED A. LOTT

121 Campus Hall (o):101.555.0101 (c):193.876.0034 reedalott@psu.edu

DEGREES

Ph.D. Religious Studies (History of Asian Religions), The University of Chicago, 201x
M.A. Library and Information Science (ALA-accredited), University of Virginia, 200x
M.A. Humanities, University of Kentucky, 200x
B.A. Philosophy, Peking University, Beijing , China, 200x

LANGUAGES

Chinese (native proficiency, with research-level classical reading competence)
English (proficiency)
Japanese (working knowledge)
French (reading knowledge)
German (reading knowledge)

CURRENT PROFESSIONAL APPOINTMENT

Curator, East Asian Collection, Brown University Library, Providence, RI. (March 201x-present)

Chiefly responsible for administrating all aspects of 150,000-volume Chinese-Japanese-Korean collections, including collection development and management, technical services, reference and research consultation, outreach activities, preservation and stewardship, and supervision of staff. Also play a role in scholarly resources budget planning and priorities. Successfully fundraising for East Asian Collection, nearly $600,000.

PROFESSIONAL/SCHOLARLY ACTIVITIES

Associate in Research, Fairbank Center for East Asian Research, Harvard University. (201x-present)

Founding Member, the Society for Chinese Studies Librarians (SCSL), and serve on the Committee for Scholarly Activities. (March 201x- present)

Organizer and Designer, East Asian Book Art Exhibition, John Hay Library. (October 201x-March 201x)

Participant, International Symposium on Collection Development, Research and Service on Chinese Studies, National Library of China, Beijing, China. (September 201x)

Supervisor, Professional Field Experience Program, School of Library and Information Studies, University of Rhode Island. (Fall 201x)

Organizer, *Exhibition on Chinese Coins in the Song Dynasty and Traditional Chinese Handcrafts*. (July 200x)

Panelist, "East Asia Studies: Challenges of Complex Reality in an Era of Globalization and Digitization," Cornell University. (November 200x)

Organizer, "Cultural Essence over the Centuries: An Exhibition from East Asian Collection," Brown University. (Fall 200x) URL: http://worf.services.brown.edu/exhibits/archive/EAC/index.html

Discussant, Panel of Inner Alchemy and Quanzhen Daoism, International Conference on Daoist Studies, Boston. (June 200x)

Chief Instructor, Chinese Tai Chi Chuan (Taijiquan) Program, Recreational Services. (200x-200x) Created and taught one of the most comprehensive Tai Chi programs in North America for all levels.

Religious Studies CV; Library and Information Science CV, page 2

Reed A. Lott, page 2

PUBLICATIONS

"The Study of Bai Yuchan: Review, Deliberation and Outlook" "Guanyu Bai Yuchan yanjiu de kaocha, sisuo yu qianzhan." In *Tianlu luncong (Collected Essays on Chinese Studies by East Asian Librarians in North America)* (Guilin: Guangxi Shifan Daxue Chubanshe, 201x), 100-115.

"A Textual Research on Bai Yuchan's Works and the Formation of the Resources of Daoist Southern Lineage" "Bai Yuchan zhuzuo ji daojiao nanzong jingji wenxian de xingcheng kaolue." In *Tianlu luncong (Collected Essays on Chinese Studies by East Asian Librarians in North America)* (Guilin: Guangxi Shifan Daxue Chubanshe, 200x), 5-24.

Brown's East Asian Collection. *BiblioFile: Newsletter of the Brown University Library*, 30 (Fall 200x): 5.

"The Characteristics of Buddhism at Mount Wutai." *Mount Wutai Researches,* 14 (March 19xx): 27-32.

PUBLISHING PROJECTS IN PROGRESS [BOOKS & ARTICLES]

Golden Elixir and Transcendence: Bai Yuhcan's Dao of Inner Alchemical Cultivation (in process)

A Study of Bai Yuchan (Bai Yuchan yan jiu) (forthcoming)

The Sourcebook of Daoist Cultivation of the Southern Lineage (daojiao nanzong xiulian wenxian) (forthcoming)

"Inner Alchemy and Thunder Rites: Bai Yuchan's Spiritual Experience in Daoist Ritual Practice" (under editorial review)

PRESENTATIONS

Workshop on Scholarly Resources for East Asian Studies, Department of East Asian Studies, April 201x

"East Asian Studies: Resources, Access, and Communication," New England Association for Asian Studies (NEAAS) Regional Conference, Brown University, October 201x

"Thinking Globally: A Librarian's Professional Trip to China," Brown University Library, September 201x

"Scholarly Resources and Services in North American East Asian Libraries" (invited lecture), Beijing Foreign Studies University, Beijing, China, September 201x

"Introduction to Chinese Tai Chi Chuan" (Taijiquan), Sumer Chinese Program (invited workshop), May 201x

"Group Decision Making," Everyday Leadership Programs, Brown University, March 201x

"Introduction to East Asian Collection," for International Teaching Assistants, Brown University, August 200x

"An Overview of Trends in Developing and Accessing Chinese Scholarly Resources," Association for Asian Studies (AAS) Annual Meeting, Boston, March 200x

PROFESSIONAL DEVELOPMENT ACTIVITIES

Workshops:
NACO Workshop for Name Authorities, Brown University, July-August. 201x
East Asian Library Management Program, China Focus (Certificate), Luce Summer Institute, July 201x
CEAL XML Workshop for East Asian Libraries, San Diego, March 201x
Library of Congress-CEAL East Asian Art Cataloging Workshop and CJK Rare Book Cataloging Sessions, Washington, DC. April 201x
NELINET OCLC CJK Workshop, Amherst, January 201x

Memberships:
Association for Asian Studies (AAS)
Council on East Asian Libraries (CEAL)
American Library Association (ALA)
Society for Chinese Studies Librarians (SCSL)

School Psychology CV

Strategic Features: School Psychology CV

Review this CV if you are seeking an internship in a clinical, academic, or research setting.

CV BASICS:

Highest Degree:	Doctoral studies underway
Experience:	Teaching & research assistantship Clinical experience
Job Target:	Internship at APA approved pediatric or psychiatric hospital Post-doc appointment

CONTENT FEATURES:

- Academic Background is presented first to emphasize academic preparation required for an internship or residency.
- *Clinical Training* category includes the type of training; Site Description; Responsibilities; and Client Population. This style is the convention in this specialty. Both the *Extern* training and the *Practica* experiences are included in one category to show the variety and intensity of training.
- The clinical experiences highlighted on the first page demonstrate diversity of placement sites.
- Page two presents several critical areas of productivity and professional involvement in service activities and key memberships.

DESIGN FEATURES:

Font:	Corbel condensed font, size 10
Margins:	.75" top, bottom; .75"left, right
Layout:	Insert table with two columns.
Line spacing:	One line space between categories.
Enhancements:	Use of a graphic line to separate name and contact information. Italics are used for organizational emphasis.

School Psychology CV

IMA SAMPLE

#225 Academic Hall, Any University, Any City, State 12345
c: (101)555-1110 o: (102)555-1998 ima-sample@UK.edu

ACADEMIC PREPARATION

University of Kentucky, Lexington
Doctoral Candidate, School Psychology, 201x – present (Full APA Accreditation)
Dissertation Proposal: MMPI-2 Profiles of Adolescents with ADHD
Advisor: Bea Fine, Ph.D.

Master's Degree, Psychology, May 201x
Thesis: Analysis of Measures Assessing ADHD

Macalester College, St. Paul, Minnesota
Bachelor of Arts Degree, Psychology and Mathematics, June 200x
graduated with high distinction *Phi Beta Kappa*

CLINICAL TRAINING

Extern:
Psychology Extern, Assessment and Therapy, Kosair Children's Hospital, Louisville, KY, 10/201x – present.
Responsibilities: psychological assessments; group psychotherapy; consultation with multidisciplinary treatment teams; in-service seminars; and research critical pathways for treatment of eating disorders and treatment outcome studies.
Client population: in-patient/out-patient children and adolescents with pediatric and/or psychological concerns.

Practica:
Therapy Practicum, Bluegrass County Services, Lexington, KY, 09/201x – 06/201x.
Responsibilities: crisis intervention at community mental health center, long and short-term individual, group, couples, and family therapy; intake termination reports; diagnosis/case conceptualization; progress notes & supervision of students.
Client population: community-based clinic treating all ages with a wide range of psychopathology.

Therapy Practicum, University of Kentucky Counseling Center, 09/201x – 05/201x.
Responsibilities: personality and vocational testing and interpretation, short-term individual therapy, session and termination notes, case conceptualization and presentations, and weekly didactic seminars.
Client population: university students whose presenting problems included college adjustment and psychiatric disorders.

Assessment Practicum, Hope and Health Clinic, Lexington, KY, 10/201x – 04/201x.
Responsibilities: intakes; completion of psychological evaluations including administration/interpretation of test data and writing of assessment reports; case presentation; supervision from advanced students.
Client population: community-based clinic for underserved children with a wide range of presenting issues.

RESEARCH ACTIVITIES

Supervised Projects:
Self-ratings of competence in children diagnosed with ADHD
Predictor variables of drop out in ADHD parent training
Childhood depression inventory validation study

School Psychology CV, page 2

Sample, page 2

GRADUATE RESEARCH APPOINTMENTS	Research Assistant, Department of Educational School, and Counseling Psychology, University of Kentucky, 201x – present. Research, collect, and analyze data for a federally funded project on implications of behaviors of ADHD adults in employment settings. Collaborative team project supervised by Will B. Fine, Ph.D. and Bea Goode, M.D., Ph.D. Project Assistant, ADHD Parent Training Research Team- Southeast Region, Psychology Department, University of Kentucky, 201x. Organized and co-led parent training groups with an emphasis on behavior management techniques. Reviewed neuropsychological testing results and compiled data into research reports.
UNIVERSITY TEACHING	Teaching Assistant, College of Education, University of Kentucky, Fall 201x – present. *Introduction to Computer Technology in the Helping Professions:* responsibilities include planning course content, presenting course material in conjunction with hands-on experience using appropriate digital applications for practitioners in counseling areas. Offer individual help sessions and evaluate student performance in course papers, projects, and examinations. Instructor, Bluegrass Technical and Community College, Lexington, 200x – 201x. *Psychological Foundations:* developed syllabus and materials for use in undergraduate level psychology course. Utilized online course materials and distance education based web components to facilitate course goals.
PUBLICATIONS	Sample, I. (201x). *Towards a more positive framework for parent training modules.* American Psychology Quarterly, (2) 245–260. Sample, I., Fine, W.B. (201x). *ADHD college students and assistive technology. A case study.* Assistive Technology Review, 30–41.
PRESENTATIONS	Sample, I. (April 201x). *Assistive technology and the ADHD student*. Poster session, annual meeting, Kentucky Psychological Association, Louisville, Kentucky. Sample, I., Example, A. & Fine, W.B. (November 201x). *Depression and ADHD in college students.* Paper presented at annual meeting, American Psychological Association, New York, New York.
SERVICE	Affiliations: Psi Chi Association for the Advancement of Behavior Therapy American Psychological Association; Kentucky Psychological Association Boards & Committees: Student Services Committee, University of Kentucky, Fall 201x – 201x Board member, Assistive Technology/ADHD Project, Kentucky Cares, Lexington, 201x Client Advocate Committee, Neighborhood Centers, Lexington, 200x – 200x Facilitator: Workshop Facilitator, ADHD College Initiative, UK Office of Student Life, Fall 201x Co-facilitator, Relational Aggression in Girls Workshop, Lexington Schools, April 200x
EMPLOYMENT	Diagnostician, ADHD Treatment Center, St. Paul Hospital, St. Paul, MN, 200x Behavior Interventionist, Star Treatment Center, Austin, MN, 200x

Science Education CV

Strategic Features: Science Education CV

Review this CV if you have international degrees and experiences and are pursuing a doctoral degree and employment in the U.S.

CV BASICS:

Highest Degree:	Ph.D. nearly finished
Experience:	Teaching and assistantships Grant participation Secondary teaching experience
Job Target:	American universities, especially research institutions

CONTENT FEATURES:

- The categories represented on the first page show – at a quick glance – the current educational attainment of the candidate including degrees earned outside the United States. Research (interests and experiences) is the main focus on page one, primarily because the job objective is to be considered for an appointment in a research-based university. By providing short annotations in the *Summary of Teaching and Supervision* category, the reader is aware of prior teaching experience with the focus on level of instruction rather than the location of instruction.
- Page two shows considerable scholarly experience in the areas of publications, presentations, and service. International experience is highlighted with appropriately titled subcategories.
- A separate category is designed to demonstrate knowledge and integration of technology.

DESIGN FEATURES:

Font:	Palatino Linotype font, size 10
Margins:	.75" top, bottom, left, right
Layout:	Insert table with two columns.
Line spacing:	One line space between categories.
Enhancements:	Bullets used as an organizational tool.

Science Education CV

WILL B. FINE PO Box 21101, City, State, Zip (c) 123.765.8876 (o) 321.8745.0980 willbfine@csu.edu

ACADEMIC PREPARATION

Colorado State University, Fort Collins, Ph.D., Science Education, May 201x
Dissertation: *inquiry-oriented science environments: case study of a middle school*
Comprehensive areas: *teaching/ learning sciences, rhetoric of inquiry, literacy, physics*

Colorado State University Center for Inquiry Certificate, 201x
An interdisciplinary program exploring the historical, social, and political aspects of paradigm of knowledge and rhetoric of inquiry

Sharif University of Technology, Tehran, M.S., Physics, October 200x

Sharif University of Technology, Tehran, B.S., Physics, October 200x

RECOGNITION

Awarded Fellow, Graduate Institute on Engagement and the Academy (201x)
Graduate Teaching Award: Colorado State University (201x)
Action Research Award, Graduate Student Competition (201x)

RESEARCH INTERESTS

Application of holistic learning theories on science classroom practices
Teacher and student learning throughout inquiry-oriented classroom practices
Dialogic aspects of science literacy in classroom practices
Analysis of evidence-based classroom language
Mixed methods:
- Mediated discourse analysis
- Ethnographic analysis
- Corpus analysis of language and discourse

SUMMARY OF TEACHING AND SUPERVISION

200x - present
Five years: • teaching physics at high school level
Four years: • designing and implementing professional development courses for in-service elementary/secondary teachers
Three years: • teaching and supervising pre-service science students

RESEARCH APPOINTMENTS

Graduate Research Assistant, CSU Science Education Department, 201x – 201x
- International Institute for Science Inquiry Grant
  Responsibilities: Designing discourse analysis tools for qualitative and quantitative measurement of teachers' and students' learning

Course Designer and Researcher, Tebyan Educational Center, 200x – 200x
- National Science Grant, Iran
  Responsibilities: Designed a virtual inquiry-oriented course for in-service teachers; completed comparative study of effect of the course on different cultural environments.

Principal Researcher, National Education Center, 200x – 200x
- Responsibilities: Designed ninth-grade inquiry-oriented physics curriculum. Over 1,000 students use this package to learn physics.

Science Education CV, page 2

Will B. Fine., page 2

TEACHING AND SUPERVISION

University Teaching:
Designing and teaching Science Methods, Colorado State University (201x)
- Physics application for elementary/secondary pre-service teachers

Directing and teaching PD workshops for in-service teachers, Tehran (200x)
- Helping teachers become familiar with inquiry-oriented approaches

PUBLICATIONS

Articles in Referred Journals:

Fine, W.B., & Goode, I.M. (201x). Making effective collaborative classroom inquiries. Physics Education, 62(5), 22-26

Fine, W.B. (200x). Criteria for assessing students' ability to apply physics to daily-real life. Iranian Physics Education Journal, 10(70), 48-59 (in Persian)

PRESENTATIONS

International Conference Papers:

- Fine, W.B., & Goode, I.M. (201x). Effects of inquiry-oriented practice. Accepted paper; to be presented at ASTE. London
- Goode, I.M., & Fine, W.B. (201x). How teaching practices foster creativity and learning. Paper presented at NARST. Frankfurt

International Poster Sessions:

- Fine, W.B. (201x). Creating effective classroom inquiry lessons. Poster presented at GRIEP. Amsterdam.
- Fine, W.B. (201x). Photography as an integrated part of a physics course. Poster presented at ICPE. Tokyo.

SERVICE

Membership in Professional Organizations:
- American Educational Research Association (AERA)
- Association for Science Teacher Education (ASTE)

Volunteer:
- Science Curriculum Review Board, area school districts
- Tutor, Neighborhood Centers, Fort Collins United Way

TECHNOLOGY

Multi-media and technology integration:
- Knowledge of multiple technologies and software considered primary in the domain of research and science education. Command of data management software and analysis using Ms EXCEL, SPSS.
- Use Web-based course management and site development software for distance education and campus-based courses.
- View blog contributions at: www.sciencetimes.blog.com/inquiry
- Teaching Portfolio at: www.willbfineteachingportfolio.com

Second Language Acquisition CV

Strategic Features: Second Language Acquisition CV

Review this CV if you are nearing completion of your doctoral program and have an extensive record of teaching experience, graduate appointments, and fellowships as well as rich technology integration.

CV BASICS:

Highest Degree:	Ph.D. in final stages
Experience:	Teaching experience Graduate assistantships Technology/new media experience
Job Target:	Academic teaching positions

CONTENT FEATURES:

- The five categories on page one–*Formal Education, Honors & Grants, Research Interests, Languages,* and *Graduate Appointments involving Technology,* presents the candidate's strengths at first glance on page one. These categories will set this candidate apart from others competing for the same jobs.
- A slightly different format is used to list *Research Interests & Languages;* instead of listing each research area and each language, a symbol was inserted to divide items thus eliminating large areas of empty white space. Again on page two, space was saved and redundancy avoided by listing three teaching positions with one descriptive section.
- Page two shows considerable teaching and scholarly experience by using just two category headings – *Graduate-level Teaching Experiences* and *Scholarly Activities.* Substantial scholarly production is broken into subcategories to demonstrate breadth of efforts.

DESIGN FEATURES:

Font:	Gill Sans MT font, size 10
Margins:	.75" top, bottom, left, right
Layout:	Open new document; use tabs to indent.
Line spacing:	One line space between categories.
Enhancements:	Italics and bold are used for organizational emphasis. Select use of bullets in sections that detail teaching and multifaceted experiences.

Second Language Acquisition CV

HIREM E. SOON

21 College Street, Any Place, State ZIP (201)565-2321 hiremesoon@mc.edu
Blog: germanhirem.blogspot.com

FORMAL EDUCATION

CARNEGIE MELON UNIVERSITY, PITTSBURGH, PA
Doctor of Philosophy Candidate, Second Language Acquisition, September 201x - present
Thesis: *The effect of multimedia advance organizers on comprehending authentic German video*

WBS-Training AG, Leipzig, Germany
Certificate as Multimedia Designer for E–Learning/Learning Software, 201x

Universität Leipzig, Leipzig, Germany
Magister in DaF (equivalent to M.A. in Teaching German as a Foreign Language), 200x
Thesis: *Anglizismen in der deutschen Gegenwartssprache unter besonderer Berücksichtigung der Sportberichterstattung der Leipziger Volkszeitung sowie der Lernerwörterbücher von Langenscheidt und de Gruyter*

HONORS & GRANTS

Barnard Dissertation Year Fellowship, Carnegie Melon University, 201x–201x
Outstanding Teaching Assistant Award, Carnegie Melon University, 201x
Fulbright Grant, FLTA-program *(Fulbright and IIE - International Institute for Education)*, Juniata College, Huntingdon, 200x–200x
DAAD Grant, University of Otago (New Zealand); University of Queensland (Australia), 200x; 200x
PAD Research Grant (Pädagogischer Austauschdienst), Fareham College, Fareham, UK, 200x–200x

RESEARCH INTERESTS

Computer-assisted and computer-mediated language learning | Second language acquisition theories
The role of technology in second language acquisition | Teaching methods in second language learning
Curricular development | Foreign language pedagogy | Educational multimedia

LANGUAGES

German: native | English: near native fluency | Russian: near native fluency | Spanish: basic knowledge

GRADUATE APPOINTMENTS INVOLVING TECHNOLOGY

Graduate Assistant in the Multimedia Language Studio, 201x-201x
- Advised and assisted professors and graduate students in using a range of multimedia development software and hardware

Graduate Research Assistant for Flash-based Animation Phonetics Project, summers 201x; 201x
- Developed German module for Phonetics project; produced and edited video segments; worked with Flash animations

Graduate Research Assistant for 1st year Content Modules Project, summer 200x
- Developed web-based reading and cultural activities using Dreamweaver, Fireworks, WebCT

Translator and Project Associate for Development of Alternate Assessment in Reading and Mathematics for English Language Learners, 200x
- Assisted in the development of IAARM: translated English reading tests into German; scored student responses; revised tests based on student responses; provided feedback for revision of scoring protocol

Second Language Acquisition CV, page 2

HIREM E. SOON, page 2

GRADUATE-LEVEL TEACHING EXPERIENCES

Carnegie Melon University: Assistant Course Coordinator and Teaching Assistant, 201x–present

- Designed and administered the course management system for the German courses; provided support, guidance and leadership to teaching assistants; created teaching material on WebCT; helped revise reading pedagogy and design reading comprehension questions; taught Intensive Elementary and Intermediate German; authored and integrated multimedia teaching materials; added significant online learning components for the German Department.

Juniata College (Huntingdon, PA): German Language Instructor, 201x–201x
University of Otago (Dunedin, NZ): German Language Instructor, 200x
Fareham College (Fareham, Hamshire, UK): German Language Instructor, 200x–200x

- For above positions, conducted "A-Level" oral proficiency preparation classes; performed oral exams to measure student language proficiency; taught undergraduate German language, literature, and culture courses; judged Annual Goethe Verse-Speaking Competition; designed innovative course materials incorporating technology and new media.

SCHOLARLY ACTIVITIES

Publications:

The use of L1 in a L2 online chat activity. *Canadian Modern Language Review*, 62 (201x), 161–182 (with B. Fine & V. Goode).
Der Terminus Anglizismus: Was steckt dahinter? (The term Anglicism: What lies behind it?) *Estudios Filológicos Alemanes*, 2 (200x), 135–142

Conference Presentations (refereed):

Advance organizer support for comprehending foreign language video—Do language and modality matter?. International Association of Applied Linguistics/AILA, Essen, Germany, 201x (forthcoming).
Using multi-modal advance organizers to support learner comprehension of foreign language video. CALICO, University of Hawaii, Manoa, Oahu, 201x.
Phonetics: the sounds of spoken language. CALICO, University of Hawaii, Manoa, Oahu, 200x.

Poster Presentations (refereed):

Uses of the first language in online chat activities in a second language. ACTFL Meeting, Chicago, 201x.
Bringing study abroad home: Peer advisers and the process of study abroad. Internationalizing the Curriculum Conference, University of Minnesota, Minneapolis (with Fred Kevin), 200x.

Workshops:

Leader, Oral Proficiency Interviewing, 201x
Co-chair, Content Modules Project, 201x
Vice chair, E–Learning/Learning Software NE Regional Meeting, 201x
Facilitator, Center for New Teaching Institute, 200x

Affiliations:

American Association for Applied Linguistics (AAAL)
Computer Assisted Language Instruction Consortium (CALICO)
American Association of Teachers of German (AATG)
American Council on the Teaching of Foreign Languages (ACTFL)

Professional Materials:

Teaching Portfolio: www.interfolio.com/portfolio/hiremesoon
Course Websites: www.germancourses.com
Podcasts: iTunesUniversity (under Hirem E. Soon)

Student Affairs/Advising Résumé

Strategic Features: Student Affairs/Advising Résumé

Review this résumé if you want to emphasize specific competences without using a "Job Objective" statement.

RÉSUMÉ BASICS:

Highest Degree:	Master's degree in progress
Experience:	Practica Graduate assistantships
Job Target:	Community college, 4-year college, or university-level student services position

CONTENT FEATURES:

- *Competences* lead off this résumé to immediately identify multiple strengths; useful alternative to Job Objective category and provides more flexibility than a traditional objective statement. This section is easy to edit by changing one or two phrases that more closely represent an advertised opening.
- *Degree* section clearly states that the individual has attended a community college. By including this degree in the résumé it implies that you are interested in this population and understand the mission of community colleges.
- Annotations in the *Professional Skills and Accomplishments* category accentuate a broad base of skills and achievements from technology to presentations to portfolio materials. Combining these different areas into one category makes it possible to save space and create a one-page résumé.

DESIGN FEATURES:

Font:	Garamond font, size 11
Margins:	1" top, bottom; 1" left, right
Layout:	Open new document.
Line spacing:	One line space between categories.
Enhancements:	Graphic line to highlight category headings.

Student Affairs/Advising Résumé

HIREM E. SOON

21 University Avenue, Any City, State 12345 (201)565-1111 hiremesoon@cgu.edu

COMPETENCIES

Academic and Career Advising	Organizational Behavior	First Generation Retention
Community College Leadership	College Student Development	Spanish Language and Culture
Adult Development	Adaptive Technologies	Advanced Psychotherapy

DEGREES

Claremont Graduate University, Claremont, California, M.A. Degree expected May 201x
Emphasis in Higher Education/Student Affairs *Thesis Topic: Career Choices for First Generation College Students*

University of Northern Iowa, Cedar Falls, Iowa, B.S. Degree, Computer Science, May 201x

Kirkwood College, Cedar Rapids, Iowa, A.A. Degree, Liberal Arts, December 201x

UNIVERSITY EXPERIENCE

Graduate Assistantships:
Program Assistant, Orientation, Claremont Graduate University, Fall 201x – Spring 201x.
Hired and trained student staff; planned and implemented orientation for 4,000 new students and families. Collaborated with faculty to deliver orientation programs for transfer students.

Teaching Assistant, Introductory Psychology, Community College Online Courses, Summer 201x.
Created instructional materials for online delivery, led online chat and discussion boards, and evaluated papers. Advised students who were enrolled in first online course.

Practica:
Career Advisor for Transfer and Nontraditional Students, Pamona College, Fall semester 201x.
Participated in presentations, orientation seminars focused on transfer/nontraditional students. Stressed success of past transfer students, employment choices, study skills, service and volunteerism.

EMPLOYMENT

Specialist, Technology Innovative Center, IC Technical Labs, Culver City, California, 201x – 201x.
One-year contract focused on subsystems and technologies testing and data analysis.

PROFESSIONAL SKILLS AND ACCOMPLISHMENTS

Technology Applications:
Statistical Programs: SAS, SPSSx, SPSS/PC, Languages: C++, FORTRAN, COBOL
Design Software: Dreamweaver, FrontPage, Collaborator, Adobe Photoshop, Fireworks, HTML5

Presentations:
Poster Session, "First Generation Success," ACPA National Conference, San Diego, June 201x
Workshop Leader, "Advising Pitfalls," Student Advising Meeting, Los Angeles, May 201x

Affiliations and Portfolio:
Campus: Graduate Student Development Association - President, 201x; Member, 201x – present
www.interfolio.com/portfolio/hiremsoon (scholarships, campus activities, special recognition, abstracts)

Student Development/Higher Education CV

Strategic Features: Student Development CV

Review this CV if your experience includes administrative, teaching and/or student services responsibilities in a college and university setting. This CV is a good model to review if you have considerable professional, academic, and community experiences to share.

CV BASICS:

Highest Degree:	Ph.D. in progress
Experience:	Research and teaching assistantships Student services position
Job Target:	Administrative position in student services Leadership institute for college students

CONTENT FEATURES:

- Presenting a number of categories on page one paints a portrait of multiple talents and leadership skills. A reader can quickly see the progression of education by isolating *Ph.D., M.S.* and *B.A.* A separate category was included to bring attention to attendance at professional academies.
- Including a *Professional Overview* category can distinguish one with considerable experience. At a glance, reader recognizes career track.
- Selecting a format that uses graphic lines to divide categories clearly delineates each particular section.
- Annotations provide detailed and accurate descriptions of the professional experience listed on page two. Including details allows the reader to get a clear picture of duties and responsibilities, and significance of experiences.

DESIGN FEATURES:

Font:	Gill Sans MT font, size 10
Margins:	1" top, bottom, left, right
Layout:	Open new document; use tabs to indent.
Line spacing:	One line space between categories.
Enhancements:	Use of a graphic line to separate categories.

Student Development/Higher Education CV

IMA SAMPLE
16 University Avenue, Any City, State 12345 (101) 555-0101 i-sample@uw.edu

DEGREES

Ph.D. University of Wisconsin-Madison, December 201x
Student Affairs Administration and Research Minor: Athletic Administration
Dissertation title: *Female student athletes: A study of graduation rates: 1995 & 2005*
Advisor: Dr. Vera Goode

International Exchange: South Africa Study Tour, Participant, Summer 201x
Guadalajra, Mexico Adminstrative Exchange, Participant, Fall 201x

M.S. Hofstra University, Hempstead, May 201x
Counseling
Master's Thesis: *Study habits of first-year students at Ball State University*

B.A. University of Wisconsin-Madison, August 199x
English Education and Finance

INSTITUTES AND PROFESSIONAL ACADEMIES

Dealing With Difference Summer Institute, Participant and Panel Member, May 201x, June 201x
Madison Leadership Academy and Performance Institute, Participant, September 201x-January 201x

PROFESSIONAL OVERVIEW

Instructor, 2 years
Research and Teaching Assistant, 4 years
Student Affairs Administration, 5 years
Athletic Student Services Graduate Assistant, 4 years

HONORS AND GRANTS

Bev Kane Promising Scholar Award, University of Wisconsin-Madison, 201x
Lawrence Quinn Scholarship Award, University of Wisconsin-Madison, 201x, 201x
Educational Leadership Fund Grant, American College Personnel Association, 201x
Presidential Minority Graduate Student Scholarship Award, 201x
President's Excellence in Multicultural Leadership Affirmative Action Award, 200x
Outstanding New Professional, New York Annual Conference, 200x

TEACHING EXPERIENCE SUMMARY

Multi-cultural Counseling, Instructor, Hofstra University, Spring 201x, Fall 201x
Citizenship in a Multicultural Society, Online Instructor, Beloit College, Fall 201x
Multiculturalism in the Helping Professions, Online Instructor, Beloit College, Spring 200x
Inequality in Sport, Teaching Assistant, University of Wisconsin, Fall 201x
Financial Management: Leadership 101, University of Michigan, Winter Interim 200x
English Teacher, East High School, Madison, 199x-200x

SELECTED CONFERENCE PRESENTATIONS

"A study of the graduate rates of female athletes," 200x, ACPA Annual Conference, March 201x
"Multicultural Social Justice Education Curriculum." Research Symposium, Hofstra University, May 201x
"Inequality in sports: who is paying attention?" NCAA Research Forum, Indianapolis, September 201x
"Negotiations and Networking." ACPA Regional Conference, November 200x

Student Development/Higher Education CV, page 2

Ima Sample, Page 2

PUBLICATIONS/RESEARCH

Sample, Ima. (in press). Graduate rates of female athletes, 201x. *Journal of College Student Development.*
Seal, T. A., Sample, I., & Min, G. (201x) Methods for assessing graduation timelines and a sense of personal success. *Journal of College and Character, 13(7)*, 1-8.
Sample, Ima. (201x). *Supporting student athletes. About Campus*, 14(6), 26-29.
Sample, Ima. (200x). *Staff and Student Diversity Climate Survey Department of Athletics.* Unpublished raw data, University of Wisconsin-Madison.

PROFESSIONAL EXPERIENCE

Director, Learning To Lead Institute, Student Services, Hofstra University, 201x-201x
Responsibilities included: curriculum development for learning to lead institute; fiscal agent and budget manager for $200,000 budget; recruitment and program development and expansion; developed marketing and promotional materials; supervised training, and evaluation graduate assistants; acted as faculty liaison; developed and implemented service learning component in Washington, DC; conducted assessment processes for Institute.

Co-Coordinator, College Student Personnel MA Program, Department of Educational and Interdisciplinary Studies, Illinois State University, 200x-200x
Responsibilities included: coordinated interview process for academic department, approximately 20 assistantship sites, 10 Greek houses; conducted program assessment; coordinated travel, volunteers, housing, food, and special events during recruitment period; arranged conference recruitment at ACPA & NASPA; lead planning team of 10 graduate students in recruitment efforts of minority applicants.

ASSOCIATION MEMBERSHIPS

National Association of Academic Advisors for Athletics
Association for The Study of Higher Education
American Education Research Association
American College Personnel Association

INSTITUTIONAL SERVICE

Student Affairs Vision Task Force, Hofstra University, October 201x-December 201x
Affirmative Action Equity Council, Chair, Hofstra University, August 201x-August 201x
Professional Staff Recruitment Committee, Chair, Illinois State University, August 200x-May 200x
University Programming Committee, Illinois State University, August 200x-May 200x

PROFESSIONAL DEVELOPMENT

ACPA Commission-Campus Recreation and Athletics, Inaugural Directorate, December 201x
Diversity Dialogues, University College of Medicine, Facilitator, August 200x-May 201x
Sigma Lambda Sigma, Faculty Advisor, September 200x-September 200x
Beloit College OPE Interview Team, Chair, February 200x

COMMUNITY INVOLVEMENT

American Cancer Society Fundraiser, Chicago Marathon, Runner/Fundraiser, October 201x
Minority Community Health Committee, University Representative, April 201x-May 201x
Audio Information Services For the Blind, Volunteer Reader, 200x
St. Louis Rams Training Camp, July 201x, 200x, 200x

Professional Portfolio: www.interfolio.com/portfolio/imasample

Studio Art CV

Strategic Features: Studio Art CV

Review this CV if you are seeking an academic position that requires a specialized studio art background.

CV BASICS:

Highest Degree:	MFA
Experience:	Studio instructor Adjunct positions
Job Target:	College/university studio positions with teaching load

CONTENT FEATURES:

- *Teaching Interests* lists undergraduate and graduate courses that the individual can teach immediately upon hiring. Use of bullets draws one's eye just briefly to the list. Emphasis is on multiple areas.
- Exhibitions and juried/group shows provide evidence of recognition as a productive artist, with strong and unique community connections.
- *Current Teaching Experience* on page two divides the duties into three areas for the reader: teaching, studio, and committee responsibilities. This design quickly places emphasis on the three major commitments of the position.
- A category was created to describe *Studio Work;* this employment is directly related to the type of position sought. Descriptive phrases are used to quickly give the reader an overview of work and accomplishments.

DESIGN FEATURES:

Font:	Book Antigua font, size 11
Margins:	1" top, bottom, left, right
Layout:	Insert table with two columns.
Line spacing:	Two line spaces between categories.
Enhancements:	Use of bullets for emphasis. Italics are used to create subcategories.

Studio Art CV

IMA SAMPLE

16 University Avenue Any City, State 12345 ima-sample@niu.edu (101) 555-0009
Art portfolio: www.ImaSampleArtPortfolio.com
Teaching portfolio: www.ImaSampleTeachingPortfolio.com

EDUCATION:

M.F.A. Studio Art, University of Illinois at Urbana-Champaign, May 201x
B.F.A. Studio Art, Kansas City Art Institute, Kansas City, Missouri, 200x

INTERNATIONAL STUDY FELLOWSHIP:

Milan and Florence Italy International Fellowship for Arts, 201x
Selected for 12 month fellowship to study ceramics-3rd century Italy
Invited to examine relics held in reserve in the Italian National Museum.

TEACHING INTERESTS:

Teaching undergraduates and graduate students in the following courses:

- Exploring Forms in Clay
- Problems in Design: Form and Structure
- Sculpture (Undergraduate and Graduate level)
- Art in Entrepreneurial Settings

TEACHING OVERVIEW:

Adjunct, Studio Art, 201x – present, Northern Illinois University, DeKalb
Instructor, Studio Art, 201x – 201x, Lake Forest College, Lake Forest
Teaching Assistant, 201x - 201x, Studio Art, University of Illinois
Ceramics Instructor, 200x, University Memorial Union Craft Center
Careers in Art Entrepreneurial Instructor, 200x, University of Illinois

JURIED SHOWS:

- Kansas City Artists Exhibit & Review, Kansas City Art Gallery, 201x
- Missouri Clay/Paper Regional Show, St. Louis, May 201x (Purchase Prize)
- Northwest Ceramic & Sculpture Show, Boise, Idaho, 201x (Grand Prize)
- 5th Annual Michigan Artists' Show, Detroit Art Center, 201x
- Mid-Mississippi Annual Exhibition, Davenport, 200x (Student Award)
- Minnesota Artists' Exhibition, Hamline University, 200x

INVITATIONAL EXHIBITIONS:

- Ceramic Revelations and Relics, Millard Memorial Gallery, Chicago 201x
- Alaska Sculpture Invitational, Gallery ShowPlace, Anchorage 201x
- Contemporary Ceramics Invitational, Cooper Gallery, Cleveland 200x

GROUP SHOWS:

- Graduate Student Art Show, University of Illinois, Champaign, 201x
- Cook County Art Show, Chicago Public Library, 201x
- Florida Ceramics Arts Show, West Palm Beach, 200x
- Summer Art Fair, Montana State University, Bozeman, 200x

Studio Art CV, page 2

Sample, page 2

CURRENT TEACHING EXPERIENCE:	*Teaching Responsibilities:* Adjunct Instructor, Studio Art, Northern Illinois University, DeKalb, 201x – present. Responsibilities include working with non-major and major undergraduate students and M.A. students in Art Education. *Courses:* Introduction to Sculpture and Advanced Sculpture. *Course content:* Basic sculptural concepts, processes, investigation of materials (clay, wood, plaster); emphasis on developing formal language, acquiring basic skills; understanding spatial, conceptual, technical issues. *Studio Responsibilities:* Supervise graduate students who assist undergraduates in the studio; meet with graduate assistants in a weekly seminar to discuss needs and materials. *Committee Responsibilities:* Undergraduate Accreditation Review Committee Member, 201x Course Review Committee, College of Liberal Arts, 201x Faculty Selection and Interview Team Member, 201x
PRESENTATIONS:	"Arts and Community Pride," State of Illinois Economic Development Conference, Springfield, Illinois, May 201x "Ceramics and Rehab," Midwest Penal Conference, Des Moines, Iowa, October 201x "Removing Barriers with Art," Motivation and Rehabilitation Conference, Evanston, Illinois, February 200x
PUBLICATIONS:	"Arts and Prison: Making a New Start with Art." *Journal of Prison Reform.* (in press) "Hands and Hearts: Art in Prison," *State Health Bulletin*, vol. 6, 32-41, May 201x
RELATED EXPERIENCE:	Artist in Residence & Volunteer, Illinois State Prison, Springville, 201x - Freelance Graphic Artist, 200x - present Matting and Framing, Contemporary Art Supplies, Chicago, 200x
STUDIO WORK:	Proprietor, Ceramics and Serenity Shop, Naperville, Illinois, 201x – present Own and operate a ceramics production studio; operate a hands-on studio hosting small and large groups; design specialty items. Awarded Chamber of Commerce New Business Award for 201x.
SERVICE:	Board President, Community Cares, Inc, DeKalb, Illinois, 201x – present Volunteer, Free Medical Clinic, Kansas City and DeKalb, 201x – 201x Membership in College Art Association & Midwest Sculptors' Association
DOSSIER:	References and portfolio of art productions, studio work, syllabi, student evaluations, shows, exhibitions, presentations and publications available in paper or online at: www.ImaSampleTeachingPortfolio.com

Teaching (K-12) Résumé

Strategic Features: Academe CV to Teaching Résumé

Review this résumé if you are interested in pursuing secondary teaching opportunities.

RÉSUMÉ BASICS:

Highest Degree:	Master's degree; Ph.D. in progress
Experience:	College assistantships, tutor, Peace Corps
Job Target:	Teaching in a secondary setting: private or public schools, charter or boarding schools *Note:* seeking a position that does not require teaching certification/state licensure

CONTENT FEATURES:

- An objective statement, rarely used in a CV, pinpoints type of position sought.
- *Related Teaching Experiences* category demonstrates that previous experiences were sought working with teaching materials and students.
- In *Education,* a chronological format is used that stresses undergraduate training in Spanish and Global Studies. The Master's Degree and Advanced Studies make the connection to the English teaching area.
- Annotations provide detailed and accurate descriptions of teaching interests and related teaching experience. Including details helps to convince the reader that your first priority is to teach high school students, not college-level students. Potential training in specific area mentioned to further substantiate this.

DESIGN FEATURES:

Font:	Calibri font, size 10
Margins:	1" top, bottom; 1" left, right
Layout:	Insert table.
Line spacing:	2.5 line spaces between categories.
Enhancements:	Limited use of bullets for emphasis.

Teaching (K-12) Résumé

ALEC SAMPLE
16 University Avenue, Any City, State 12345 (101) 555-0101 a-sample@IU.edu

---

TEACHING OBJECTIVES

Classroom teaching:
- Spanish, Global Studies, English

Instructional skills:
- Integrating technology and new media into curricula
- Incorporating research skills into unit plans and projects
- Clearly communicating goals for learning

RELATED TEACHING EXPERIENCE

Instructor/teaching assistant, Indiana University, 201x – present
Non-profit online writing service, (www.writing.com) 201x – present
Tutor, Hispanic Learning Center, Chicago, summers, 201x – 201x
Peace Corps Volunteer, Kingston, Jamaica, 200x – 200x
- Worked with students of all ages in diverse settings
- Established meaningful learning projects incorporating reading, writing, reporting, and self-evaluation/reflection
- Expected quality work by establishing high expectations

EDUCATION

Spanish and Global Studies, B.A., June 201x, Butler University
Comparative Literature, M.A., May 201x, Purdue University
Comparative Literature, Advanced Studies, 201x – present, Indiana University
Licensure: Interested in pursuing alternative secondary licensure

ACTIVITIES

Community:
Translator, Charity Hospital and Clinic, Bloomington, 201x –present
Website builder/fundraiser, Lake Charities, South Bend, 201x
Reader for vision impaired, Grace Center, South Bend, 201x

Campus:
Chair, Course Review Committee, 201x – 201x
Student member, Search Committee for the Vice President, 201x
Member, University Music and Lecture Series Committee, 201x

Publications:
Articles published and presentations given on the topic of intercultural expectations and retention of international students

PORTFOLIO

Portfolio available from *Interfolio* at: www.interfolio.com/portfolio/asample (letters of recommendation, writing samples, abstracts, conference presentations, language audio, campus activities, and community service)

Teaching (K-12)/Adult Education Résumé

Strategic Features: Teaching Résumé/Adult Education (without state certification/license)

Review this résumé if you are seeking a teaching position in K-12 settings or in adult education. The sample deemphasizes doctoral work and emphasizes strengths in a particular skill area. This format is very valuable for career changers.

RÉSUMÉ BASICS:

Highest Degree:	Master's degree (doctoral studies halted)
Experience:	Military, advisor, industry
Job Target:	Secondary or adult teaching in public/private settings

CONTENT FEATURES:

- First category emphasizes the three strengths the candidate can bring to the employment setting: teaching areas, activity sponsorship, and skills. The format isolates the strengths and draws attention to how this candidate will help students become successful.
- The focus of the résumé is to highlight experiences and skills—not necessarily an academic pedigree with the promise to publish.
- The Ph.D. program is listed in the *Academic Background* section as "graduate studies" because doctoral studies have been discontinued at this time.
- The *Professional Summary* category saves space by listing three areas: Work, Military and Volunteer. Not only does this strategy save space, it provides the reader a quick overview of your experience.

DESIGN FEATURES:

Font:	Candara font, size 11
Margins:	.75" top, bottom; .75" left, right
Layout:	Open new document and set tabs.
Line spacing:	Two line spaces between categories.
Enhancements:	Single descriptive words are used as focal points to introduce topics.

Teaching (K-12)/Adult Education Résumé

VERA GOODE 21 College Ave, City, State Zip 321.101.8765 veragoode@gmail.com

OBJECTIVE:

Teaching: Language instruction to non-native speakers-youth to business professionals
Computer programming instruction: C++ to basic website design

Activities: Mentor, advisor, coach, club sponsor

Skills: Adapt to new situations, cultures, and surroundings quickly
Ability to assist students with basic or advanced technology skills
Able to collaborate with staff, parents, students and other stakeholders

PROFESSIONAL SUMMARY:

Work: Counselor, Latino Cultural Center, West Hollywood, June 201x-present
Academic Advisor, UCLA Athletics, Los Angeles, August 201x-present
Computer Specialist, Abler Technologies, Beverly Hills, May 201x-201x

Military: United States Air Force, Air Borne Division, Second Lieutenant, 200x-201x

Volunteer: Tutor, Community House, West Hollywood, December 201x-present
Table-to-Table driver, west LA area, April 201x-201x
Youth Soccer Coach, Beverly Hills Youth Soccer Club, 201x-201x

ACADEMIC BACKGROUND:

University of California-Riverside, Graduate Studies, September 201x-December 201x
Second Language Acquisition

Cornell University, Ithaca, Master of Arts Degree, May 201x
Spanish

University of Michigan, Ann Arbor, Bachelor of Science Degree, June 200x
Computer Science and Spanish

INTERNATIONAL EXPERIENCE:

Service:
Reading for Peace Project, Amman, Jordan, Summers 201x -201x
Collaborated with volunteers from numerous countries
Worked directly with youth to enhance reading strategies

Study:
Summer Language Institute, Barcelona, Spain, 201x
Universidad de San Jordi, Spain, August 200x -201x
AFS Student, Lima, Peru, Junior Year, 200x

Travel:
Leisure and study trips to South & Central America, Middle East, Europe
Led Outward Bound trips to Canadian Boundary Waters & Little Big Horn Mountains

Technology/Communications Résumé

Strategic Features: Technology/Communications Résumé (Comparative Lit CV to résumé)

Review this résumé if you are seeking a position that requires specialized skills in a particular area that does not call for a doctorate.

RÉSUMÉ BASICS:

Highest Degree:	Ph.D. in progress
Experience:	Tutor Instructor Peace Corps Volunteer
Job Target:	Creative or administrative position in collegiate setting, small business or related organization

CONTENT FEATURES:

- A *Competencies* category clearly identifies specific proficiencies and areas of expertise. Creating this category serves a number of functions—it tells the employer what you can do and it prepares you to answer key interview questions such as: What are your strengths? What can you bring to our organization? Why should we hire you?
- *Accomplishments* draw on several categories from the CV; concise action phrases send quick and clear messages.
- The résumé omits descriptions about dissertation, research, teaching and related activities (full descriptions can be reviewed on CV) to avoid academic stereotyping.
- *Professional Activities* category allows a number of topics to be presented in one distinct category.

DESIGN FEATURES:

Font:	Calibri font, size 11
Margins:	1" top, bottom; 1" left, right
Layout:	Insert table.
Line spacing:	Two line spaces between categories.
Enhancements:	Bold font to highlight category heading; limited use of italics for sub-category headings.

Technology/Communications Résumé

ALEC SAMPLE
16 University Avenue, Any City, State 12345 (101) 555-0101 a-sample@IU.edu

---

COMPETENCIES

Technology—new media, web 2.0, software evaluation
Communication—writing, speaking, persuasion, translation
Supervision—evaluation, project development, on-time delivery
Research—documenting, validating, experimenting, reporting

ACCOMPLISHMENTS

Integrated new media into existing and new projects
Proficient in three languages; translating/writing experiences
Selected for prestigious fellowships and scholarships
Instructed and evaluated 400+ graduate/undergraduate students
Generated start-up costs for an small non-profit business

RELATED EMPLOYMENT

Instructor/teaching assistant, Bloomington, Indiana 201x – present
Non-profit online writing service, (www.writing.com) 201x –present
Tutor, Hispanic Learning Center, Chicago, summers, 201x – 201x
Peace Corps Volunteer, Kingston, Jamaica, 200x – 200x

EDUCATION

Spanish and Global Studies, B.A., Butler University, June 201x
Comparative Literature, M.A., Purdue University, May 201x
Comparative Literature, Advanced Studies, Indiana University, 201x –

PROFESSIONAL ACTIVITIES

Community:
Translator, Charity Hospital and Clinic, Bloomington, 201x – present
Website builder/fundraiser, Lake Charities, South Bend, 201x
Reader for vision impaired, Grace Center, South Bend, 201x

Campus:
Chair, Course Review Committee, 201x – 201x
Student member, Search Committee for the Vice President, 201x
Member, University Music and Lecture Series Committee, 201x

Publications:
Articles published and presentations given on topic of intercultural expectations and retention of international students

PORTFOLIO

Portfolio available from *Interfolio* at: www.interfolio.com/portfolio/asample (letters of recommendation, writing samples, abstracts, conference presentations, campus activities, and community service)

Women's Studies CV

Strategic Features: Women's Studies CV

Review this CV if you have extensive experiences in international settings or wish to apply for positions requiring a strong international/multi-cultural, theoretical/practical background in policy and social issues.

CV BASICS:

Highest Degree:	ABD (all but dissertation)
Experience:	Fellowship experience Professional positions
Job Target:	Research institution top priority Master's level considered

CONTENT FEATURES:

- To highlight international experience, the first category, *International Overview*, provides a quick overview of both intellectual and practical experiences; this information is relevant for positions with an advertised international component.
- In the *Academic Background* section it is clear that the dissertation is in progress, the topic chosen, and a projected date for completion has been established.
- Research and teaching abilities are highlighted by giving brief annotations of skills used in both areas. Research competencies are required for advancement in this field and are included on page one for emphasis.
- The categories on page two demonstrate both the interest and ability to publish and present and to contribute to myriad groups in academic and community settings.

DESIGN FEATURES:

Font:	Calibri font, size 10.5
Margins:	1" top, bottom, left, right
Layout:	Open new document; use tabs to indent.
Line spacing:	One line space between categories.
Enhancements:	Selected use of bullets to highlight research, teaching, & service; indentations to draw emphasis.

Women's Studies CV

IMA SAMPLE

#5 Academic Hall, Any University, Any City, State 12345
c: (101)555-1110 o: (102)555-1998 ima-sample@uw.edu

INTERNATIONAL OVERVIEW

- Fellowship — Peru Educational Institute for International Research
- Languages — Spanish, Portuguese, Italian
- Research — Ford Foundation Research Dissertation Award:
  Social networks and women activism in Peruvian villages
- Grant — Women's Health Resources, Pan American Health Organization, 201x
- Peace Corps — Senior Trainer, Peace Corps Training Center, Lima, Peru, 200x-200x
  Volunteer, Honduras, 200x – 200x
- Study — Undergraduate exchange – Fundación Ortega y Gasset, Summer 200x
  Study Abroad: Toledo, Spain, 200x
  Spanish Language Training, Cuernavaca, Mexico, 200x

ACADEMIC BACKGROUND

Global Studies, Georgetown University, M.A. 201x; B.A. Spanish and Portuguese, 200x

Women's Studies, University of Washington, Seattle, (ABD) 201x – present (expected May 201x)

Concentration: Women's health policy in developing countries

Doctoral examination areas:

Politics of Health Education
Women in Development Studies
International Education

Dissertation topic:

Working women, child care and social supports in rural Peru: social networks and activism as a mediating factor (projected completion: May 201x)

UNIVERSITY RESEARCH AND TEACHING EXPERIENCE

Research Assistantships and Internships:

Center for International Rural and Environmental Health, Costa Rica & University of Washington, 201x

- Assigned to CIREH's Women, Health, Employment, and Development in Central America; researched and compiled online bibliography of over 500 references for grant; assisted with preparations for international conference held in San Jose, Costa Rica.

Ford Foundation Graduate Research Intern, Ford Foundation, New York, NY, 201x-201x

- Selected on competitive basis to work with a Ford Urban Poverty Program Officer; researched the Foundation's grants and papers dealing with young childrens' care, development, and education worldwide; interviewed experts within and outside the Foundation; synthesized data and published results in the Ford Foundation Review.

Teaching Assistant:

Global Studies I, Georgetown University, Spring 201x and Fall 201x (undergraduate course)
International Issues in Rural Development, Georgetown University, Fall 201x (graduate course)
Cross-Cultural Perspectives, Georgetown University, Distance Education Unit, 201x

- Created syllabi, presented lectures and monitored discussion groups; encouraged students to examine social and political implications of governmental decisions; assessed tests and examinations and evaluated research proposals and papers.

Women's Studies CV

Ima Sample, page 2

PRESENTATIONS AND PAPERS

"Women, Health, and Employment in Central America," invited address, Conference of The Pan American Health Organization, October 31, 201x, San Jose, Costa Rica.
Paper: "Working Women and Health Support Networks in Limon Region of Costa Rica"

"Women's Health: At the Crossroads of Development," presentation, Third World Foundation Conference, Kansas, City, KS, November 20, 201x. Conference recordings in *Crossroad Journal*, Vol 34, pages 129-136.

WORKSHOPS

"Multicultural Workshop for Health Providers," Seattle Community Center, May 201x

"Women and Political Indecision: Finding Remedies." Women's Political Action Consortium, Washington, DC, September 201x

"Development and Health Policy," NE Women's Group, Boston, MA, July 201x

SERVICE

Senior Trainer, Center for Human Potential, U.S. Peace Corps Training Center, El Coyal, Alajuela, Costa Rica, October-April, 201x.

- Designed, planned and implemented over 100 hours of technical training for U.S. Peace Corps trainees in the Integrated Child Development and Community Development Program; worked closely with experienced trainers in developing technical program.
- Utilized non-formal adult education and participatory methodology during training sessions conducted in English and Spanish.
- Facilitated on-going trainee support group incorporating cross-cultural counseling and evaluation of trainees' progress.

U.S. Peace Corps Volunteer, Integrated Development Program, Honduras, 200x-200x

- Worked with a non-governmental development agency, UNISA, in establishing cooperative family centers in both rural and urban areas of Honduras.
- Collaborated in developing and designing curriculum appropriate to the rural/urban environments; trained adolescent females as preschool teachers and adult women in the management of family centers and child-care centers.

HONORS AND AWARDS

International Dissertation Research Fellowship, 201x
S.M. Royal Dissertation Grant, 201x-201x
University of Washington Graduate Teaching Award, 201x

PROFESSIONAL TRAINING (Brown University)

"Cross-Cultural Training and Development," International Programs, 10/15/201x
"Writing Seminar," University Graduate College, 6/10/201x
"From Research Paper to Journal Publication," Graduate Center for Teaching Seminar, 9/1/200x

AFFILIATIONS

OMEP, World Organization for Young Children
Association for Women in Development
Society for International Development

References and writing samples available upon request

Index of CVs & Résumés

*Represents professional résumés and CVs that have been transformed into résumés.

8810414R0

Made in the USA
Charleston, SC
16 July 2011